Water
A Source For Future Conflicts

Water
A Source For Future Conflicts

By

Major General (Retired) AK Chaturvedi, AVSM, VSM

Published in association with
Centre for Joint Warfare Studies (CENJOWS)
New Delhi

Vij Books India Pvt Ltd
New Delhi (India)

Published by

Vij Books India Pvt Ltd
(Publishers, Distributors & Importers)
2/19, Ansari Road, Darya Ganj
New Delhi - 110002
Phones: 91-11-43596460, 91-11- 65449971
Fax: 91-11-47340674
www.vijbooks.com

e-mail : vijbooks@rediffmail.com

Copyright © 2013, Centre for Joint Warfare Studies (CENJOWS),
New Delhi

Paperback Edition 2015

Contents

List of Appendices, Annexures, Figures And Tables

Chapter-3

Figures

Tables

Chapter-4

Figures

Tables

Chapter-6

Foreword

Water is one of the most important elements for the survival of life on the planet of Earth. While there is enough of water on Earth, the quantity of fresh water is quite limited. The quantity of fresh water is finite and is gradually getting reduced in terms of per capita availability, due to a host of reasons, like; exponential rise in population, pollution of fresh water resources, erosion in the quantity of fresh water due to global warming and above all human greed. Criticality of fresh water can be appreciated by the fact that all through the history, a large number of battles have been fought for the control/ denial of water sources. In India the problem is assuming far greater criticality because; on one side; due to reasons mentioned above, as it is the availability is getting reduced, what makes the problem even more serious is that we are surrounded by countries where situation is even worse, the relationship with many of them for historical reasons is far from pleasant and either the necessary legally binding dispute resolution mechanism is not in place (case of People's Republic of China (PRC)) or the existing treaty does not meet the aspirations of the stake holders (case of Indus Water Treaty-1960 (IWT) . Therefore a tension on account of water relations in the overall context of a trust deficit is likely to escalate into a major crisis. In this connection another factor which merits consideration is that the water resources within the Indian Subcontinent are monolithic due to geography of the region and the partition on account of political consideration has rendered their division quite inviable, Also an uneven distribution of the water resources and the lack of infra structure for optimal utilisation of these resources within the country may result into internal conflicts (a common feature in India and also within Pakistan presently), which may pose threat to the integrity of a young nation like India (though India has been a geographical entity but as a nation it emerged only post independence in 1947). Therefore it is absolutely important for the security establishment and the perspective planners of the country, that this problem is analysed in its correct perspective comprehensively across the entire spectrum of the issues so that a long term strategy is evolved to deal with the issue.

Keeping in view the importance of the subject, CENJOWS took up the subject for the research. Major General (Retired) AK Chaturvedi, AVSM, VSM who has been working in the field of Water Security issues, was tasked to take a fresh look on all aspects of water and related subjects. In this research, he has done an extensive survey of all relevant issues with respect to water and has tried to establish a co-relation between availability versus requirement and based on his work, he has recommended a 'Way Ahead'. I hope that the work will be able to stimulate many a minds to further deliberate on the issue and steadily we will be able to provide workable options to decision makers.

(KB Kapoor)
Maj Gen (Retd.)
Executive Director, CENJOWS

New Delhi
April 2013

Acknowledgement

"I dedicate this book to the Armed Forces of India, who are entrusted to ensure the Natioal security and have helped the author to develop a capacity to underatke such an analysis."

I am extremely thankful to Major General KB Kapoor, VSM, the Executive Director, CENJOWS for considering me worthy of being able to shoulder the responsibility to do this research which is so very important for the safety, security and survival of mankind in general and India in particular. I am also indebted to Col AK Singh, the Secretary CENJOWS for all sagacious and energetic assistance which he was ever willing to extend.

I am thankful to all the authors and analysts whose work helped me to do my research and whom, I have quoted. A very special thanks to Professor KD Sharma of the Planning Commission for his very insightful suggestions with respect to the issues that he recommended to form part of the research and the material on the subject that he shared with me. I am also thankful to Lt Gen (Retired) Gautam Banerjee, PVSM, AVSM, YSM for encouraging me to take up this research.

Finally a special thanks to my wife Mrs Renu Chaturvedi and my daughters; Miss Medha and Miss Pragya for helping me to provide directions to my research with their suggestions, helping me in compilation/ proof reading and finally providing me the IT support; an area where I am reasonably challenged.

Lucknow   (AK Chaturvedi)

April 2013   Major General (Retired)

Abbreviations

BCM	Billion Cubic Metres
CUM	Cubic Meters
CGIAR	Consultative Group on International Agricultural Research
FAO	Food and Agriculture Organisation
FoEME	Friends of the Earth Middle East
GIS	Geographical Information System
GAP	Guneydogu Anadolu Projesi (South Eastern Anatolia Project) on the River Euphrates in Turkey
GDP	Gross Domestic Product
GOI	Government of India
HWs	Head Works
IGNP	Indira Gandhi Nahar Pariyojna
IEEEP	Institute of Electrical and Electronics Engineers, Pakistan
IWT	Indus Water Treaty
IRSA	Indus River System Authority
ILC	International Law commission
KRB	Kabul River Basin
Laos PDR	Laos People's Democratic Republic
MCM	Million Cubic Meters

MDGs	Millennium Development Goals
Mha	Million Hectare
MAF	Million Acre Feet
NCIWRDP	National Commission for Integrated water Resource Development
NJP	Nathpa Jhakri Project
NWMP	National Water Management Plan.
PLA	People's Liberation Army
ppb	Particle Parts per Billion
PRC	People's Republic of China
SADC	Southern African Development Community
Sq Kms	Square Kilometers
SqM	Square Meters
SYL	Sutlej-Yamuna Link.
TAR	Tibet Autonomous Region.
UNDP	United Nations Development Programme.
WASSA	Water and Security in South Asia
WAPDA	Water and Power Development Agency

Chapter-1
Introduction

"The consequences for humanity are grave. Water scarcity threatens economic and social gains and is a potent fuel for wars and conflict."

Ban Ki Moon
Secretary General
United Nations Organisation

Water along with sunlight and wind is one of the most important resources for the sustenance of life because it is a fundamental human need. Its criticality makes it a vital national asset for any country. In view of its all pervasiveness, it is the key to the socio-economic development of any society and as such of the quality of life for the society. With the ever rising population and consequent increase in the economic activities in the overarching envelope of increased energy intensive mechanisation, the water requirement is rising exponentially. This dynamics of the social and economic transformation will continue to spur the demand for fresh water and as such pose a challenge to national planners to find ways and means to bridge the demand-supply gap in the water sector. In this connection role of rivers assumes great importance. Rivers are a crucial source of water resources and physically link upstream and downstream users. While their flow offers ample opportunity for water harnessing, but it also creates barriers and tensions due to certain non-equitable uses and difference in perceptions of the upper and lower riparian about the rationality of each other's view point due to rising needs of both upstream and downstream users without any accretion in the quantum of available resource. The management of rivers in the context of inter-state relations cannot take place in a vacuum but need a rather complex political and economic framework which should be evolved by a mutual consultation between the stake holders or by coercive methods used by one of the users against other users.

Because of the criticality of the water for the human survival, no wonder, from time immemorial water has had a major bearing on the evolution of civilisations. History is witness to the fact that all human settlements from the time immemorial have come up along the river valleys or have been based on oases in the deserts. All ancient civilisations, of the world, to name a few; Nile Civilisation, yellow river valley civilisation, Indus Valley civilisation and finally Tigris-Euphrates River valley civilisation, have all been river valley civilisations. These civilisations even today are alive and thriving in the form of Egypt, China, India-Pakistan-Bangladesh, Turkey, Iraq and Syria, although it is a separate issue that some of their geographical and political contours have changed with the passage of time.[1]

In addition, many a fights between adversaries through the history have either been to deny access to the water or to gain unhindered access to the water. Water has played a central, albeit usually overlooked, role in conflicts throughout the human history, more than even precious energy resources. During the past 50 years alone, there have been over 500 conflicts pitting a country against another country, and 21 instances of actual hostilities as a result of disagreements over water. It is being anticipated that many of the wars of the 21st century will be fought over water. Water" and "war" are two topics being discussed together with increasing frequency. The problem, each time is as to who owns the water, how the water should be shared between different countries and under what conditions. In this connection it is appreciated that, though partly, water has also played a critical role in the Israeli-Palestinian conflict and other wars in the region but it was much under reported. The 'Six-Day' war, which pitted Syria, Jordan and Egypt against Israel, had partly to do with a disagreement over water. One of the reasons (there were of course many others) as to why Israel has been reluctant to pull out of the Golan Heights and the West Bank; because it fears losing control of water flows by handing over control of them to hostile forces. Even nearer home;

Pakistan's one of the important interest in Kashmir is the water of Jhelum and Chenab. Similarly China's, one of the main interest, in Tibet is its water based resources. It may be appreciated that the 261 international watersheds[ii] , covering a little less than one half of the land surface of the globe, affect about 40% of the world's population. During the past 15 years, there have been armed conflicts over water in Bangladesh, Tajikistan, Malaysia, Yugoslavia, Angola, East Timor, Namibia, Botswana, Zambia, Ecuador and Peru. Several terrorist groups have threatened to poison water systems and water distribution has been regularly targeted in Iraq. However it would be interesting to examine the role of water in the initiation of a conflict or perpetuate/aggravate a conflict or be used as a force multiplier in deciding the outcome of a conflict. In recent times, the British Non Profit Organisation, International Alert released a study,[iii] identifying 46 countries—home to 2.7 billion people—where water and climate stresses could ignite violent conflict by 2025, prompting UN Secretary-General Ban Ki-moon to say,

"The consequences for humanity are grave. Water scarcity threatens economic and social gains and is a potent fuel for wars and conflict."

Case of International Water Channels. Quantum of available usable water in these rivers is increasingly becoming lesser and lesser due to a host of reasons. Though some of the reasons are; population growth, political instability, and conflict, however these reasons need to be examined in detail. Implication of scarcity of any resource which has a cross boundary relevance is part of a resource geopolitics and as such results into a conflict. Main issue remains ownership of water. The Trans boundary Freshwater Dispute Database, needs to be generated which can provide a framework for quantitative, global-scale explorations of the relationship between freshwater resources availability, its augmentation, need for international cooperation to manage these resources and absence of such cooperation & resultant conflict. It has been established by a number of researchers that as scarcity increases, so does the potential for conflict.[iv] There are many examples of internal water conflicts ranging from interstate violence and death along the Cauvery River in India, to California farmers blowing up a pipeline transporting water to Los Angeles to much of the violent history in the Americas between indigenous peoples and European settlers.[v]

and Popular press[vi] point to water not only as a cause of historic armed conflict, but as the resource which will bring combatants to the battlefield in the 21st century. The problem, each time, is who owns the water, how the water should be shared out between different countries and under what conditions. The fundamental problem is that access rights to water are often badly defined. Unlike with other commodities, the institutions of modern capitalism - property rights, private companies, free market prices – have rarely been applied to water, and especially not to water flows that cross different countries. The result is that countries all too often use non-commercial methods to arrange their water supplies – such as finders-keepers, war, or diplomatic deals.[vii] Indian Subcontinent is endowed by nature, because two of the five river systems by discharge in the world are in Indian Subcontinent:-

Table-1.1 Five Largest Rivers By Discharge

Ser No	River	Average Disharge at the River Mouth (CUM / Sec)
1.	Amazon	212,000
2.	Congo	40,000
3.	Yangtze	22,000
4.	Brahmaputra	20,000
5.	Ganges	19,000

Water Stress by International River Basin

Source: UN Environment Programme and Oregon State University, 2002.

Fig-1.1 Water Availability Per Capita By Basin

Water Security

Before nuances of the water security are studied, it would be pertinent to slightly go back into the matrix of broader human security from where the water security emanates. Security studies have increasingly included in their ambit the domestic factors that can lead to destabilization of a national government and as such there is a need to understand the broader concept of "Human Security", which considers "security of people not just of territory". A link between the two was established by Ullman (1983),[viii] who evolved the concept of national security, which is as follows:-

> *"A threat to National security is an action or sequence of events that threatens drastically and over a relatively brief period of time to degrade the quality of life for the inhabitants of a state, or threatens significantly to narrow the range of policy choices available to the government of a state or to private, non government entities (persons, groups, corporations) within a state".*

Human Security has been defined by Meyers (1993) and in a broad sense it goes as follows:-

> *".... Security applies most at the level of the individual citizen. It amounts to human well being: not only protection from harm and injury but access to water, food, shelter, health, employment and other basic requisites that are the due of any person on earth. It is the collectiveity of these citizen needs-overall safety and quality of life-that should figure prominently in the nation's view of security."*

Centrality of Water in the Security Matrix of a Nation. This linkage as explained above clearly establishes the centrality of the Water in a nation's security matrix. Water security can be defined as the capacity of a set of people to ensure that they continue to have access to potable water. It will be in terms of time and duration. It is an increasing concern which is a function of population growth, drought, climate change, oscillation between El Niño and La Niña effects, urbanisation, salinity, upstream pollution, over-allocation of water licences by government agencies and over-utilisation of groundwater from artesian basins for needs other than basic sustenance. Also non availability of water on account of various tangible and intangible factors has a major bearing on the production of food grains, industrial output and to meet the demands of the service sector. All these aspects enlarge the scope of the water security which, with all these aspects borne in mind, now can be defined as the capacity of a society to the affordable access to clean water for agricultural, industrial and household usage besides for drinking purposes. This revised interpretation of the water security makes it an important part of human security. Historically also it can easily be concluded that water or lack of it caused the collapse of defences in battles where defences were invested but lack of water forced the defenders to accept terms which were less than favourable. In modern times also countries like Israel and Singapore have declared their water sources as national vital interests and have formulated their policies to ensure their safety and security. It will also be not far from truth that one of the major interest of Pakistan in Kashmir and China's interest in Tibet is the water assets of these two places respectively.

Finite Nature of Water. There is another question which is relevant and calls for a serious examination is; whether quantity of water or more importantly usable water be increased. It is indeed a complex problem and has its co-relation in the availability of energy, capacity to do pollution control, address global warming among many other relevant aspects. Thus Water along with food, pollution control, global warming and energy forms a critical part of the 'new security agenda' and redefines the understanding of security as a basis for policy-response and long term planning.

Need to Evolve a Timely Response to Water Shortage. Water security for India implies effective responses to changing water conditions in terms of quality, quantity and uneven distribution. Unheeded it can affect relationships at the inter-state level and equally contribute to tensions at the intra-provincial level. Water security is rapidly declining in many parts of the world.[x] According to the Pacific Institute "While regional impacts will vary, global climate change will potentially alter agricultural productivity, freshwater availability and quality, access to vital minerals, coastal and island flooding, and more. Among the consequences of these impacts will be challenges to political relationships, realignment of energy markets and regional economies, and threats to security".[xi] It impacts regions, states and countries. Tensions exist between upstream and downstream users of water within individual jurisdictions.[xii] There are a number of examples in History wherein conflict over use of water from rivers such as the Tigris and Euphrates Rivers has been recorded.[xiii] Another highly politicized example in history is Israel's control of water resources in the Levant region since its creation,[xiv] where efforts of Israel to secure (to reduce the possibility of its water sources falling into the hands of Arabs) its water resources was one of several drivers for the 1967 Six Day War. Water security is sometimes sought by implementing water desalination, pipelines between sources and users, water licences with different security levels and war. More than 50 countries on five continents are said to be at the risk of getting embroiled into conflict over water.[xv] & [1] Turkey's South Eastern Anatolia Project (Guneydogu Anadolu Projesi, or GAP) on the Euphrates has potentially serious consequences for water supplies in Syria and Iraq.[xvi] *In 1987 India recognised water security as an overriding national objective.*[xvii]

Migration and Conflict. With several parts of the India, becoming increasingly water scarce, especially in North India, millions of people will be forced to move away from their homes (internal migration) in search of work and water supply with attended problems of tensions in the region of deficit and also in the new emerging areas of water shortage in areas where these internally migrated people move to. This trend will worsen the tensions that are already prevalent in parts of the country over migrant workers. These tensions will further exacerbate existing ethnic & social divides and increase crime rates especially in urban areas where most rural migrants are likely to gravitate. It is estimated that in the next two decades, more and more rural residents will be forced to abandon their hometowns due to the lack of water resources, and the increase in extreme weather events such as floods. Lack of job security in the agriculture sector due to water shortages will also force many farmers to leave their villages and move towards urban areas. With an increased number of people competing for scarce resources and jobs, an anti-outsider mentality will start to take over, and create a backlash against migrant workers. This tension could

---

[1] http://en.wikipedia.org/wiki/Water_security#cite_note-9

manifest itself violently, given the appropriate circumstances and external pushes. While this 'locals versus outsiders' conflict is already prevalent in certain parts of the country, and to a large extent in most urban centres, future water shortages will push these conflicts to the forefront of national dialogue. This phenomenon, known as environmental migration, will not be restricted to the Indian territories. *Migrants from countries like Nepal and Bangladesh are also likely to move into India due to a serious shortage of water within their own countries, creating a serious human security problem.*[xviii]

With water becoming an increasingly scarce resource, its importance in any discussion on national security has started becoming increasingly more and more regular and significant. Today non-traditional threats are assuming greater importance in the security grid. The 'securitisation move' of an existential issue such as water generates political attention, public awareness and policy-initiatives. Human security, as various definitions suggest, is based on access to clean food; basic health care and education; environment, water security and energy security. In this connection it needs to be appreciated that the quantity of water and its regeneration is finite. Gradually its availability per capita is steadily reducing and that is the reason for its criticality.

Scarcity versus Conflict. Due to growing scarcity, water has become a resource of contention and conflict among the regions of a state/ states/ countries sharing the resource and the nature of conflict gets reduced to the question of who has the 'good' and how much of it, who needs and how much of it. From an inter-state perspective, an analysis of water security would essentially entail an investigation as to why and when states choose to cooperate over water or why and when states tend to use water as a 'bargaining tool' and an 'instrument of politics'. Finally it is essentially a question of survivability. " It is also true that the water resources have rarely been the sole cause of conflict" but should be viewed as a "function of the relationships among social, political, and economic factors, including economic development."

Most Affected Countries

Based on a map published by the Consultative Group on International Agricultural Research (CGIAR),[xix] the countries and regions suffering most water stress are North Africa, the Middle East,[xx] India, Pakistan, Central Asia, China, Chile, South Africa and Australia. Water scarcity is also increasing in other parts of South East Asia.[xxi] South East Asia as a whole covers 3.20% of the surface area but accounts for 21% of population (1995 Census). The annual average replaceable water resources are 6.8% of the total replaceable water resources (Report of the FAO 1997 a[xxii]). The average per capita availability of fresh water in the entire South East Asia region in 1995 was 2265 CUM as against world average of 7000 CUM per capita.[xxiii] As far as India is concerned the major reason for declining water availability in the country is the substantial increase in the population. The annual per capita availability in the country was 6008 CUM per year in 1947 which has declined to 2246 CUM per capita per year in 1997.[xxiv] The pattern of the change with a likely trend up to 2027 has been as tabulated below:-

Table-1.2: Water Availability In India		
Ser No	**Year**	**Availability of water (CUM/Capita/Year)**
a.	1947	6000
b.	1957	5300
c.	1967	4200
d.	1977	3500
e.	1987	3000
f.	1997	2246
g.	2007	2100
h.	2017	2000
j.	2027	1800
Source: Engleman & Roy 1993		

Legal Framework

The problems of water management are compounded in the international realm by the fact that the international laws that govern it are poorly developed, contradictory, and unenforceable as such international laws on allocating water within river-basin are difficult to implement. The United Nations (UN) Convention on the Non-Navigational Uses of International Watercourses approved in 1997 by a vote of 104-3 (though not yet ratified), requires watercourse nations (Article 5) to participate in the use, development, and protection of an international watercourse in an equitable and reasonable manner. In spite of the UN Convention, riparian nations pitch their respective claims and counterclaims based on their interest and interpretation. This raises a fundamental question on whether formal arrangements on long lasting peaceful sharing of river waters can be achieved particularly in regions where the political climate is hostile to co-operative endeavours. In this situation, such long-negotiated instrument of international water law as the 1997 UN Convention on the Non-Navigational Uses of International Watercourses, is of little help as it provides for equally contradictory 'equitable use' and 'no significant harm' principles: while the former is favoured by upstream countries, downstream riparian states insist on emphasising the latter because it protects their own rights. It is also difficult to enforce the Convention in the absence of any international enforcing mechanisms. More importantly, the Convention hardly weighs out a variety of political, social, economic, demographic and environmental factors that encompass each shared river basin.

Water as a Human Right. *Access to at least 20 litres of clean water daily is considered fundamental for the "human right to water" to be respected.* Water is the second most important natural resource (first being air) for human survival. It, however, needs to be noted that legally water has not been recognized as a human right under the international law. The United Nations Development Programme's (UNDP) Human Development Report 2006 focused on the continuous and widespread global water crisis, that over 1 billion people are without access to drinking water[xxv] and another 2.5 billion people worldwide do not enjoy access to basic sanitation. (*Where people are forced to defecate in fields, ditches or buckets, they are deemed to be deprived of access to proper sanitation*).[xxvi] According to the latest Human Development Report; many countries resisted the "Declaration on the Rights of Indigenous People" (DRIP) over the years due to fears of secession threats and loss of state power. Nevertheless, after over two long and tortuous decades of formal debate and discussion it was adopted by the UN General Assembly on 13 September 2007. The Declaration reaffirms that Indigenous People, both; individually and collectively, enjoy all rights already recognized at the international level, and that the special circumstances of their existence as discriminated peoples and long dispossessed of their ancestral resources, demand particular attention by States and by the international community.[xxvii] The Millennium Development Goals (MDGs), born out of the United Nations Millennium Declaration, set out eight specific commitments to be met by 2015, which if fulfilled, would significantly enhance the human condition worldwide. Goal 7, entitled `Environmental Sustainability', was created with the aspiration to reduce by 50 per cent the more than one billion people who lack access to safe drinking water and 2.5 billion who live without basic sanitation. Such deprivation is likely to escalate tensions between states which have competing requirements and a pie to share which is not adequate for both of them. Such a state may lead to water wars.

Case of Surface Water Vs Ground Water: India- A Case Study. A challenge to India's water policies has been the weak legal regime. For example, legislation on ground water extraction is absent in many parts of the country. Under the present framework, which dates back several decades, the land owner is given the right to capture an unlimited amount of ground water without considering the needs and requirements of adjacent land owners. A major constraint in evolving a uniform water management policy is that water is a state subject, included in Entry 17 of the List II in the 7 Schedule of the Constitution. Water issues are politically sensitive with many unresolved issues between the states of the Indian Union. Though Entry 56 in the List I empowers the Centre to legislate on inter-state rivers, but so far political expediency has not allowed inter state issues to get resolved. The Cauvery water dispute between Tamil Nadu and Karnataka is a case in point. Likewise, the Sutlej-Yamuna Link (SYL) canal issue between Punjab and Haryana has been equally emotive and serious challenge to the federal nature of the Indian polity and raise a debate about the control of resources. Taking advantage of the federal structure, states have overplayed the autonomy card and by constantly sniping at the Centre have resisted the idea of river basin organisations. The River Boards Act

1956, for all purposes, is a dead letter. As a result there has been unviable exploitation and short sighted management practices by both upper and lower riparian states resulting in irreversible ecological damage. Similar is the issue within Pakistan (where the dispute over the surface water between various provinces is becoming a major issue; in fact an issue of survival on which the integrity of the nation is coming under a serious threat due to aspirations of various states which are at variance). Even Bangladesh is also suffering on account of over exploitation of the ground water which is due to a serious shortage of surface water because of a long outstanding dispute between India and Bangladesh. Therefore whenever water crisis of a country; internally or with neighbouring countries, is to be tackled, this issue needs to be reflected on and this dichotomy within a country needs to be addressed.[xxviii]

Impact of Rising Population

There is a very strong co-relation between growth of population and the availability of fresh water. Water being finite, its availability gets adversely affected with a rise in population. Since the first civilizations arose in the Nile, Tigris, and Euphrates river basins, population growth and distribution have been intimately linked to the availability of freshwater. Today, nearly 40 percent of the world's food supply is grown under irrigation,[xxix] and a wide variety of industrial processes depend on water. In the last half of this century, population growth and urbanization, together with changes in production and consumption, have placed unprecedented demands on water resources. Already, humans use more than one half of all accessible surface water runoff. This proportion is expected to increase to 70 percent by 2025, thereby reducing the quantity and quality of water available for aquatic ecosystems.[xxx] These ecosystems are critical for a range of life-supporting functions, including the cleaning and recycling of water itself. More than 1 billion people today lack access to an adequate supply of safe water for household use. In next 30 years, as many as 5.5 billion people may live in areas suffering from moderate to severe pressure on water resources, rendering the provision of safe water even more difficult. [xxxi] Figure 1.2 provides a simplified diagram of the relationship between population dynamics and water resources. Population dynamics includes growth, distribution, migration, and other characteristics as shown.

Population dynamics and water resources interact through human uses of water. For example, population growth leads to increased use of water for food production and household use, which, in turn, may exacerbate water shortages, food insecurity, and ultimately lead to economic and social crises. Conversely, naturally scarce water supplies, poor water quality, or uneven distribution of water resources may have adverse effects on the health and ultimately the growth and distribution of populations.

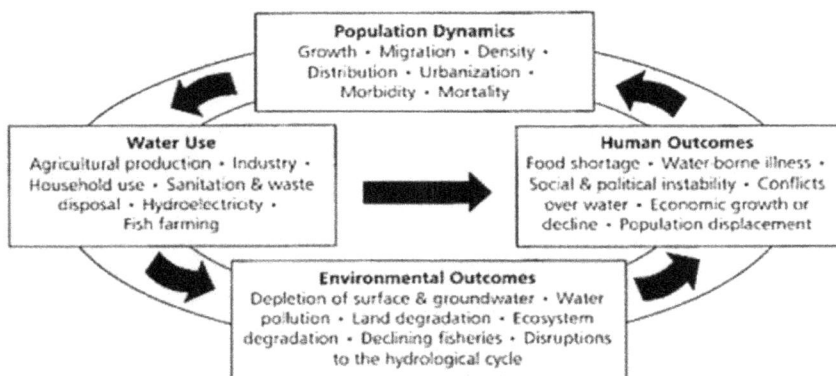

Source: Water and Population Dynamics: Local Approaches to a Global Challenge

Fig-1.2: Water And Population Dynamics

By far the most important demographic trend affecting water resources is population growth. The past two centuries have seen dramatic increases in world population, from one billion in 1800 to six billion at the close of the 20th century. More people and increasing consumption of food, consumer goods, and water for domestic use have created demands for clean freshwater that in many areas exceed nature's capacity to deliver through the hydrological cycle. Figure-1.3 shows how people use freshwater in various parts of the world. Agricultural production accounts for an average of 69 percent of freshwater use worldwide, whereas industry uses 23 percent and households eight percent. The dependence of our food production systems on irrigation, links freshwater with food security, and therefore with human nutrition and well-being.

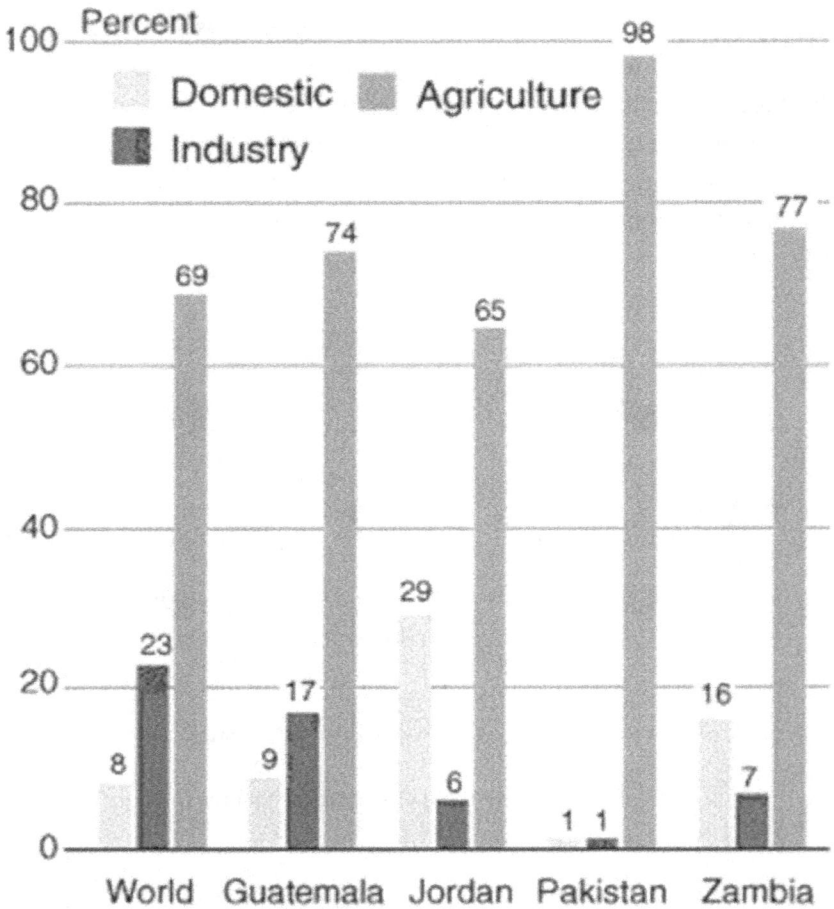

Fig-1.3: Fresh Water Use By Sector

Large dams are a major part of the water-population equation. Dams are most often constructed for hydroelectricity, but they are also used to divert water for irrigation or domestic water supplies and also to control floods. Worldwide, there are some 40,000 large dams (those higher than 15 meters), most of these have been built since 1950. A direct demographic impact of dam building has been the displacement of an estimated 30 million to 60 million people by reservoirs and irrigation works.[xxxii] Population growth and migration often lead to changes in land cover that can affect water resources. For instance, population growth contributes to increased demand for agricultural land, fuel wood and timber, resulting in deforestation. Forests act as water regulators by reducing water runoff and soil erosion and by helping replenish groundwater. They also release moisture into the atmosphere. Therefore, when forests are cut, the hydrological cycle is irrevocably altered unless regeneration occurs. Transformation of forests into pasture or croplands, especially in hilly areas, can lead to soil erosion, siltation of major water courses, flooding, and reductions in groundwater reserves. Water resource issues and population dynamics are not linked adequately in research, policy, and practice. Water resource management can benefit from a multidisciplinary team approach involving hydrologists, engineers, social scientists, and ecologists who, together with local stakeholders, collaborate in all phases of problem identification and analysis, policy dialogue and formulation, program design and implementation, enforcement, and monitoring and evaluation. As urban areas grow, the demand for water resources is likely to grow because urban populations, on average, use more water for domestic and industrial purposes than rural populations. A case study of Jordan brings out that the rapid growth of country's two largest cities, namely; Amman and Zarqua, has led to the unsustainable pumping of a major aquifer. This has reduced water availability for local farmers, and resulted in the desiccation of a wetland of international importance. On the other hand, urbanization can also present opportunities through economies of scale for more efficient and cost-effective water management.

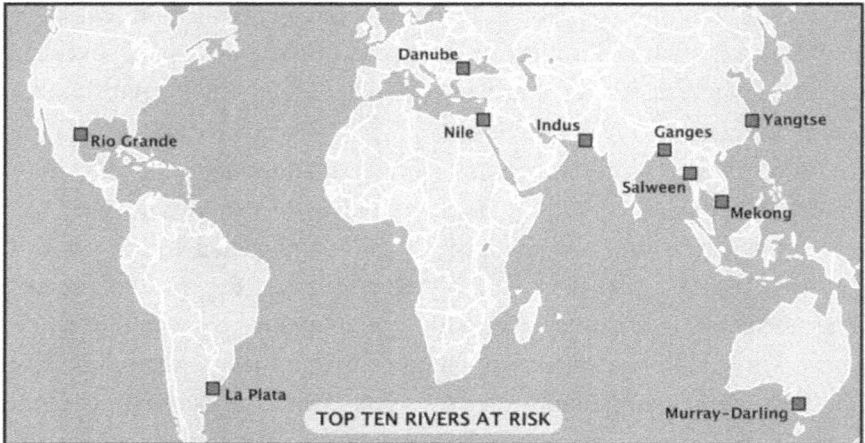

Of the world's top ten rivers at risk, five are sourced on the Tibetan plateau, according to a WWF-UK report published in March 2007. The major risk factors identified include: dams, pollution, shipping, climate change, over-extraction, over-fishing, and invasive species.

Fig-1.4: Major Rivers At Risk Due To Various Environmental And Human
Factors

Food Security and Water Scarcity: India- A Case Study. Rising population world over, especially in the under developed countries, is resulting into increasing demand of food. To produce various types of food matter, water is one of the most important input element. Thus water has a major bearing on the food security of a nation. Over-extraction of water from the underground sources by the farmers trying to grow more to meet the nation's food requirement, is depleting the water stock. If we consider the case of India; recent research shows that in six years starting from 2002 and ending in 2008, more than 109 cubic kilometres of underground water has depleted. This is double the capacity of India's largest reservoir and three times the capacity of the largest reservoir in the US. More significant aspect is that the average replenishment during a year during that period was 30 per cent less than the withdrawals.[xxxiii] Similar/ worse is the situation in many other countries including many of those in South Asia. Thus the gap between demand and supply will continue to rise and also will contribute to rising tension among those countries which compete for the same pie. There are other contributory factors like over exploitation of scarce water resource which results into the source getting polluted which further affects the availability of potable/ usable water. The impact of pollution on the availability is being analysed later in chapter three in detail.

Impact of Climate Change

The water resources have been heavily affected by the global warming phenomenon. Sea levels have risen, glaciers are melting faster and as such retreat of glaciers has accelerated. The most harmful effect of global warming is the shrinking of the Arctic Circle. This phenomenon has caused concerns among all the sectors. Putting it in simpler terms it means that the water bodies would be affected during the long and scorching summers since the rate of evaporation would increase with warmer summers. Water cycle is important for any kind of human activity and global warming would adversely affect this cycle causing a turmoil in the human activities as well as the climactic changes. Global warming is likely to cause excessive floods. The world has already been witnessing this change in last couple of years in the form of heavy floods in Pakistan, China, Europe and North America. The water levels in many regions would go down due to excessive evaporation and this would cause torrential downpours increasing the chance of a deluge. The acceleration in the phenomenon of global warming has caused the ice sheets in the West Antarctic Circle and Greenland to shrink. Carbon sediments have been released in the air and due to the increase of carbon emission the reduction in the ice sheets has taken place. This reduction might cause a huge flood around the world. By the end of twenty first century the water in the sea is expected to rise by 7.1-23.2 inches. Due to the augmentation of global warming effects the Thermohaline circulation might as well get disrupted. The fresh water from the Polar Regions would interrupt the Gulf Stream causing this distress. The implication of a change of course of the gulf stream would have worldwide effect that would drastically accelerate climate change and extremes. The imbalance created in the water cycle by global warming has far reaching effects. Some places on the earth would face extreme temperatures along with torrential rainfall while others would face scarcity of water and drought. In fact, according to the scientists this phenomenon of global warming might even cause desertification in the extreme Tropical areas like Africa. The glacier rich areas like Western North America, Asia, Alps, Indonesia and Africa are suffering badly due to global warming. The melting of glaciers in these regions has raised concerns regarding the increase in water levels. Ocean circulation also suffers due to global warming. The oceans act as the absorber of carbon dioxide and when it reaches the saturation point it fails to absorb any more carbon dioxide. As a result the ocean surface becomes warm.

Acidification of ocean is caused due to the concentration of carbon dioxide in the atmosphere. This is an indirect effect of global warming causing distress to people worldwide. The rise in sea level would cause infiltration of the saline water into the groundwater. This will pose as a potential danger for the health of the living organisms.[xxxiv]

An additional 1.8 billion people would be living by 2080 in water scarce areas if the impacts of climate change are not properly mitigated. [xxxv] "As climate change and adverse water impacts increase in politically charged areas, conflicts are likely to intensify, requiring new and rapid adaptive security strategies." [xxxvi]

Water Pollution

Water pollution poses a significant health risk, especially in heavily industrialized, heavily populated areas like China. In response to a worsening situation in which entire cities lacked safe drinking water, China passed a revised Water Pollution Prevention and Control Law. [xxxvii] The possibility of polluted water making its way across international boundaries, as well as unrecognized water pollution within a poorer country brings up questions of human rights, allowing for international input on water pollution. There is no single framework for dealing with pollution disputes local to a nation.

Potential for Water Disputes

There are 261 international rivers, covering almost one half of the total land surface of the globe, and untold numbers of shared aquifers. The number of international basins has grown from 214 in 1978 to 263 today. These international basins cover 45.3% of total land surface, affect about 40% of the world's population, and account for about 60% of the global river flow. Nineteen basins are shared by five or more riparian countries, with only the Danube being shared by 17 riparian states, whereas five basins – the Congo, Niger, Nile, Rhine and Zambezi – are shared by countries numbering between 9 and 11 (Wolf, 2001). Water has been a cause of political tensions between Arabs and Israelis; Indians and Bangladeshis; Americans and Mexicans; and all ten riparian states of the Nile River. Thus potential for water disputes is correspondingly large, though probability may not be that large,[xxxviii] because besides life, water is necessary for proper sanitation, commercial services, and the production of commercial goods. Thus numerous types of parties can become implicated in a variety of water disputes. For example, corporate entities in a country may pollute water resources shared by a community with the resultant tension, or governments, both; national as well as local may argue with attended probability of disputes over who gets access to a river which because of its location is trans boundary in nature. The broad spectrum of water disputes because of their locale and their complex nature due to commercial interests, environmental concerns, and human rights question, make them difficult to address within the existing frame-work of local and international laws. The problem gets further compounded because many a times the sheer number of potential parties to a single dispute can leave a large list of demands to be met by courts and lawmakers. As a resource, some consider water to be as valuable as oil, needed by nearly every industry, and needed nearly every day.[xxxix] Water shortages can completely cripple an industry just as it can cripple a population, and is capable to affect developed countries as much as it can affect countries with lesser developed infrastructure for water management. Water-based industries are more visible in water disputes, but commerce at all levels can be damaged by lack of water.

Inter-disciplinary Nature of the Resource. Water, by its nature, is an interdisciplinary resource. The attendant disputes can only be resolved through active dialog among various stakeholders across disciplines. Just as the flow of water totally ignores political boundaries, so does it's management strain the capabilities of institutional boundaries. While water managers generally understand and advocate the inherent power of the concept of a watershed as a unit of management, where surface- and groundwater, quantity and quality, are all inexorably connected, the institutions developed to manage the resource follow these tenets only in exception.[xl]

Role of Proactive Diplomacy. Negotiators whose task is to provide timely diplomatic intervention, or apply means of the so-called 'preventive diplomacy', in order to avoid the escalation of a dispute into an open conflict need to build capacity for scenario building to identify areas vulnerable to future conflicts related to water. To do that, they need to identify potential indicators of conflict that incorporate a wide range of physical, social, economic and environmental variables, including those which can be analysed within a Geographic Information System (GIS), and to develop a comprehensive model to explore specific linkages between them. In particular, this method can be applicable in those cases of internationally shared rivers where progress towards successful resolution of a dispute was slow or unachievable. Considering all factors having influence on river basin regime, it is becoming crucial to elaborate meaningful and workable framework to provide resolution to the growing number of water conflict.[xli]

Aim

To analyse the impact of water/ water related differences between the nations on the conflicts/ disputes between the neighbouring countries.

Development Of The Contours Of The Research

Research Question. Is Water a 'Flash Point' for "Future Wars"?

Terms Of Reference. Water from time immemorial has been a cause of disputes between nations all over the world. However attempting to focus on issues over the time span from ancient to modern period and also across the entire globe would be a tall order. Therefore to keep the research focussed in this research it has been kept limited to Asia in general and South Asia in particular. Also the research is limited to examine the issues related to fresh water and not the water as a whole.

Hypothesis. Water related issues may not always be the only cause for the disputes. These may at times act as an stimulant for the problem to explode. Problem may be on account of reasons ranging from boundary disputes to cross border terrorism to illegal migration and many other reasons. In view of these possible reasons following hypothesis has been set to be examined:-

"Water based conflicts are not only on account of water based disputes but are also associated with other disputes between the two adversaries and also among those who have their own internal problems. Water based issues would result into further aggravating the already vitiated environment and cause conflict to become more violent, more decisive and finally may make the conflict more one sided."

Scope

The research shall attempt to examine following aspects:-

► Importance of water in the human life and its criticality for the survivability of a group/ country dependent on it.

► Historical conflicts between the nations which had water related issues at the base of these conflicts.

► An analysis of water availability versus water requirement and reasons for the gap between the two- this will entail an analysis for the entire world with a view to identify the water deficient areas and the conflicts which may be bedevilling them.

► An analysis of Asian conflicts- with a view to identify the direct or indirect causes which have caused them and their impact on the international relations of the concerned country with her neighbours and the region. Also an attempt will be made to identify future flash points.

► Case of South Asia- issues in general, bilateral issues, reasons for them, contributory factors for them, interests of outside powers, their own internal pulls, pressures and contradictions. An attempt will also be made to identify issues which can be solved or which are potential flash points finally examine aspects which need addressing to ease the tensions. Water problems are not only between nations but also between stake holders within a country. Especially in the context of India and Pakistan this issue will be analysed.

► A Way Ahead to address the issues, both; common and bilateral.

► Conclusion.

Chapter-2
Water As A Source of Conflicts Through Ages

"The crisis of our diminishing water resources is just as severe (if less obviously immediate) as any wartime crisis we have ever faced. Our survival is just as much at stake as it was at the time of Pearl Harbor, or the Argonne, or Gettysburg, or Saratoga."

-Jim Wright, U.S. Representative,
The Coming Water Famine, 1966

Water has historically been a source of tension and generally a factor in conflicts that may have started for other reasons,[xlii] including territorial disputes, a fight for resources, and strategic advantage.[xliii] As freshwater is a vital, yet unevenly distributed natural resource, its availability often impacts the living and economic conditions of a country or region. Conflicts occur mostly over freshwater; because freshwater resources are necessary, yet limited, they are the centre of water disputes arising out of need for potable water.[xliv] There have been hundreds of instances of water wars through the ages, involving just about everybody from legendary Assyrian king Nebuchadnezzar to French Emperor Louis XIV and famous military operations such as the Dam Busters raid during the Second World War. In 1503, Leonardo da Vinci and Machiavelli planned to divert the Arno River away from Pisa during hostilities between Pisa and Florence.

Astonishingly, Arizona and California almost went to war in 1935 over the construction of the Parker Dam and diversions from the Colorado River. Water historian Peter Gleick, director of worldwater.org and the author of a unique chronology of water wars, has discovered a huge history of conflict and tension over water resources. The earliest known example dates back to 3,000 BC. Well before the remarkably similar accounts of the Great Flood to be found in the Bible, ancient Sumerian legend tells the tale of the deity Ea, who punished humanity for its sins with a devastating six-day storm.

As mentioned earlier; conflicts on account of water are as old as human history. One of the earliest recorded water war was some 4,500 years ago, when the two Mesopotamian city-states, Lagash and Umma, went to war.[xlv] In ancient Greece, Spartans have known to have poisoned the wells during the Peloponnesian War. Closer home first known battle, in Indian Subcontinent over water, was between the kingdom of Kapilvastu and Licchavis during the period 500 BCE. It would be interesting to note that, one of the most legendary conflict in the Islamic History, The Battle of Karbala was finally reduced to a battle for water when Ibn Sa'ad the local commander of the forces of the Umayyad Caliph Yazid I blocked the access to Euphrates waters to Imam Hussein and a small group of his followers. In fact Yazid I who had usurped the power by dubious means, had ordered his commanders to seize the Imam's allegiance of loyalty at any cost, even by brutal force. The commanders had to assemble a relatively large army, surrounding Imam Hussein's camp in a desert called Karbala in Iraq (See Fig 2.2).Then they cut off the basic necessities to the camp, including access to water.[xlvi] The Battle of Karbala took place on the Muharram the 10th day of Muharram, in the year 61 AH of the Islamic calendar[xlvii] (October 10, 680)[xlviii] at Karbala, in present day Iraq (See Fig 2.1). The battle was between a small group of supporters and relatives of Muhammad's grandson Hussein ibn Ali, and a much larger military detachment from the forces of Yazid I, the Umayyad caliph, whom Hussein had refused to recognise. Ubayd Allah ibn Ziyad local governor of the region of the Calif, appointed Umar ibn Sa'ad to command the battle against Hussein ibn Ali. Ibn Ziyad sent a brief letter to Umar ibn Sa'd that commanded, "Prevent Hussein and his followers from accessing water and do not allow them to drink a drop [of water]. Ibn Sa'ad followed the orders, and 5,000 horsemen blockaded the Euphrates. One of Hussein's followers met Umar ibn Sa'ad and tried to negotiate some sort of access to water, but was denied. The water blockade continued up to the end of the battle on the 10th day of Muharram, (October 10, 680 CE).[xlxi] Al-Abbas ibn Ali, a member (a brother) of Husain's entourage, in a desperate move, advanced towards a branch of the Euphrates along a dyke and managed to reach the water line. Umar ibn Sa'ad, commander of Yazid's Forces, while giving orders for an all out assault on Al-Abbas ibn Ali, is believed to have said that if he (Al-Abbas ibn Ali) succeeded in taking water back to his camp, they would not be able to defeat them till the end of the time stipulated. A massive enemy army blocked his (Al-Abbas ibn Ali) way and surrounded him. He was ambushed from behind a bush and showered with arrows and other weapons. Finally, Al-Abbas ibn Ali was felled to death in his heroic effort to bring water to the thirsty women and children of Imam Husain's party without success. In the words of Hussein ibn Ali this setback broke the back of the team. Hussein ibn Ali said: "Abbas your death is like the breaking of my back". Hussein and all his supporters were killed, including Hussein's six month old infant son, Ali al-Asghar ibn Husayn, and the women and children were taken as prisoners. The dead are regarded as martyrs by Muslims, and the battle has a central place in Shia history and tradition, and has frequently been recounted in Shia Islamic literature.

Fig-2.1 Battle Of Karbala

There had been 200 known conflicts in the history for water and the number is growing.[1] (See Appendices A and B attached). In recent times Battle of Beersheba (1917) during World War I was for the water sources of Palestine.[2] Since 1948 close to 40 incidents of hostilities have taken place over water resources, most of which have taken place in the Middle East; Jordan Basin & Tigris- Euphrates and Africa; Nile, Volta and Zambezi River. David Zhang of Hong Kong University published a study linking water shortages to violence throughout history. Analyzing half a millennium's worth of human conflict—more than 8,000 wars—Zhang concluded that climate change and resulting water shortages had been a far greater trigger than previously imagined. "We are on alert, because this gives us the indication that resource shortage is the main cause of war," Zhang told the London Times.[2] Even in India during medieval period outcome of many a battles of forts were for access or denial of the water. Also battles in the desert terrain had always been for the water sources.

---

[1] http://www.islam.org/karbala
[2] UNESCO publishes first world map of underground trans boundary aquifers accessed Nov 21, 2008.

Asia is home to 57 basins and a large number of them are likely to emerge as flash points. Important likely regions are Central Asia, South Asia and Mekong Sub Region. Some of the other important known conflicts over the years are as mentioned in subsequent paragraphs.

West Asia. Invariably, writings on "water wars" point to the arid and hostile Middle East as an example of a worst-case scenario, where armies have, in fact been mobilized and shots fired over this scarce and precious resource. Elaborate, if misnamed; "hydraulic imperative" theories have been developed for the region, particularly between Arabs and Israelis, citing water as the prime motivator for military strategy and territorial conquest. It is worth noting that the region has only 01% of water for a population which is 5% of the world's population.[3] Important conflicts have been as follows:-

▶ **Rivers: Euphrates and Tigris-** Both the Tigris and Euphrates Rivers originate in the mountains of eastern Turkey with the majority of their water head is generated from annual rainfall and snowmelt. Approximately 98% of the waters of the Euphrates is generated within Turkey,[li] with the remaining two percent gets added as the river flows through Syria. A negligible amount is contributed to the annual flow of water in the river as it passes through Iraq, The Tigris receives almost half of its waters initially from Turkey and a negligible amount as it forms border firstly between both Turkey and Syria, and thereafter between Syria and Iraq, and is then fed nearly half its remaining waters from tributaries in Iraq, many of which originate in the mountains of western Iran. The rivers join at the Shatt al-'Arab north of Basra and flow together for a little more than 160 kilometres miles to the Persian Gulf. The rivers have several small tributaries which feed into the system from shallow freshwater lakes, swamps, and marshes, all surrounded by desert. It needs to be noted that the Tigris–Euphrates Basin is primarily shared by Turkey, Syria and Iraq, with many Tigris tributaries originating in Iran. The construction of numerous dams, hydroelectric plants, and irrigation canals on the Tigris and Euphrates Rivers over the past

---

[3] Sutherland, Ben (Mar 18, 2003), "water shortages Foster Terrorism", BBC News, retrieved Ja 14, 2010.

30 years as part of the Southeast Anatolian Development Project (known as the "GAP") has given Turkey, the upper riparian, ability to unilaterally control all water flow of the Euphrates and almost half of the flow of the Tigris. The extensive quantities of water being harnessed through the dozens of projects that constitute GAP have the overarching goal of increasing the standard of living and economic development in the South Eastern portion of the country. In this connection a statement of Suleyman Demirel, Turkish Prime Minister during July 1992 is quite significant. He said, "We do not say we share their oil resources. They cannot say they share our water resources. This is a right of sovereignty. We have the right to do anything we like." Syria is the middle riparian and has historically relied on waters from the Yarmuk, Banyas and Orontes Rivers to satisfy the majority of its water needs prior to 1970s. Syria has, over the years, drastically increased its use of Euphrates through construction of the Tabqa Dam in 1973, and a series of dams in recent decades, to supply irrigation waters for a vast region of Syria. Iraq is the lower riparian and has historically been the heaviest user of waters of both rivers for irrigation of agricultural lands. They invested heavily in construction along both rivers in the 1950s and 1960s to harness these resources for power generation production and irrigation and continued to invest capital in water storage projects in recent decades. The altered river flow and increased water use by the other two riparian states, coupled with their continued need and heavy use of freshwater resources, has placed them in the most precarious position of the three major players. Since 1960s and 1970s, when Turkey began the GAP project in earnest, water disputes have regularly occurred in addition to the associated dams' effects on the environment. In addition, Syrian and Iranian dam construction has also contributed to political tension within the basin, particularly during a drought. A number of conflicts; through ages have taken place over water and water related issues among upper riparian; Turkey and lower riparian states; Iraq and Syria. Iraq has historically practiced heavy use of the waters of both rivers for agricultural irrigation, with little diversion of waters from Syria or Turkey. In recent decades, however, both Turkey and Syria have

undertaken significant projects to alter, store, and use flows from both rivers. Turkey's projects have been much more significant to the region and have established its position of power to use or abuse the waters of these rivers with relative impunity. Iran, although a riparian, is not given significant focus due to its limited role in the current politics of the basin. The issue of water rights became a point of contention for Iraq, Turkey and Syria beginning in the 1960s, when Turkey implemented a public-works project (the GAP project) aimed at harvesting the water from the Tigris and Euphrates rivers through the construction of 22 dams, for irrigation and hydroelectric energy purposes. Although the water dispute between Turkey and Syria was more problematic, the GAP project was also perceived as a threat by Iraq. The tension between Turkey and Iraq about the issue was further aggravated due to Syria and Turkey's participation in the UN embargo against Iraq following the Gulf War. However, the issue had never become as significant as the water dispute between Turkey and Syria.[lii] The 2008 drought in Iraq sparked new negotiations between Iraq and Turkey over trans-boundary river flows. Although the drought affected Turkey, Syria and Iran as well, Iraq complained regularly about reduced water flows. Iraq particularly complained about the Euphrates River because of a large number of dams on the river. Turkey agreed to increase the flow several times, beyond its means in order to supply Iraq with extra water. Iraq has seen significant decline in water storage and crop yields because of the drought. To make matters worse, Iraq's water infrastructure has suffered from years of conflict and neglect.[liii] In 2008, Turkey, Iraq and Syria agreed to restart the Joint Trilateral Committee on water for the three nations for better water resources management. Turkey, Iraq and Syria signed a memorandum of understanding on September 03, 2009, in order to strengthen communication within the Tigris–Euphrates Basin and to develop joint water-flow-monitoring stations. On September 19, 2009, Turkey formally agreed to increase the flow of the Euphrates River to 450 to 500 centi metres, but only until October 20, 2009. In exchange, Iraq agreed to trade petroleum with Turkey and help curb Kurdish militant activity in their border region. One of Turkey's last large GAP dams on the Tigris – the Ilisu Dam – is strongly opposed by Iraq and is the source of political strife.[liv]

Fig-2.2 River Basin Of Rivers Tigris And Euphrates

- **Jordan River-**The Jordan River is a major water source that flows through the Jordan Rift Valley into the Dead Sea. The River Jordan is only 20 yards wide in some places, and its deepest point is around 17 feet. It extends from tributaries at the base of Mount Hermon to its main source, the Kinneret, and then down to the Dead Sea. The river forms the boundary between the country of Jordan and the West Bank. The Jordan River is a key water source for Israel, Jordan, Syria, and Lebanon; water remains a central issue to the Middle East conflict.[lv] The cultural and religious significance of the Jordan River is equal to that of its modern practical uses. It is the place where Joshua and the tribes of Israel crossed into Jericho, and also the scene of many biblical battles. In Christian tradition, the Jordan is the scene of the baptism of Jesus by John the Baptist. Christian pilgrims can today visit the traditional site of the baptism at a place called Yardenit, at the point where the Jordan River flows out of the Kinneret. Israel and Jordan have signed treaties on Jordan River-related matters. For Israel, the water of the Jordan River is an absolute necessity for the purposes of drinking water and for irrigation. In the Tanakh, the Jordan River is mentioned several times as a source of fertility for Israel. The Jordan was crossed by Judas Maccabeus and his brother Jonathan Maccabaeus during their war with the Nabataeans[lvi] (1 Maccabees 5:24). A little later the Jordan was the scene of the battle between Jonathan and Bacchides, in which the latter was defeated[lvii] (1 Maccabeus 9:42-49).

Fig-2.3: Jordan River

▶ The Jordan River basin, some 18,300 Sq Kms in area, straddles the territories of four separate modern Arab political entities, and a Jewish one. These are Lebanon, Syria, the West Bank (represented by the Palestinian Authority), and the Hashemite Kingdom of Jordan on the Arab side, and Israel (see Fig 2.3) respectively. Before these entities were created and became separate and independent of one another, unilateral designs for the utilization of the basin waters were laid down.

▶ The conflict over the waters of the Jordan basin dates back to the late 1800s when the Zionist Organization chose Palestine to establish a national home for the Jews. Several water plans were prepared to harness those waters for the benefit of the side that prepared them. The Zionist Organization had plans prepared as early as 1899 and it continued working until Israel was established and the new state took over the chores of more detailed planning and implementation.

▶ The indigenous societies, primarily the Hashemite Kingdom of Jordan, came up with competing plans starting in 1939 and had a Master Plan prepared for the development of the Jordan Valley. Several water plans were prepared under the mandate to utilize the waters of the Jordan basin[lviii] (Naff and Matson, 1984). Two plans were prepared by Mavromatis and by Henriques of Great Britain in 1922 and 1928 respectively. A concession was awarded by the Ministry of the Colonies in 1921 to the Jewish engineer Pinhas Rutenberg for the utilization of the Jordan and its major tributary the Yarmouk for power generation, and to drain the Huleh marshes.

▶ The power concession was sanctioned by the Transjordan Cabinet on January 8 1928 and a power station was put into operation in 1932. In 1935, the Palestine Land Development Company, an arm of the Zionist Organization, prepared a plan for the transfer of water from the Jordan to the Upper Galilee.

▶ The British government dispatched a commission in 1936, headed by Lord Peel to find a solution for the mounting unrest in Palestine, and followed it with another headed by Mr Woodhead. The commissions recommended among other measures, a partition of Palestine between the Palestinian

Arabs and the Jews, and setting an upper limit for the quota of Jewish immigrants.

▸ In the wake of those missions, the government of Transjordan initiated a study for the utilization of the Jordan waters to determine their capacity to support three states: Jordan, Palestine, and a Jewish state. The study was conducted by a British engineer, Michael Ionedis, who had worked on the Tigris and the Euphrates in Iraq earlier and later became the Director of Development in the government of Transjordan.

▸ Water projects soon became a cause for military clashes, as Israel attempted to implement unilaterally its National Water Carrier project, whose intake on the Jordan River was originally located in a demilitarized zone between Israel and Syria close to Jisr Banat Ya'coub (see Fig 2.4). The Israeli project was meant to transfer Jordan River waters to irrigate as much as possible of its arid south and make room for more Jewish immigrants to the new state, something that Arabs strongly resented; they gave priority to the return of Palestinian refugees over receiving more Jewish immigrants.

▸ One of the most volatile region in the world through the ages has been Jordan River Basin where conflicts on account of water between Israel, Lebanon, Jordan and Palestine Territories had been quite regular through ages. In this connection the caveat laid by the late King Hussein of Jordan while signing the Peace accord with Israel in 1979 was quite telling. The Late monarch said that Jordan will never go to war with Israel again except to save her water resources.[4]

---

[4] http://www.mideastnews.com/waterwar.htm

Fig-2.4: The Ceasefire Line Between Syria And Israel (1949)

Africa.

Nile River[5] -The Nile is a major north-flowing river in North Eastern Africa, generally regarded as the longest river in the world. It is 6,650 km (4,130 miles) long. It runs through ten countries of Sudan, South Sudan, Burundi, Rwanda, Democratic Republic of the Congo, Tanzania, Kenya, Ethiopia, Uganda and Egypt.[lxi] It has two major tributaries; the White Nile and the Blue Nile. The White Nile is longer and rises in the Great Lakes region of the Central Africa, with the most distant source still undetermined but located either in Rwanda or in Burundi. It flows north through Tanzania, Lake Victoria, Uganda and South Sudan. The Blue Nile is the source of most of the water and fertile soil. It begins at Lake Tana in Ethiopia at12°02′09″N 037°15′53″E and flows into Sudan from the South East direction. The two rivers meet near the Sudanese capital of Khartoum. The Nile basin is along a region which is water deficient and as such has been a source of conflicts through the history between Ethiopia the upper riparian and the lower riparian states of Egypt and Sudan. Egypt is essentially dependent on waters of River Blue Nile and the present dispute

---

[5] " Water Conflict and Cooperation: Lessons from Nile River Basin", Kaneri-Mbote, Patricia (Jan 2007)Navigating Peace (Woodrow Wilson International Centre for Scholars).

between Egypt and Ethiopia is on account of the construction of the GIBE III Dam by Ethiopia. In this connection statement of the then President of Egypt Anwar Sadat, after signing the Peace Accord with Israel in 1979, is significant. He said that Egypt will never go to war again, except to protect her water resources.[6]

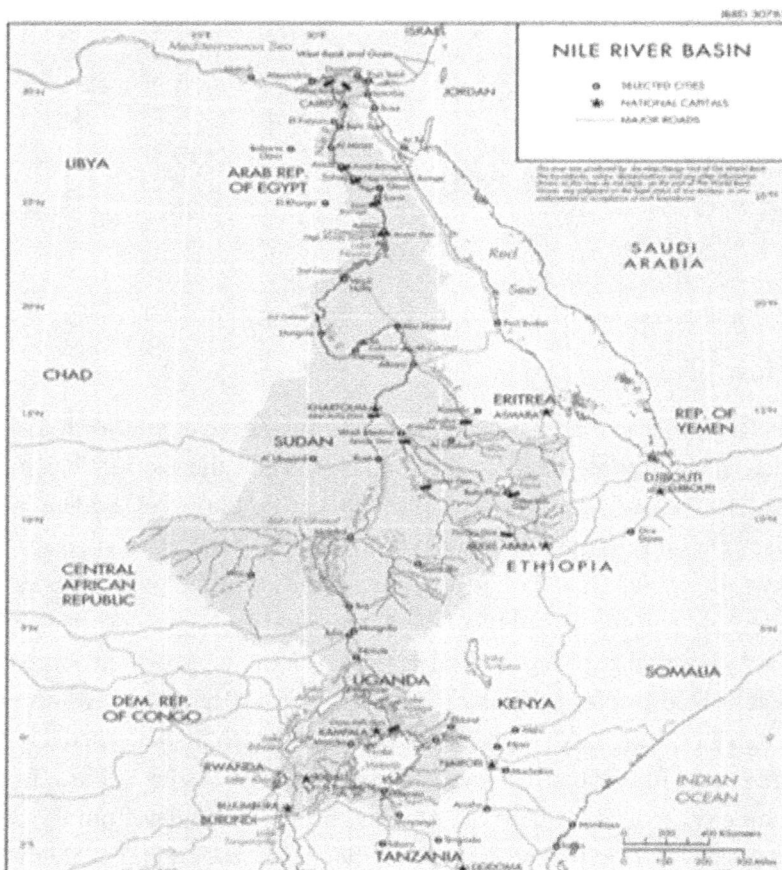

---

[6] Ibid 5.

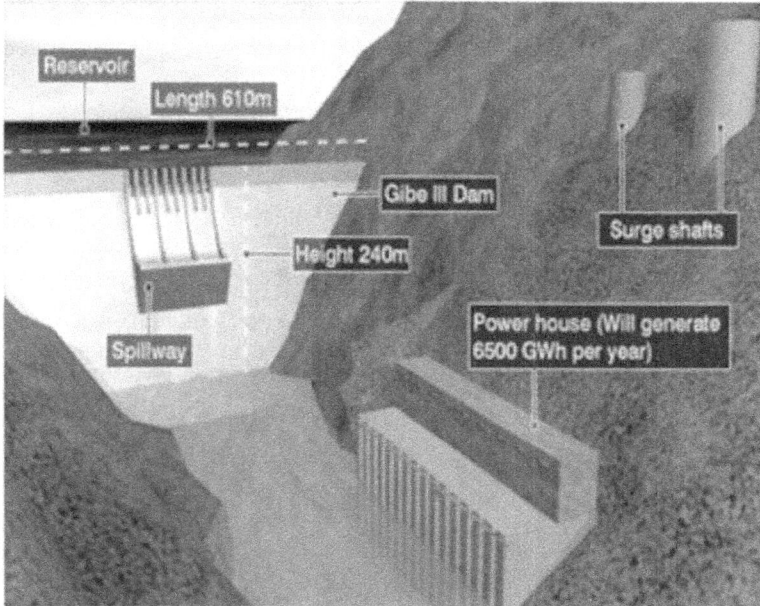

Fig-2.5 River Nile Basin And Gibe III Hydro Electric Project

▶ The other possible flashpoints in Africa had been; the Niger, Volta and Zambezi basins.[7]

▶ In 2007 an 18-month study of Sudan by the UN Environment Program concluded that the conflict in Darfur had its roots in climate change and water shortages. According to this report, due to disappearing pasture and evaporating water, and holes the rainfall is down by 30 percent over 40 years in some parts of the Sahel which had sparked dispute between herders and farmers and threatened to trigger a succession of new wars across Africa.[lxii]

▶ Recent humanitarian catastrophes, such as the Rwandan Genocide of 1994 have been linked back to water conflicts.[lxiii]

Central Asia. Central Asia lies in the heart of the Eurasian continent and comprises of the five former Soviet republics, namely: Kazakhstan, Kyrgyzstan, Tajikistan, Turkmenistan and Uzbekistan, as well as of northern Afghanistan and China's Xinjiang Uighur Autonomous Region. The climate in Central Asia is hot and dry, with low and irregular precipitation. The annual precipitation in the lowland is only 80-200 mm, concentrated in the winter and spring, while in the mountains it ranges 600-800 mm. The region has very different climatic zones with distinct water demands for irrigation.

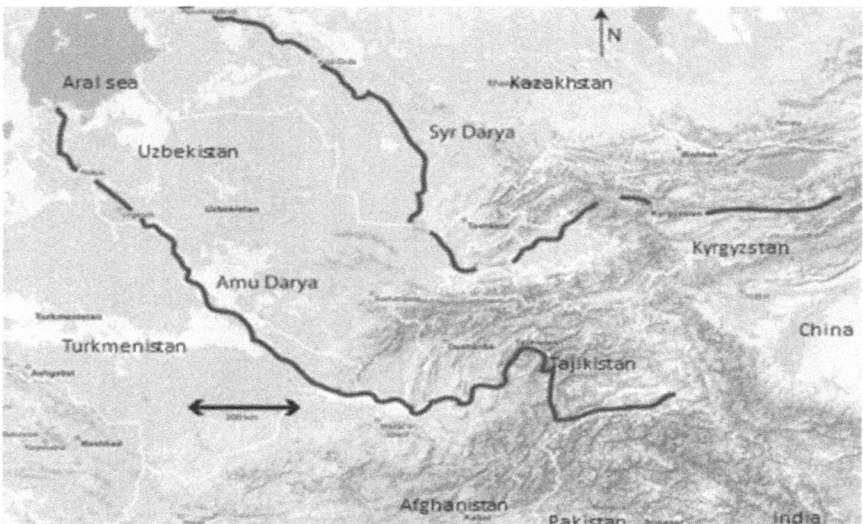

Fig-2.6 Central Asia River Basins

---

[7] http://news.bbc.co.uk/2/hi/africa/454926.stm

▶ **River Basins-**All the countries of the Central Asia share basins of the two major rivers in the region: the Amu Darya and the Syr Darya. The basins of these rivers form the Aral Sea Basin. The Amu Darya catchment basin constitutes 62% of the region's surface water resources and the Syr Darya forms the remaining 30%. The Basin's population of over 35 million occupies about 1.5 million Sq Kms and population density varies from about 10 persons per Sq Kms in the desert plains to over 300 in the valleys and foothills of the mountains.[lxiv] Agricultural, industrial and personal needs can only be satisfied through diversion of water from the Syr Darya, Amu Darya and Zeravshan rivers and their tributaries. The Amu Darya is Central Asia's largest river and has the highest water bearing capacity of the region draining the catchment of 692,300 Sq Kms. It originates in the Pamir Mountains and forms the Pyandj river at the Tajik-Afghan border. Near town of Termez in Uzbekistan the Pyandj is joined by the Surkhandarya to form the Amu Darya. The Pyandj is augmented by a number of major tributaries including the Vaksh and Kafirnigan. From its origin, the Amu Darya flows 2540 km west across Tajikistan, Uzbekistan and Turkmenistan and finally crosses the Uzbek region of Karakalpakstan to discharge into the Aral Sea. Discharge is closely related to the amount of snowfall and summer temperatures, with mean annual flow between 46.9 and 108.4 Cubic Kms per annum with an average of 78.5 Cubic Kms.[lxv] The Syr Darya is the longest (2,212 km) river in Central Asia, having less catchment of 219,000 Sq kms. It rises in the mountains in Kyrgyzstan and has two major tributaries: the Naryn fed by over 700 glaciers in the Tien Shan, and the Kara Darya sourcing in the Ferghana and Alay mountains. After confluence in eastern Uzbekistan, these form the Syr Darya which crosses into Tajikistan and then re-enters Uzbekistan and finally flows into Kazakhstan where it discharges into the Aral Sea. Its discharge is smaller than the one of the Amu Darya, ranging from 21.4 to 54.1 Cubic Kms per annum, with the average of 37.2 Cubic Kms.[lxvi]

▶ **History of the Area-** The major states of the 19th century's Central Asia, the Bukhara Emirate, the Khiva and the Kokand Khanates, were put under the control of the Russian Empire by the end of the century, when the Anglo-Russian Agreement curtailed further Russian expansion in the vicinity of the Northern borders of British India. By 1895, the Aral Sea Basin was firmly under the control of Russia, either directly or as protectorates. Thus, the scene for the future colonial relationship was set that persisted under the Soviets and indirectly led to the Aral Sea environmental catastrophe. The 1917 Bolshevik Revolution toppled the Provisional Government (in power between March-November 1917) and proclaimed Russia the Soviet Republic, eventually to be replaced by the Union of Soviet Socialist Republics. The creation of Central Asian States, in their modern borders, was finished by 1924. In fact, the USSR established modern-day Central Asian States set to become independent nations in future.[lxvii]   In 1991, after the Belovezh Agreement was signed by the leaders of the three most powerful Soviet republics – Russia, Ukraine and Belarus, the Soviet Union ceased to exist and the Soviet Republics became independent. The independence appeared somewhat of a shock for the five Central Asian Republics, as there was little domestic pressure for them to leave the Soviet Union and also there was no real history of these republics as independent nations.

▶ **Water Sharing Problems Post Breakup of Soviet Union-**Post breakup of the Soviet Union, the irrigation system which was a command irrigation system in the Central Asian republics is now being used by the individual republics to suit their immediate requirements. As such Syr and Amu Darya are not even reaching Aral Sea which is almost getting dried up. Such a situation has created enough tensions between Tajikistan and Kyrgyzstan as upper riparian states and Turkmenistan, Uzbekistan and Kazakhstan as lower riparian states. Although, Central Asian Republics went for an accord, for water sharing, but the problem is far from over. Central Asia has become notorious worldwide, as a site of the most dramatic environmental disaster, the Aral Sea Crisis. Once, it was the fourth largest lake in the world, but now the Aral Sea has shrunk by more than half, over the last forty years. [lxviii] The major reason for that was increased discharge of inflowing water for irrigation. Grand Soviet schemes for the production of cotton, rice and other irrigated cultures required huge amounts of water. Despite that, water consumption goes at the same pace as before. The most populated nation in the region Uzbekistan (25 million in 2002), alone uses three-fifths of regional water supplies. In fact, industrial consumption of water in Uzbekistan and Turkmenistan is twice that of the consumption in Kyrgyzstan and Tajikistan.[lxix] Wasteful use of water on Uzbekistan's very large irrigated area has contributed to a dramatic decline of the combined flow of Amu Darya and Syr Darya and acted as a major factor in the Aral Sea Crisis. Not surprisingly, this situation has already led to numerous small-scale local conflicts, beginning in the late 1980s when the central authorities weakened their grip on Central Asia. In 1990, the outbreak of conflict in the Kyrgyz town of Osh, on the border with Uzbekistan, claimed over 300 lives and was provoked by fierce competition for water together with high population density, limited arable land and ethnic dimension (large population of Uzbeks living in the area).

► **Water Conflicts-**Since summer 1993, there have been serious water tensions between Kyrgyzstan and Uzbekistan. Kyrgyzstan was blamed by the Uzbek authorities for releasing excessive water from the Toktogul Reservoir. Extra water did not reach the Aral Sea but was dumped instead into the Aydarkul depression, the large 'sinus' which has developed as a result of years of negligence. [lxx] In 1997, Uzbekistan has deployed 130,000 troops on the Kyrgyz border to guard the reservoirs straddling the two countries.[lxxi] In June 2001, the Kyrgyz parliament adopted a law classifying water as a commodity, and the government followed up by announcing that the downstream countries would be charged for the water they use. Uzbekistan's response was to cut off all deliveries of gas to Kyrgyzstan and accuse Kyrgyzstan of failing to honour the barter agreement to provide Uzbekistan with water in return for oil and gas. Although weaker in political and military terms Kyrgyzstan acknowledged this failure, Uzbekistan would be emboldened to behave in a more aggressive manner towards its neighbours. The two were on the verge of violent conflict for several times.[lxxii]

United States of America. Even a country like USA, which is otherwise surplus in water resources, had its share of water problems. But most of these were within the states of the Union. In 1901, the year when Queen Victoria died and Rudyard Kipling wrote Kim, the State of Kansas sued the State of Colorado for diverting so much water from the Arkansas River in the central United States that it ran dry in summer. The two States eventually signed a contract with each other, but they became embroiled in a dispute over the interpretation of the terms of the agreement. Legal battles continued intermittently until the U.S. Supreme Court issued a decision in 2004.[lxxiii] Another conflict in USA was known as The California Water Wars. It was a series of conflicts between the city of Los Angeles, farmers and ranchers in the Owens Valley of Eastern California, and environmentalists. As Los Angeles grew in the late 1800s, it started to outgrow its water supply. Fred Eaton, mayor of Los Angeles, realized that water could flow from Owens Valley to Los Angeles via an aqueduct. The aqueduct construction was overseen by William Mulholland and was finished in 1913. The water rights were acquired through political fighting and, Farmers in the Owens Valley may not have received fair value for their water rights.[lxxiv] By the 1920s, so much water was diverted from the Owens Valley that agriculture became difficult. This led to the farmers trying to destroy the aqueduct. Los Angeles prevailed and kept the water flowing. By 1926, Owens Lake at the bottom of Owens Valley was completely dry due to water diversion. The water needs of Los Angeles kept growing. In 1941, Los Angeles diverted water that previously fed Mono Lake into the aqueduct. Mono Lake, north of Owens Valley, is an important ecosystem for migrating birds. The lake level dropped after the water was diverted, which threatened the migrating birds. Environmentalists, led by David Gaines and the Mono Lake Committee engaged in a series of litigation with Los Angeles between 1979 and 1994. The litigation forced Los Angeles to stop diverting water from around Mono Lake, which has started to rise back to a level that can support its ecosystem.[lxxv]

Fig-2.7: The Los Angeles Aqueduct In The Owens Valley

Historical Perspective of Water based conflicts in Europe. Europe is generally a continent where the water disputes have been minor in nature. Credit substantially goes to good conflict resolution mechanism being in place. River Rhine and River Danube are two international rivers. The riparian states of Rhine River have a common historical back ground. Throughout the history parts of the Rhine river have functioned as the border between the states. The Rhine regions are connected through several conflicts, part as aggressor and part as conquered region. Some Rhine regions were hard hit by violent conflict especially in Alsace-Lorraine (Border between Germany and France) and the Netherlands. The conflict resolution in the riparian states is through The Central commission for Navigation on the Rhine which dates back to1815 Congress of Vienna. Today it is based on the so called Mannheim Act (revised Rhine Navigation Act of 1868), in its 1963 version. The Central Commission for Navigation on the Rhine is the oldest European Organisation that is still active. It success since nineteenth century, has made the idea of European integration a reality. The other known dispute, since 1980 are as tabulated below:-

Table 2.1: International Water Resources And Recent International Conflicts In Europe (Since 1980).

Ser No	River/Lake System	Countries Involved	Main Cause of Dispute
1.	Rhine	Switzerland, Germany, France, The Netherlands	Industrial pollution
2.	Szamos,Tisza	Hungary, Romania, Yugoslavia	Pollution from mining
3.	Danube	Hungary, Romania, Yugoslavia	Pollution from mining
4.	Danube	Yugoslavia, NATO	Pollution from military activities
5.	Danube	Slovakia, Hungary	Dam, water flow
6.	Danube	Bugaria, Romania	Agricultural pollution
7.	Drava	Croatia, Hungary	Dam project
8.	Neretva	Bosnia-Herzegovina, Croatia	Flooding, protection of estuary and marine areas, water supply
9.	Evros/Maritza/ Merec	Greece, Bulgaria, Turkey	Dam, reduced water flow
10.	Nestos/Mesta	Greece, Bulgaria	Irrigation, pollution
11.	Aoos	Greece , Albania	Dam
12.	Axios/Vardar	Greece, FYR Macedonia	Dam, irrigation

Sources: Gleick, 1998; Horsman, 2001; and, Vlachos and Mylopoulos, 2000.

Growth of Rules and Laws on Sharing of International Water Channels[lxxvi]

The multi-dimensional uses of international rivers and lakes have been classified, for legal purposes, into navigational and non-navigational uses. The main reason for such a distinction is that a separate set of international rules has emerged for each of the two uses.

Rules Regulating Navigational Uses. The rules to regulate water of the international rivers started emerging as early as the beginning of the 19th century. At that time, navigational uses were more important than non-navigational uses, and it was also relatively easier to get an agreement on rules regulating such usage. Indeed, the first treaty on navigational usage was concluded at the beginning of the 19th century, and that treaty was followed by a number of other agreements. In this connection it needs to be noted that by the beginning of the 19th century, navigation had became the single largest user of rivers in Europe, virtually turning such rivers into international highways. The extensive use of rivers for navigation necessitated some form of regulation, and prompted the major European powers to conclude a treaty in 1815, named the Act of the Congress of Vienna. The Act established the principle of freedom of navigation for all riparian states on the rivers they share, on a reciprocal basis, as well as its priority over other uses. The trend towards freedom and priority of navigation established by the Act of the Congress of Vienna continued to prevail, and was confirmed and expanded in 1885 by another treaty, the General Act of the Congress of Berlin with regard to the Congo and Niger Rivers in Africa. The purpose of that Act was to facilitate the movement of the colonial powers in Africa by opening some of its rivers for all of them. As a result, this Act extended the freedom of navigation to non-riparian states as well. The 1919 Peace Treaty of Versailles continued the liberalization trend in navigation by opening all the navigable rivers in Europe to all the European countries.

Rules Regulating Non Navigational Uses. Although some basic customary rules have emerged over a period of time, yet there is still no universal treaty in force that regulates the non-navigational uses of international watercourses. The United Nations Convention on the Law of the Non-Navigational Uses of International Watercourses (the UN Convention), which was adopted by the United Nations General Assembly on 21 May 1997, after 23 years of preparatory work by the International Law Commission (ILC), and extensive deliberations by the General Assembly thereafter, has yet to enter into force and effect. non-navigational uses of rivers, such as irrigation and hydropower, were not major competitors with navigation at that time. The steady growth in population also rendered other uses, such as domestic and irrigation, more demanding and necessary. The Barcelona Convention (Convention and Statute on the Regime of Navigable Waterways of International Concern), which was concluded in 1921, reconfirmed the principle of freedom of navigation, but recognized other uses of rivers as well. Two years later in 1923, the Geneva Convention (General Convention Relating to the Development of Hydraulic Power Affecting More than One State) was adopted. That Convention dealt with the right of any riparian state to carry out on its territory any operations for development of hydraulic power that it may consider desirable, subject to "the limits of international law". Further necessitated by the increasing and heavy reliance on rivers and lakes for non-navigational purposes as a result, largely because of the reconstruction and development efforts after the Second World War. The steady growth in population was another important factor. However, this increased reliance on rivers and lakes was not accompanied by the adoption of any official rules to regulate such non-navigational uses. One of those principles is that of absolute territorial sovereignty which is also known as the Harmon Doctrine. Judson Harmon was the Attorney General of the United States of America when he gave an opinion in 1895 regarding the uses of the waters of the Rio Grande that the United States and Mexico share. His opinion concluded that a state is free to dispose, within its territory, waters of an international river in any manner it deems fit, without concern for the harm or adverse impact that such use may cause to other riparian states. However, this opinion and the principle it entailed were criticized and discredited, for obvious reasons, by subsequent decisions of international tribunals and writings of experts in this field. The basic principles of international law, contrary to the Harmon Doctrine, prohibit riparian states from causing harm to other states, and call for cooperation and peaceful resolution of disputes. A Second Principle that emerged is about the absolute territorial integrity. It establishes the right of a riparian state to demand continuation of the natural flow of an international river into its territory from the upper riparian or riparian states, but imposes a duty on that state not to restrict such natural flow of waters to other lower riparian states. At most, this principle tolerates only minimal uses by an upstream state. In essence, this principle is the exact opposite of the principle of absolute territorial sovereignty as it is intended to favour downstream riparian states, often by protecting existing uses or prior appropriation. This principle has also been criticized and, like the Harmon Doctrine, is not recognized as a part of contemporary international water law. The Third Principle, that of limited territorial sovereignty or limited territorial integrity, asserts that every riparian state has a right to use the waters of the international river, but is under a corresponding duty to ensure that such use does not harm other riparian states. Accordingly, this principle restricts both principles discussed above, and asserts the equality of all riparian states in the utilization of the waters of an international river. The Fourth Principle is regarding the community of co-riparian states in the waters of an international river. The basis of this principle is that the entire river basin is an economic unit, and the rights over the waters of the entire river are vested in the collective body of the riparian states, or divided among them either by agreement or on the basis of proportionality. As such, this principle is a further extension of the third principle, but goes beyond the third principle by vesting the rights over the river in a collective body. This principle did not gain wide acceptance because riparian states believe that it forces them into reaching an agreement. Clearly, this is an ideal principle that overlooks sovereignty and nationalism, and the competing demands of the different riparian states. New York Resolution which was adopted by the ILA in 1958, stated that each co-riparian state is entitled to a reasonable and equitable share in the beneficial uses of the waters of the drainage basin. The principle of equitable utilization was the essence of discussion by the ILA at the Tokyo Meeting that was held in 1964, as well as the Helsinki Meeting in 1966. The latter meeting (Helsinki Meeting) established the principle as the guiding rule for the work of the ILA in the field of international rivers. The Helsinki Rules The statements and resolutions adopted by the ILA in Dubrovnik and New York and the discussion in Tokyo in the first 10 years since it started working on international rivers paved the road for the comprehensive rules issued by the ILA in its meeting in Helsinki in 1966. Those rules are known as the 'Helsinki Rules on the Usage of the Waters of International Rivers'. Although the title of the Rules refers to international rivers only, Article I states that the Rules are applicable to the use of the waters of an international drainage basin. Such a drainage basin is defined as "a geographical area extending over two or more States determined by the watershed limits of the system of waters, including surface and underground waters, flowing into a common terminus". As such, the Helsinki Rules also apply to groundwater connected to surface water. This is the first time that a trans boundary groundwater was addressed by any international legal instrument. The Helsinki Rules established the principle of "reasonable and equitable utilization" of the waters of an international drainage basin among the riparian states as the basic principle of international water law. For that purpose, the Helsinki Rules have specified a number of factors for determining the reasonable and equitable share for each basin state. Article V of the Helsinki Rules state that the relevant factors to be considered include, but are not limited to following:-

- ► The geography of the basin, including in particular, the extent of the drainage area in the territory of each basin state.

- ► The hydrology of the basin, including in particular the contribution of water by each basin state.

- ► The climate affecting the basin.

- ► The past utilization of the waters of the basin, including in particular, existing utilization.

- ► The economic and social needs of each basin state.

- ► The population dependent on the waters of the basin in each basin state.

- ► The comparative costs of alternative means of satisfying the economic and social needs of each basin state.

- ► The availability of other resources.

- ► The avoidance of unnecessary waste in the utilization of waters of the basin.

- ► The practicability of compensation to one or more of the co-basin states as a means of adjusting conflicts among uses.

- ► The degree to which the needs of a basin state may be satisfied, without causing substantial injury to a co-basin state (ILA, 1966).

Helsinki Rules. The Rules devote a separate chapter each for the aspects of; pollution, navigation and timber floating. With regard to navigation, the Rules incorporate the customary international law principle that grants each riparian state the right of free navigation on the entire course of the river or lake on a reciprocal basis. It is noteworthy that this is the first international legal instrument to include rules for both navigational and non-navigational uses of international rivers. Article VI of the Helsinki Rules confirmed the decline of the primacy of navigation by stating that a use or category of uses is not entitled to any inherent preference over any other use or category of uses. The Article, as such, equates all uses of international drainage basins. The Rules also include a chapter on procedures, not only for settlement, but also for the prevention of disputes. The latter part of the chapter deals with notification of other riparian states of any proposed construction or installation that would alter the regime of the basin or give rise to a dispute. As such, the Helsinki Rules cover a wide range of issues, including both navigational and non-navigational uses of international watercourses. The Helsinki Rules have no formal standing or legally binding effect per se. However, until the adoption of the UN Convention 30 years later, they remained the single most authoritative and widely quoted set of rules for regulating the use and protection of international watercourses. Indeed, those Rules are the first general codification of the law of international watercourses. As noted by Charles Bourne, the Helsinki Rules were soon accepted by the international community as customary international law.[lxxvii] The Protocol on Shared Watercourse Systems in the Southern African Development Community (SADC) concluded in 1995 was based largely on the Helsinki Rules, and the Protocol itself made explicit references to such Rules. Some of the bilateral treaties also made specific reference to the Helsinki Rules such as the 1992 Agreement between Namibia and South Africa on the Establishment of a Permanent Water Commission. When India and Bangladesh presented their case on the dispute over the Ganges River to the United Nations in 1975, both relied heavily on the Helsinki Rules [lxxviii]. Moreover, many of the decisions of the Supreme Court of the United States of America on inter-states water disputes relied on similar factors in determining the water share of each of the riparian states.[lxxix]

Convention. On 8 December 1970, the United Nations General Assembly adopted a resolution asking the ILC to study the topic of international watercourses. The ILC is a UN body composed of legal experts nominated by states, elected by the United Nations General Assembly, and is tasked with the codification and progressive development of international law.

The ILC started working on the draft Convention in 1971. It completed its work and adopted the articles of the draft Convention in 1994, and recommended the draft articles to the General Assembly that year. After three years of informal and formal deliberations by the Sixth Committee of the UN (the Legal Committee), convened as Working Group of the Whole (the Working Group), and by the General Assembly of the United Nations, the Convention The Helsinki Rules, the UN Watercourses Convention and the Berlin Rules (Downloaded By: [World Bank Group Library] At: 19:30 25 October 2007) were adopted by the General Assembly on 21 May 1997. A total of 103 countries voted for the Convention, with three against (Burundi, China and Turkey), and there were 27 abstentions, while 52 countries did not participate in the voting. The Convention was opened for signature on 21 May 1997, and the Convention was opened for signature on 21 May 1997, and remained open for three years until 20 May 2000. By that time only 16 states signed the Convention. Although signatures closed on 20 May 2000, states can still become party to the Convention by acceding to it. This means that they can have the Convention approved or accepted through their legislative process without having signed it. The Convention is a framework convention that aims at ensuring the utilization, development, conservation, management and protection of international watercourses, and promoting optimal and sustainable utilization thereof for present and future generations. As a framework convention, it addresses some basic procedural aspects and few substantive ones, and leaves the details for the riparian states to complement in agreements that would take into account the specific characteristics of the watercourse in question. Such agreements can adopt or adjust the provisions of the Convention.

International laws on allocating water within river-basin are difficult to implement and often contradictory. The UN Convention on the Non-Navigational Uses of International Watercourses approved in 1997 by a vote of 104-3 (but not yet ratified) requires watercourse nations (Article 5) to participate in the use, development, and protection of an international watercourse in an equitable and reasonable manner. In spite of the UN Convention, riparian nations pitch their respective claims and counterclaims based on their interest and interpretation. This raises fundamental questions on whether formal arrangements on long lasting peaceful sharing of river waters can be achieved particularly in regions where the political climate is hostile to cooperative endeavours.

Chapter-3
An Analysis of Water Availability And Water Requirement

"Only one-third of the water that annually runs to the sea is accessible to humans. Of this, more than half is already being appropriated and used. This proportion might not seem so much, but demand will double in thirty years. And much of what is available is degraded by eroded silt, sewage, industrial pollution, chemicals, excess nutrients, and plagues of algae. Per capita availability of good, potable water is diminishing in all developed and developing countries."

- Marq de Villiers, Water, 2000

One of the most important issues in the analysis of water availability versus water requirement is that the requirement/demand is based on the needs at the current prices and the quantum required to be supplied is to be worked out in terms of quantity available at the consumer end.[lxxx] Total water available in the world is 1,400,000,000 cubic Km. Water covers 70.9% of earth's surface. 96.5% of water is in oceans and only 1.7% is ground water, 1.7% is in glaciers and .01% is in the atmosphere in the form of water vapour. Only 2.5% of water is fresh water and 98.8% of this fresh water is in ice and only 0.3% is in lakes and rivers. Finally 0.003% of fresh water is within biological bodies. It may also be noted that 70% of fresh water is used for agriculture. Water usage has been growing at more than twice the rate of population increase in the last century[1]. Globally water usage

---

[1] http://www.fao.org

has increased six times in last 100 years and will again double by 2050, mainly due to enhanced needs on account of requirement in the domain of irrigation and agriculture. As such an increasing number of regions are getting affected by water scarcity. By 2025, 1800 million people will be living in countries/ regions with absolute water scarcity and 2/3rd will be under water stress[2]. In 1955 there were seven countries who were categorised as the water scarce countries which included three in Middle East, namely Bahrain, Jordan and Kuwait. In 1990, 13 more countries got added to this list including Algeria, Israel including Palestine territories, Qatar, Saudi Arabia, Somalia, Tunisia, UAE and Yemen. It is anticipated that by 2025, ten more countries will be added to this group, including Egypt, Ethiopia, Iran, Libya, Morocco, Oman and Syria. It is apprehended by an estimate that by 2046 there will be a drop in food grain production because of water shortage, which will result into starvation, which will further trigger mass migration and violence. Water availability per capita, in the region of Himalayan rivers' Basins of Bangladesh, China, Nepal and India, is set to decline by 2030. According to a report[3] changes from 2010 to 2030 are going to be as tabulated below:-

Table – 3.1: Water Availability In Himalayan Basin Region

Serial Number	Country	Water Availability (BCM)	
		2010	2030
(a)	Bangladesh	7320	5700
(b)	China	2150	1860
(c)	Nepal	8500	5500
(d)	India	1730	1240

It can easily be appreciated that in totality, India, Nepal and Bangladesh will be required to cope with a shortage of 275 BCM of water within next 20 years, as against the requirement assessed as per current usage, which is more than the total amount currently available in Nepal. [4]

---

[2] ibid
[3] http://www.strategicforesight.com/water_riverbasins.htm
[4] An assessment by Strategic Foresight Group

South Asia houses 1/5th of the world's population and same is likely to increase to 1/4th by 2025. The economies of the countries of the region heavily depend on agriculture which contributes on an average of 40-50% to the GDP of the nations of the region and provides nearly 70% of the rural employment. A large proportion of the food grain production comes from irrigated agriculture and irrigation is the major user of the fresh water supply. Main limitation for increasing the food production is the availability of the water.[lxxxi]

The India's Union Ministry of Water Resources has estimated that the country's water requirements would be around 1093 BCM for the year 2025 and 1447 BCM for the year 2050. With projected population growth of 1.4 billion by 2050, the total available water resources would barely match the total water requirement of the country. In 1951, the annual per capita availability of water was 5177 CUM, which got reduced to 1342 CUM by 2000. The facts indicate that India is expected to become 'water stressed' by 2025 and 'water scarce' by 2050. In India and for that matter even in Bangladesh the contamination of the ground water is adding to the reduction of the available water. Studies conducted in last few years by a host of scientific institutions have found very high level of arsenic pollution across the Gangetic plains. In Bangladesh almost 90 per cent ground water is contaminated, in India in last five years the problem has become highly acute in Jharkhand, Bihar, Uttar Pradesh, Assam and other parts of North East besides parts of West Bengal which in any case was badly affected even earlier. This problem, though a part of natural hydrological system typical of Indo Gangetic plains, has been accentuated because of indiscriminate pumping of the ground water. Against a WHO norm of 10 micro grams/ litre in some of the districts, it has gone up to 4500 micro grams/ litre. Recent studies reveal that even deep aquifer also has started getting affected.[lxxxii]

Table-3.2: Water Availability In Different Continents

Ser no	Continent	Per Sq Kms of Territory	Per Capita (Thousands of CUM Per Year)
a.	Europe	277	4.24
b.	North America	324	17.40
c.	Africa	134	5.72
d.	Asia	311	3.92
e.	South America	672	38.30
f.	Oceania	268	83.60

Source: United Nations, The State of Environment in Asia and the Pacific 2005 (Bangkok: United Nations Economic and Social Commission for Asia and the Pacific, 2006) based on "Assessment of Water Resources in Asia and the Pacific in the 21 st Century", by Igor A Shiklomanov (unpublished, 2004).

Availability Of Water Per Capita In The World.

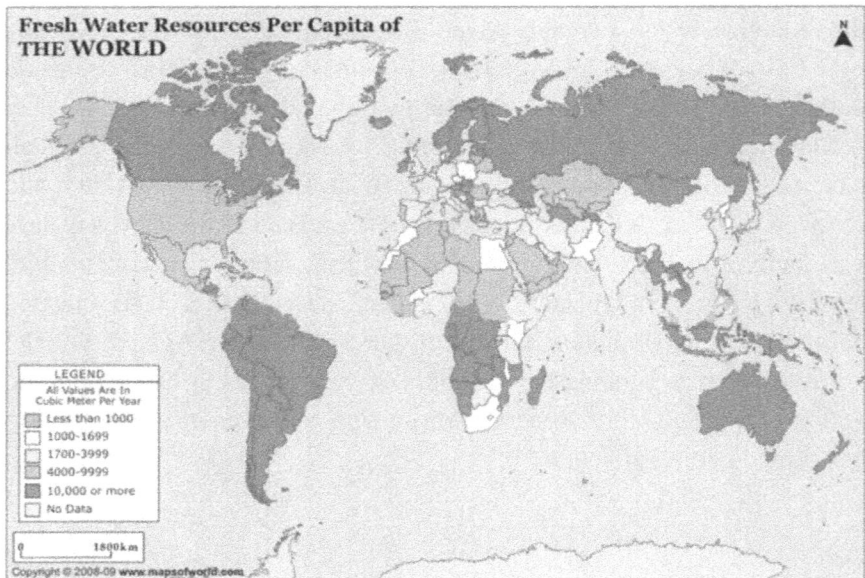

Fig- 3.1 World Wide Water Availability

Annual Renewable Water Resources in Selected Asian Countries.

South Asian Countries have problem in terms of their dependence on the external sources, which is a source of tension on account of a resource which otherwise is short in availability. Countries like china and Turkey which are upper riparian states have an inherent advantage. Following table brings out this aspect quite clearly. Situation with respect to countries of the Indian Subcontinent and Mekong region is specially serious so far as their water security is concerned.

Table-3.3: Water Dependency Of Selected Countries

Ser No	Country	External (MCM)	Total (MCM)	External Dependency Ratio (in %)
a.	Bangladesh	1,105,644	1,210,644	91.3
b.	People's Republic of China	17,169	2,840,000	0.9
c.	India	647,220	1,907,760	33.4
d.	Indonesia	0	2,838,000	0.0
e.	Japan	0	430,000	0.0
f.	Malaysia	0	580,000	0.0
g.	Myanmar	165,001	1,045,601	15.8
h.	Nepal	12,000	210,200	5.7
J.	Pakistan	170,300	225,300	75.59
k.	Philippines	0	479,000	0.0
l.	South Korea	4,850	69,700	7.0
m.	Sri Lanka	0	50,000	0.0
n.	Thailand	199,944	426,744	47.4
o.	Vietnam	524,710	891,210	58.9

Source: Based on FAO's Aquastat online data, 2011, www.fao.org/nr/water/aquastat/main/index.stm

Water Shortage, Stress, Scarcity and Insecurity

"Water Shortage" refers to an absolute deficiency where the level of available water cannot meet basic societal and economic needs. In this connection actual quantity determining a per capita minimum will vary from place to place, depending on the environment. "Water Stress" as a term was popularised by the Swedish hydrologist, Malin Falkenmark, who in 1989 developed the water stress index,[lxxxiii] which divided the volume of available fresh water resources in a country with its population. By factoring in water requirements for food self sufficiency, the index treated countries with 1,666 CUM of water availability per capita per annum or less as water stressed. Countries; with less than 1000 CUM of water per capita per year, were said to be chronically water stressed or in a state of water scarcity.[lxxxiv]

Water Scarcity Versus Water Stress. UN has defined these states and these are as follows[5] :-

'Water Stressed' - availability <1700 CUM/ capita.

'Water Scarce' - availability <1000 CUM/ capita.

'Absolutely Scarce'- availability <500 CUM/ capita.

Major Water Deficient Areas In The World. The countries which are water scarce are as follows[6] :-

- Somalia.

- Mauritania.

- Sudan.

- Niger.

- Iraq.

- Uzbekistan.

- Pakistan.

---

[5] "International Decade for Water for Life 2005-2015 and http://www.un.org/waterforlifedecade/scarcity.shtml
[6] Ecologist, 29 June 2010, http://www.theecologist.org/news/news_round_ufo.

- Egypt.

- Turkmenistan.

- Syria.

Reference: Above list has been compiled taking into account assured access to water, water demand and reliance on external supply.[7]

Environment of absolute physical scarcity increases the propensity for conflict—even more so if alternative means of overcoming the freshwater supply-demand gap are limited or are entirely absent. This is true for many underdeveloped, semi-arid to arid regions, such as the Sahel and parts of Central Asia. These regions are likely to experience increasingly the water stress, given our current understanding of climate change. Second, man-made scarcity fosters competition and dispute. We see this in cases where a powerful elite controls the availability and access to freshwater— for example, in watersheds where upstream riparian states deprive downstream people of access to water in sufficient quantity and quality at the right time. If not adequately dealt with, increasing freshwater scarcity could induce large-scale population migration and trigger war, especially if displacement occurs across rigid territorial boundaries.[lxxxv]

The scarcity of water in an arid and semi-arid environment leads to intense political pressures, often referred to as "water stress," a term coined by Falkenmark (1989). Furthermore, water not only ignores our political boundaries, it evades institutional classification and eludes legal generalizations. Interdisciplinary by nature, water's natural management unit, the watershed -- where quantity, quality, surface- and groundwater all interconnect -- strains both institutional and legal capabilities often past capacity. Analyses of international water institutions find rampant lack of consideration of quality considerations in quantity decisions, a lack of specificity in rights allocations, disproportionate political power by special interest, and a general neglect for environmental concerns in water resources decision-making. Water scarcity, and potential conflicts arising from it, is linked to larger issues of population growth,[lxxxvi] increasing food prices[lxxxvii] and global warming. There are two general views about how these problems could unfold. The first dates back to the work of Thomas

---

[7] Ibid14

Malthus, an eighteenth century British clergyman and author who believed that: "The power of population is so superior to the power of the earth to produce subsistence for man, that premature death must in some shape or other visit the human race." In other words, more people and scant resources will invariably lead to discord and violence.

Finite Nature of Water and Impact on Food Security. Water is renewable, but finite. As demands increase against this finite supply, competition for water is intensifying not just between countries, but also within countries—between farms and cities, states and provinces, ethnic groups, and economic interests. The escalation of these tensions poses much greater threats of civil unrest, humanitarian crises, and loss of life than do international wars over water. The most destabilizing global water-related threat is rising food prices and increased hunger. Globally, less water will be available for food production in the years ahead, even as world population climbs by 1.2 billion by 2025 and as at least that many people strive to move toward water-intensive North American–style diets. Already, we are using tomorrow's water to meet today's food demands: at least 10 percent of global food production depends on the unsustainable use of water. In India, where this figure may be closer to 15 to 20 percent, millions of tube wells have already gone dry. In China, which has 20 percent of the world's population but only 8 percent of its renewable fresh water, falling water tables, the over tapped Yellow River, and the reallocation of water from agriculture to urban-industrial uses will soon force the nation to enter the ranks of net grain importers. Indeed, China's wheat harvest (the world's largest) has declined some 8 percent since its 1997 peak. Meanwhile, this year about a quarter of the US grain harvest will be used not for food or feed, but to fuel automobiles.[lxxxviii]

Case of India

The National Commission for Integrated Water Resource Development (NCIWRD) of India has estimated that the total water requirement of India, in 2050, would be about 973 BCM on the lower side and about 1180 BCM on the higher side depending upon population growth. The Union Ministry of Water Resources, however, on the basis of other studies has estimated the country's water requirements to be around 1093 BCM for the year 2025 and 1447 BCM for the year 2050. With a projected population growth of 1.4 billion by 2050, the total available water resources would barely match the total water requirements of the country. In 1951, the annual per capita availability of water was 5177 CUM, which got reduced to 1342 CUM by 2000. The trend analysis of the falling water availability with an an analysis of reasons for the same it emerges that India is expected to become 'water stressed' by 2025 and 'water scarce' by 2050. It needs to be appreciated that Water stress results into not only in reduction of the fresh water (say surface water) but it also contributes to the lowering of the water table due over exploitation of the aquifer and the dry river beds getting damaged in search of water which has an impact on the course of the water channel during monsoon. Needless to add that the quality (eutrophication, organic matter pollution, saline intrusion, etc.) also gets affected. Eutrophication leads to shrinking/ degradation of the water body which reduces substantially the availability of potable water. In India and China this has specially become a source of serious concern.

Causes of Decline of Water Availability

Water availability is a function of cost of delivering water at the required place and time. The National Commission for Integrated water Resource Development (NCIWRD) has estimated that against a total annual availability of 1953 BCM (inclusive of 432 BCM of ground water and 1521BCM of surface water) only 1123 BCM (433 BCM ground water and 690 BCM surface water) can be put to use, i.e., only 55.6 per cent. The high-level of pollution further restricts the utilisable water thus posing a serious threat to its availability and use. India has a huge catchment area. In North and East India Ganges Brahmaputra catchment area is 1,600,000 Sq Kms and Ganges Basin is 1,100,000 Sq Kms.[lxxxix] In this size of catchment area, its vulnerability to human interference and storage arrangement. Though there are large number of reasons for the decline in the availability of the water but some of the important reasons are as follows:-

▶ **High Water Demand-** in agriculture sector both in India (it accounts for 90% usage)[8] and China (wherein it amounts to 65% of the usage). There are two main reasons[9] for the increase in the

---

[8] Ibid 11.
[9] http://www.un.org/popin/fao/water.html .

water demand for the agriculture are as follows:-

- ▸ **Massive Use of High Yield Variety of Cereals**-one ton of cereal needs as much as 400-500 tons of water.

- ▸ **Overall Increase in the Area Under Cultivation**-there is an overall increase in water demand of 17% for irrigation.

▸ **Human Practices that Contribute to Water Paucity**-Large scale development requiring impoundment of large quantities of water without factoring in the environmental considerations. One of the major intangible disadvantages is that the impoundment of water denudes nutrients of the downstream water with attended problem of lower yields of food grain and thus contributes to food insecurity. Let us consider, in this connection, the impact of Three Gorge dam constructed by China at the cost of $30 billion on Yangtze River. It is a hydroelectric dam by the town of Sandouping, located in Yiling District, Yichang, Hubei province, China.

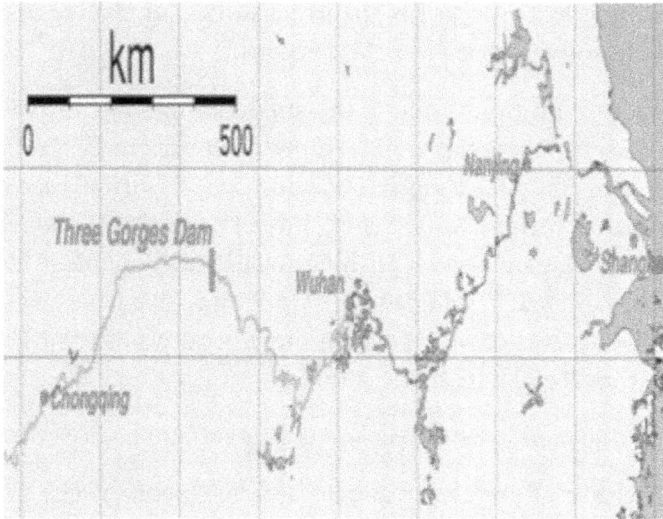

Fig-3.2: Three Gorges Dam

It is the world's largest power station in terms of installed capacity (22,500 MW) but is second to Itaipu Dam with regard to the generation of electricity annually.[xc] Except for a ship lift, the dam project was completed and fully functional as of July 4, 2012,[xci] when the last of the main turbines in the underground plant began production. However, notwithstanding the technical marvel that this dam is; it is indeed an environmental disaster. In addition to 1.4 million, officially displaced by this project another 300,000 local residents are required to be relocated and to stem a growing problem of water contamination in the river system with attended issues. [xcii] De-forestation of the river banks is another issue because it results into flood water moving unchecked due faster runoffs and reduced aquifer recharge. It is interesting to note that due to changed cropping pattern today Asia is having maximum land under irrigation. Asia has 36.9% as against America 12.5%, 8.6% Oceania, 7.7% of Europe and 5.5% of Africa area under irrigation.[xciii] Such a practice has an adverse effect on the availability of the fresh water; be it in the form of surface runoff or ground water. Therefore it is imperative that the cropping pattern needs to be reviewed to enhance the water availability. But such a conclusion is easier said than done because rise in population which is outpacing the food production with present methods of water usage does not leave any scope for reduction either in the irrigated land or change of cropping pattern easily without causing social tensions.

> ► **Water Pollution**-is one of the important reasons for the scarcity. In this connection it would be pertinent to note that Yellow river is 34% unfit and Yangtze is having her 30% tributaries polluted. Indian experience is no better; 30% of the major Himalayan rivers are biologically dead for fishing and usage by people.[10] Yamuna is 50% polluted. In Bangladesh 77 million people have been exposed to toxic level of Arsenic from the ground water supply.[11] Major reasons for pollution are as follows[12] :-
>
>> ► Squatters' 'settlements on the natural drainage of the runoff.
>>
>> ► Lack of sewage treatment and untreated sewage finding its way to aquifer or to storage facilities.
>>
>> ► Increase in the industrial usage and release of untreated industrial waste into river streams.
>>
>> ► Excessive use of pesticide and fertilizers to enhance the agricultural production.
>>
>> ► The geostrategic factors that have raised the spectre of water wars are being reinforced by the growing water stress arising from the human induced degradation of watersheds, water courses, coastal eco systems and the broader environment, which is reflected in shrinking forests and wetlands and increasing water pollution.

Effect of Global Warming- It is now experienced that in most cases where the origin of the river/ river system is a glacier, massive floods are being experienced in the downstream areas post winter. This effect is quite pronounced in the Indian Subcontinent and areas around it. Due to fast melting of glaciers, it is estimated that the Rivers; Ganges, Indus and Yellow River will become seasonal rivers by second half of the century.

---

[10] Ibid 11.
[11] Lancet Medical Journal
[12] Ibid15.

Climate change will make water less available to produce food crops in years to come, the United Nations Food and Agriculture Organization (FAO) said in a report issued Thursday. River runoff and aquifer recharges will decrease in Mediterranean, Americas, Australia and southern Africa, it said. Areas in Asia which depend on the melting of ice and mountain glaciers will also be affected, while areas with a lot of fluvial deltas are threatened by reduced water flow, increased salinity and rising sea levels, said the report entitled "Climate Change, Water and Food Security". The report also predicted an acceleration of the hydrologic cycle of the planet because high temperatures will raise the evaporation rate of the soil and sea. "The rain will increase in the tropics and at higher altitudes, but it will decrease in areas that already have dry and semi-dry characters and are located inland on the big continents," the report said. Because of this, there will be a higher frequency of droughts and flooding, which will lead to an increased use of ground water and limit the water available for agriculture even more. "The loss of glaciers, which sustain about 40 percent of the watering at world level, will finally affect the amount of available water on the surface for watering in the main producer basins," it said. The increase in temperature will prolong the growing season of crops in warmer regions, but reduce the harvest season elsewhere, adding to a higher rate of evaporation and a decrease in agricultural productivity, the report said. Rural communities and the food security of the urban population are threatened, "but the poor people in rural areas are the most vulnerable, and they could be affected in a disproportionate way," it said.[xciv] Recently some scholars, including Thomas Homer-Dixon, have analyzed various case studies on environmental degradation to conclude that there is not a direct link between scarcity and violence. Instead, he believes inequality, lack of social inclusion and other factors determine the nature and ferocity of strife.[xcv] "Unequal power relations within states and conflicts between ethnic groups and social classes will be the greatest source of social tensions rising from deprivation," said Ignacio Saiz from the social justice group. "Water too often is treated as a commodity, as an instrument with which one population group can suppress another." Bolivia, South Africa, India, Botswana, Mexico[xcvi] and even parts of the US have seen vigorous water related protests, says Maude Barlow, author of 16 books and a former senior adviser to the UN on water issues. "The fight over water privatisation in Cochobamba, Bolivia did turn into a bit of a water war and the army was called in," Barlow told Al Jazeera.[xcvii] "In Botswana, the government smashed bore holes as part of a terrible move to remove [indigenous bushmen] from the Kalahari Desert. Mexico City has been forcibly taking water from the countryside, confiscating water sources from other areas and building fortresses around it, like it's a gold mine. In India, Coke will get contracts and then build fortresses around the water sources," taking drinking and irrigation water away from local people. "In Detroit officially 45,000 people have already had their water cut off."

Effect Of Population Increase.[13] Water withdrawal globally has increased from 8% in 1970 to 11% in 2000 and it is growing rapidly. Some of the important reasons are as follows:-

- ▶ Disturbance to the runoff to reach water channel due to squatters.

- ▶ Over exploitation due to increase in the overall demand without any accretion to the availability resulting into depletion of water in the aquifer.

- ▶ Deforestation allowing runoff to run away.

Present Status of Availability

However it is heartening to note that the access to safe water is on the rise. In 1970 only 30% in the world had access to safe drinking water. The figure rose to 71% in 1990, 79% in 2000 and 84% in 2004. These figures further need to be enhanced by leveraging technology for de-contamination and desalination of sea water. In real terms in 1990, 1.6 billion people lacked access to safe drinking water which has come down to one billion people today. Also 2.5 billion people lack access to adequate sanitation. By 2025, 50% of the world will face water vulnerability. By 2030 in some of the developing regions water demand is likely to exceed supply by 50%. Another disturbing aspect is that the quality of fresh water is predicted to decrease in next 20 years.

---

[13] Ibid15.

Likely Situation in 2025

With the factors enumerated above, the situation in near to medium term is likely to further deteriorate and it is assessed that the water availability by 2025 is likely to be as depicted in the map at fig 3.2. In March, a report from the office of the US Director of National Intelligence said that risk of conflict would grow as water demand is set to outstrip sustainable current supplies by 40 per cent by 2030.[xcviii] " "These threats are real and they do raise serious national security concerns," Hillary Clinton, the US secretary of state, said after the report's release. Internationally, 780 million people lack access to safe drinking water, according to the United Nations. By 2030, 47 per cent of the world's population will be living in areas of high water stress, according to the Organisation for Economic Co-operation and Development's Environmental Outlook to 2030 report.[xcix] Some analysts worry that wars of the future will be fought over blue gold, as thirsty people, opportunistic politicians and powerful corporations battle for dwindling resources.[c] With rapid population growth, and increased industrial demand, water withdrawals have tripled over the last 50 years, according to UN figures.[ci] As per Ignacio Saiz, director of Centre for Economic and Social Rights, a social justice group. "The world's water supplies should guarantee every member of the population to cover their personal and domestic needs," but Adel Darwish, a journalist and co-author of Water Wars: Coming Conflicts in the Middle East, says modern history has already seen at least two water wars." As per him, during a discussion with him, It was admitted by the former Israeli prime minister, Ariel Sharon that "the reason for going to war [against Arab armies] in 1967 was for water," Darwish told Al Jazeera.[cii] Some analysts believe Israel continues to occupy the Golan heights, seized from Syria in 1967, to ensure control of water available there, while others think the occupation is about maintaining high ground in case of future conflicts.[ciii] Senegal and Mauritania also fought a war starting in 1989 over grazing rights on the River Senegal. And Syria and Iraq have fought minor skirmishes over the Euphrates River. UN studies project that 30 nations will be water scarce in 2025, up from 20 in 1990. Eighteen of them are in the Middle East and North Africa, including Egypt, Israel, Somalia, Libya and Yemen. Water shortages could cost the unstable country 750,000 jobs, slashing incomes in the poorest Arab country by as much as 25 per cent over the next decade, according to a report from the consulting firm McKinsey and Company produced for the Yemeni government in 2010. The Nile is another potential flash point. In 1989, former Egyptian president Hosni Mubarak threatened to send demolition squads to a dam project in Ethiopia. "The Egyptian army still has jungle warfare brigades, even though they have no jungle," Darwish[civ] said. On the Nile, cooperation would benefit all countries involved, as they could jointly construct dams and lower the amount of water lost to evaporation, says Anton Earle, director of the Stockholm International Water Institute think-tank. "If you had an agreement between the parties, there would be more water in the system," he told Al Jazeera. The likelihood of outright war is low, he says, but there is still "a lot of conflict" which "prevents joint infrastructure projects from going ahead". Darwish bets that a battle between south and north Yemen will probably be the scene of the next water conflict, with other countries in the region following suit if the situation is not improved.

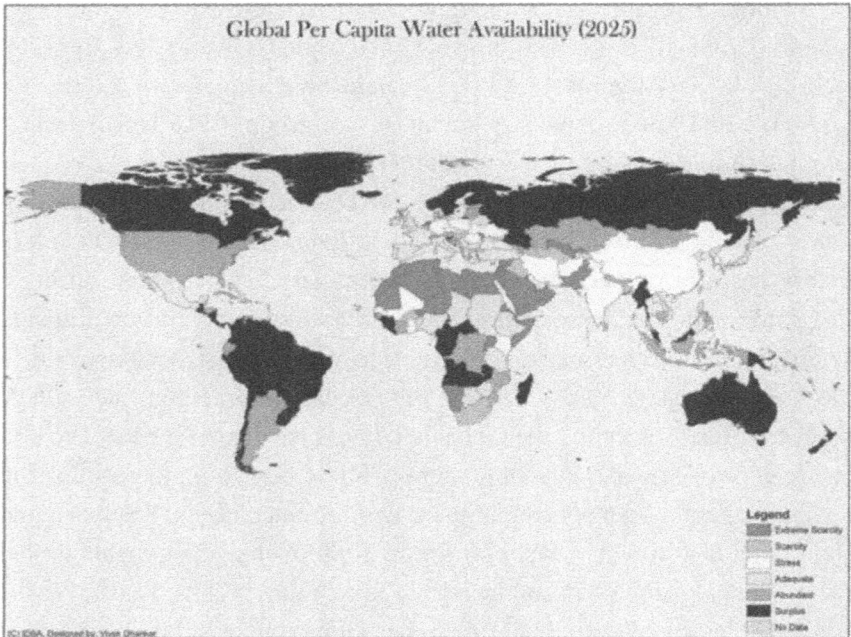

Fig-3.3: Water Availability In 2025

Chapter-4
Analysis of Some of The Potential Conflict Zones In Asia

"Whisky is for drinking and Water is fighting for."

-Mark Twain

Water is becoming increasingly a precious commodity whose control is at the core of several raging conflicts in Asia. Asia's water woes have been exacerbated by rapidly expanding economies, surging populations, rising per capita consumption levels, and continuing rural-to-urban migration. The water crisis now haunting the continent is the bitter fruit of unsustainable practices and a gross mismanagement of basin resources. It has been accentuated by the rapid spread of irrigated farming and high water consuming industries and by a growing middle class that not only uses water-guzzling comforts such as washing machines, dishwashers, water closets and many other similar appliances but is also eating more meat which is water-intensive to produce and using new variety of seeds for cereal production.

Impact of Geography. A number of rivers, flow from Chinese held territories to neighbouring countries. China has the distinction of being a source of cross border rivers flowing to the largest number of countries ranging from Russia and Kazakhstan, in North and North West to India in South and Vietnam in South East. No other country in the world matches China's position as a multi-directional, trans-boundary water provider. But, significantly the important international rivers in China all originate in ethnic minority homelands, some of which are affected by separatist movements. The traditional homelands of ethnic minorities, extending from the Tibetan Plateau and Xinjiang to Inner Mongolia and Manchuria, actually span three-fifths of the landmass of the People's Republic of China, although minority communities make up only 9% of its total Population.[cv] In recent times it is noticed that the focus of China's dam building and other water diversions are moving from internal rivers to international rivers and mega projects are moving to resource rich minority home lands. Such a development is giving rise to new tensions along ethnic fault lines over displacement and submergence issues and is fuelling deeper resentment in these poor regions. Water shortages do make a country vulnerable to international blackmail and arm twisting. The vulnerability index of selected Asian countries is as tabulated below:-

Table-4.1: Vulnerability Of Countries For Water

Ser No	Country	Internal renewable Water resource (Cubic Kms /year)	Actual Renewable Water Resource (Cubic Kms / year)	Dependency Ratio (%)	Main Source of incoming Water
1.	Kuwait	0	.02	100.0	Ground water (mostly brackish) from Saudi Arabia
2.	Turkmenistan	1.36	24.72	97.1	Amu Darya, Murghab and Tedzhen Rivers
3.	Bahrain	.004	0.116	96.6	Ground water from Saudi Arabia
4.	Bangladesh	105.0	1,211	91.3	Brahmaputra, Ganges and rivers from India's North East

5.	Uzbekistan	16.34	50.41	77.4	Syr Darya and Amu Darya Rivers
6.	Azerbaijan	8.115	34.68	76.6	Araks, Agstay, and Samur Rivers

Source: Food and Agriculture Organisation of the United Nations, Aquastat online data,2011

Effect of Growing Water Shortages. The major outcome of the Yawning gap between requirement and availability of water within Asia is adversely impacting the food security of the affected nations. As on date out of ten net importers of food grains five countries are from Asia and as on date only two countries in Asia are net exporters of the food grains.[cvi] It is anticipated that by 2050 India and China will also turn net importers essentially because production of the food grain will not be able to keep pace with the requirement mainly due growing shortage of water suitable for irrigation.[cvii] Last year regime change took place in Tunisia and Egypt. One of the reasons attributed was food shortage and Egypt is an acknowledged water scarce country. To add to the woes of countries like India the Green Revolution infact has placed greater demand on the water requirement which is difficult to meet and the solution lies in either to go back to older cropping pattern/ food habits (Coarse grain and less of meat) or find ways to enhance availability of water. Incidently People's Republic of China has already realised this correlation and has started encouraging farmers to go for food grains' farming rather than that of cash crops.[cviii] Similarly India is encouraging its farmers for dry land farming and horticulture to save on water besides encouraging people to go back to old food habits.[cix] Also a bit of crystal gazing, as far as India is concerned, would suggest a requirement of almost 450 million tons of food grains by 2050 as against the present production of 234 million tons to meet the food requirement of teeming millions and therefore it is a challenge for Indian agricultural scientists to evolve measures to economise on present rate of requirement of water to produce food grains. May be, collaboration with countries like Israel, will be of great value, to evolve technologies, which require relatively lesser quantity of water, to produce same amount of food grains.[cx]

Potential Flash Points In Asia [1]

There are as many as 57 River Basins world over, which are considered as future flash points. One of the important reasons is that out of 263 international basins in the world, 158, including most of those in Asia, lack a feasible cooperative mechanism framework. Intra state water conflicts are endemic in much of Asia. There have been 37 incidents worldwide involving water resources since 1948 that actually led to violence and out of these 30 were between Israel and her neighbour, this figure does not include potential flash point like Indo-Pakistan, Indo-China and Indo - Bangladesh. Similar situation is there in the internal water conflicts. India, Yemen and Afghanistan illustrate that the battle lines of internal wars tend to follow the lines of water courses. It can easily be concluded that while intra country water disputes are serious but inter country water disputes based on international water channels pose greater challenges to peace and stability.[cxi]

Tensions are rising in less developed regions, especially in Asia and Africa as economic development feathers the growth of intensive agriculture and imposes severe population pressure. It is anticipated by the International Water Management Institute (IWMI) that 2.7 billion people or one third of the World's population will not have access to water by 2025. It is a CATCH 22 situation, because increased population will need food security for which 15-20% more water would be needed, however water as such will be available in lesser quantity. Problem gets further compounded due to over exploitation of ground water and contamination of the surface water due to population.

Biggest risk will be in the drier basins of the Central Asia. IWMI also includes in her list Cambodia and Bhutan as the potential 'Water scarce Countries' because these countries even presently subsist only on less than 10 ltrs of water. It can therefore be appreciated that the worst affected countries are those which are at the lowest rung of the socio economic ladder of the development.

---

[1] "Asia's Potential Water Fights" by Alan Boyd pub in Asia times 25 Mar 2003

South Asia and South East Asia with five and 18 River Basins respectively have maximum disputes.[2] Maximum affected areas by the water based disputes are as tabulated below:-

Table – 4.2: Water Based Disputes

Serial No	Region	No of Disputes
(a)	Middle East	531
(b)	South East Asia	371
(c)	South Asia	273

It is anticipated that in the 21st century, Asia may emerge as the new focal point of water-related conflicts given the rapid growth of the region, which is likely to put pressure on water resources, coupled with the concentration of long-standing internal and inter-state tensions, which can act as a spark for turning water-related disputes into full-scale conflicts. Asia is home to 57 international basins, the third largest after Europe and Africa. Approximately 20% of Asians do not have easy access to water while almost 60 river basins in Asia have been identified as potential flashpoints for inter-state conflict according to a joint study by the United Nations and the University of Oregon. The rapid development, growing populations and long-standing inter-state and internal instabilities in South Asia, Central Asia, and the Mekong Sub-region in South East Asia increases the likelihood of water-related conflict in these regions and makes any water-related tensions in these areas of wider regional and potentially global significance.[3]

West Asia

Water Tension a Function of Population. The West Asia is   one of the regions where potential of eruption of a water crisis is maximum. In the last thirty years, the region's population has doubled, creating an increase in demand in a dry area where water is already a precious commodity. Use of the Jordan River's waters has been a contentious issue for decades, and water rights continue to be a major point of discussion in Israeli-Palestinian peace negotiations. The Nile has also seen its share of tension,

---

[2] Ibid 21.
[3] Asia's Coming Water Wars By Chietigj Bajpaee pub in The Asia-Pacific Journal: Japan Focus, 22 Aug 2006. http://www.pinr.com

as Egypt has been attempting to reach a water-sharing agreement with upper riparian neighbours such as Sudan and Ethiopia. United Nations Secretary General Kofi Annan on the occasion of World Water day, March 22, 2001 said, "Access to safe drinking water is a fundamental human need and therefore, a basic human right......even today, clean water is a luxary that remains out of reach of many.... more than a billion people have no access to improved water sources......"[4]

 The United Nations has suggested that around 300 potential water-related conflicts exist worldwide. A growing world population and an increasing per-capita demand have created the present tension and the possibility of a future conflict over water. In recent years, the world's water consumption has grown by 2.5% per year, while its population has grown at half that rate. Fighting over water has been dubbed "the ultimate zero-sum game" because the constantly increasing demand for fresh water is exacerbated by a fixed and limited supply. The Middle East is one of the regions where a water crisis is most likely to occur. In the last thirty years, the region's population has doubled, creating an increase in the demand in a dry area where water is already a precious commodity.

Fig-4.1: Alignment Of Tigris-Euphrates Basin

---

[4] Kofi Annan, "10 Main Uses of Water Essays", Free Research paper, dated 14 Dec 2012, uploaded on www.antiessays.com/free-essays/375427.html

Tigris- Euphrates Basin. In combined Euphrates and Tigris River basin, water rights have become a contentious issue. While the rivers are separate for most of their lengths, it is common to treat them as one hydro-political region, encompassing the states of Turkey, Syria and Iraq.

Both Tigris and Euphrates Rivers originate in the Anatolian Highlands of Turkey and flow through Syria and Iraq. Turkey contributes 88% of the water flow of the Euphrates River and 43% for the Tigris River making Syria and Iraq heavily dependent on external supplies of water. [cxii] The World Bank estimates that the total populations of these countries will grow from 96 million in 1995 to 138 million in 2010. Water from these rivers has become and will continue to be an increasingly valuable commodity as the populations of its riparian states grow.[cxiii] The main subject of controversy has been Turkey's increased use of upstream water of both rivers. In addition to Turkey's geographic advantage, its recent water management policies and large scale irrigation and hydro-energy projects, particularly the "Guneydogu Andolu Projesi (GAP, South East Anatolia Project), put Turkey in a position of great command over the river basin. Turkey first took advantage of its upstream position by completing the Keban Dam on the Euphrates in 1974. This dam was the first step in the ongoing South East Anatolian Project (Guneydogu Anadolu Projesi in Turkish, or the "GAP"), a U.S. $32 billion effort designed to accelerate the development of one of Turkey's poorest and most volatile regions. The project will eventually include twenty two dams and nineteen hydroelectric power plants on the Euphrates, Tigris, and their tributaries. The largest of these, the Ataturk Dam, was completed in 1990, and is the ninth-largest dam in the world. When the GAP would be completed in 2017, the Turkish government expects that the project would irrigate more than 1.7 million hectares of land and generate 27 billion kilowatts of power annually. [cxiv] Turkey's increased use of the Euphrates and Tigris will decrease the amount of water available to Syria and Iraq, but the exact quantum of reduction is difficult to anticipate. Following the completion of the Tabqa and Keban dams, Iraq claimed that the flow of the Euphrates had been reduced from 920 to 197 CUM per second.

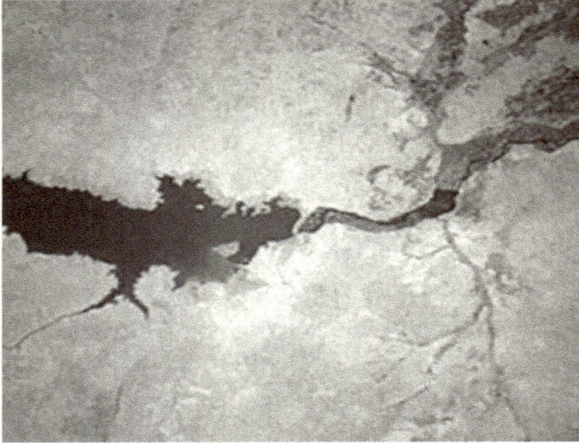

Fig-4.2: Tabqa Dam

Fig-4.3: Keban Dam

Dams On River Euphrates

One report estimates that the completion of GAP could reduce water flow to Syria by up to forty percent and flow to Iraq could diminish as much as eighty percent. Another prediction is that there would be an overall shortage of Euphrates water by 2010, if Turkey completes the GAP and population growth rates remain stable. Iraq would presumably bear the worst of this shortage because it is the farthest downstream country. Furthermore, as South Eastern Turkey becomes increasingly irrigated and cultivated, levels of salinity and pollutants in the water will increase, making the water that reaches the lower riparian countries less useful, especially for irrigation purposes. Turkish and Syrian waterworks developments have, therefore, left Iraq in a precarious position. As a country with very little rainfall, Iraq is highly dependent on the Euphrates and Tigris waters flowing in from Turkey and Syria. GAP has the potential for optimal use of land and water resources in the South East Anatolia to provide for Turkey as a whole and for sustainable socio-economic development in the poor, largely Kurdish populated region, characterised by social and economic instability. Conversely, both Syria and Iraq contend that GAP could diminish and degrade their water supply in years to come. Water shortage is especially a threat in the region due to history of drought in Syria and war torn infrastructure of Iraq.[cxv] This kind of attitude of Turkey to maximise use of water has fuelled criticism from lower riparian states of Syria and Iraq, who believe their national security will be seriously threatened if Turkey prevents water from reaching their territories. Syria and Iraq have demanded that Turkey release more water, while Turkey maintains it does not have enough for its own purposes. Despite much rhetoric and many attempts to reconcile the issue, no tripartite agreement on water sharing has so far been reached.

Fig-4.4: Area Of GAP

Fig-4.5: Ataturk Dam (1992)

The Euphrates is a relatively small river, draining a large, dry region. Measured at Hit, Iraq, the river annually averages about thirty-two BCM of water. This average discharge has ranged from 14.9 to 56.4 BCM depending on upstream rainfall.[cxvi] The Tigris originates in the same mountainous region of eastern Turkey as the Euphrates. It flows southward, forming a short stretch of the Turkish-Syrian border and later the Iraqi-Syrian border. The river then turns East across Iraq, eventually joining the Euphrates. Measured at Kut, Iraq, the average annual discharge of the Tigris is 31 BCM, with a known range between seventeen and 59 BCM.[cxvii] A key difference between the two rivers is that the Tigris receives much of its water from tributaries reaching it in Iraq, not in Turkey. Some of these rivers flow southwest from the mountains in Iran. This topography results in total water contributions of forty-three percent from Turkey, forty-two percent from Iraq, and nine percent from Iran. The addition of water to the Tigris in Iraq has two significant consequences. First, unlike the Euphrates, the Tigris makes up for the evaporation losses and actually gains water as it flows through Iraq. Second, and of more strategic importance is that, Iraq has more potential for control over the Tigris than the Euphrates because Iraq controls much of the water flowing into the Tigris. This latter fact is especially true because unlike Turkey, Syria, and Iraq, Iran has thus far not significantly exploited its waters - leaving the Tigris' Iranian tributaries open to Iraqi use once they flow into Iraq. An attempt by Iran to demand its share of ownership on a future date with consequent implication of a conflict with upper riparian states cannot be ruled out. Finally, because of its high concentration of sediments and violent nature, the Tigris has historically been less important for agriculture, and therefore, less controversial.[cxviii]

Jordan River. The Jordan River is a 251-kilometre long river located in West Asia, flowing into the Dead Sea. Currently, the river serves as the eastern border of the State of Israel and of the Israeli-occupied Palestinian Territories. The Hashemite Kingdom of Jordan takes its name from this river. It has many tributaries which feed water into this river. The important ones are; The Hasbani , which flows from Mount Lebanon, The Banias arising from a spring at Banias at the foot of Mount Hermon, The Dan whose source is also at the base of Mount Hermon, The Iyon which flows from Lebanon. The river drops rapidly in a 75 kilometre run to swampy Lake Hula, which is slightly above sea level. Exiting the lake, it drops much more in the 25 kilometres down to the Sea of Galilee. The last section has less gradient, and the river meanders before entering the Dead Sea, about 422 metres below sea level, which has no outlet. Two major tributaries enter from the east during this last section: the Yarmouk River and Jabbok River. Its section north of the Sea of Galilee is within the boundaries of Israel, and forms the western boundary of the Golan Heights. South of the lake, it forms the border between the Kingdom of Jordan (to the East) and Israel and the West Bank (to the West). In 1964, Israel began operating a dam that diverts water from the Sea of Galilee, a major Jordan River water provider, to the National Water Carrier. Also in 1964, Jordan constructed a channel that diverted water from the Yarmouk River, another main tributary of the Jordan River. Syria has also built reservoirs that catch the Yarmouk's waters. Environmentalists blame Israel, Jordan and Syria for extensive damage to the Jordan River ecosystem.[cxix] In modern times, the waters are 70% to 90% used for human purposes and the flow is much reduced. Because of this and the high evaporation rate of the Dead Sea, the sea is shrinking. All the shallow waters of the southern end of the sea have been drained in modern times and are now salt flats. Small sections of the Jordan's upper portion, near the Sea of Galilee, have been kept pristine for baptisms. Most polluted is the 96 Kms downstream stretch - a meandering stream from the Sea of Galilee to the Dead Sea. Environmentalists say the practice has almost destroyed the river's ecosystem. Rescuing the river could take decades, according to environmentalists.[cxxcxxi] In 2007, Friends of the Earth Middle East (FoEME) named the Jordan River as one of the world's 100 most endangered ecological sites, and due partially to lack of cooperation between Israel and neighbouring Arab states.[cxxii] The same environmentalist organization said in a report that the Jordan River could dry up by 2011 unless the decay is stopped. This doom's day prophecy, however, has not come true so far. The flow rate of the Jordan River once was 1.3 BCM per year; as of 2010, it has reduced to just 20 to 30 MCM per year flow into the Dead Sea.[cxxiii] For comparison, the total amount of desalinated water produced by Israel by 2012 will be about 500 million cubic metres per year. Though the gap between availability and the requirement is ever widening, but the waters of the Jordan River are as important a resource to the dry lands in the area as they ever were and no doubt that they continue to remain a source of conflict among Lebanon, Syria, Jordan, Israel and the Palestinians, which began with 1951 Syrian border clashes. Mediation by the Eisenhower administration during 1950ies failed because Arab states would not agree to Israel trying to divert 33% of water to Israel, as only 23% originated there.[cxxiv] For Israel, the River Jordan, including the Yarmouk, supplies 40% of its fresh water, of which 70% is used in agriculture, while 80% of the water derived from renewable resources of the mountain aquifers in the region are also exploited by Israel,[cxxv] The National Water Carrier Project was started in 1956 and got completed in 1964; it combined all previous water projects and delivered water to the dry Mitzpe Ramon in the South. Soon after, Syria and Jordan decided to divert the Jordan water at the source. The diversion works would have reduced the installed capacity of Israel's carrier by about 35%, and Israel's overall water supply by about 11%.[cxxvi] In April 1967 Israel conducted air raids into Syria to halt this work, and two months later the Six Days War followed. The use of Jordan River's water as a vital regional resource was the cause of the war confirmed by Ariel Sharon who said "People generally regard June 5, 1967, as the day the Six Day War began. That is the official date, but in reality it started two and a half years earlier on the day Israel decided to act against the diversion of the Jordan River."[cxxvii]

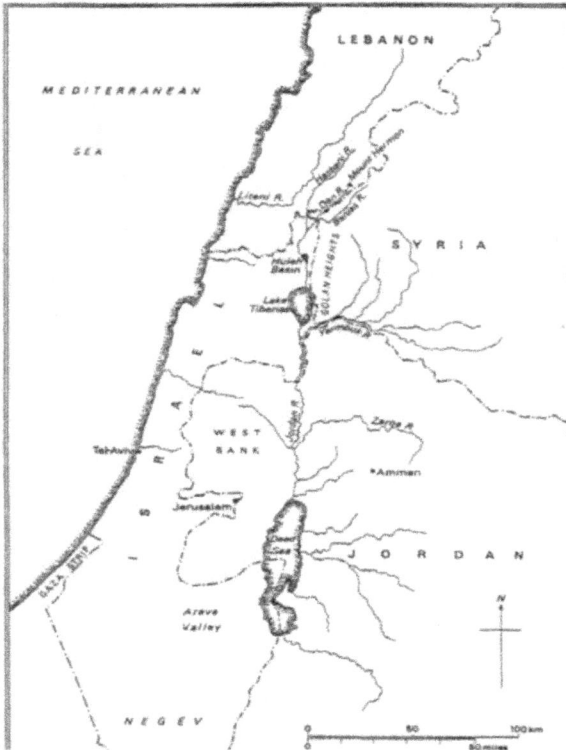

Fig-4.6: Jordan River Basin

Fig-4.7: Jordan River South Of   Bnot Ya'ako Bridge (May2009)

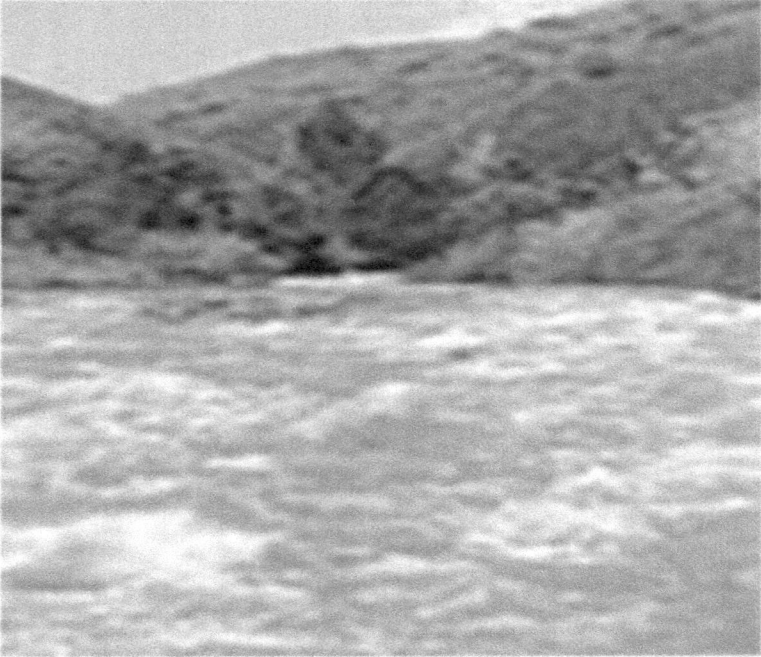

Fig-4.8: River Jordan In Spring

Central Asia

The distribution of water in Central Asia is notably uneven. While upstream Tajikistan and Kyrgyzstan enjoy water abundance, downstream nations of Uzbekistan, Turkmenistan and partly Kazakhstan experience sharp water shortages. But the problem is predominantly consumption. At the heart of economic systems of Uzbekistan and Turkmenistan is cotton, which is the major revenue earner for those countries. Cotton is a thirsty Crop which requires intensive irrigation. With plans to triple cotton and rice production and almost complete dependence on upstream water resources, water overuse is common in downstream riparian states and virtually no effort has been made to reduce the water utilization. In addition, people in Central Asia consume 110 to 120 BCM of water per annum for domestic needs, which is several times higher than in the Middle East. In Uzbekistan alone, more than two BCM of water is wasted every year.[cxxviii] Water is cheap; in some regions its price is about 65 Cents per "Olympic swimming pool".[cxxix] The consequence is some drought-prone areas grow rice and keep large areas of nothing but flooded paddy fields. Central Asia has become notorious worldwide as a site of the most dramatic environmental disaster, the Aral Sea Crisis. Once, the fourth largest lake in the world, the Aral Sea has shrunk by more than half of its original size, over the last forty years. The major reason for that was; increased discharge of inflowing water for irrigation. Grand Soviet schemes for the production of cotton, rice and other irrigated cultures required huge amounts of water. Throughout the Aral Sea's former basin, water has mobilised deep salt reserves, raised the water table and waterlogged the fields as a result of over-irrigation.

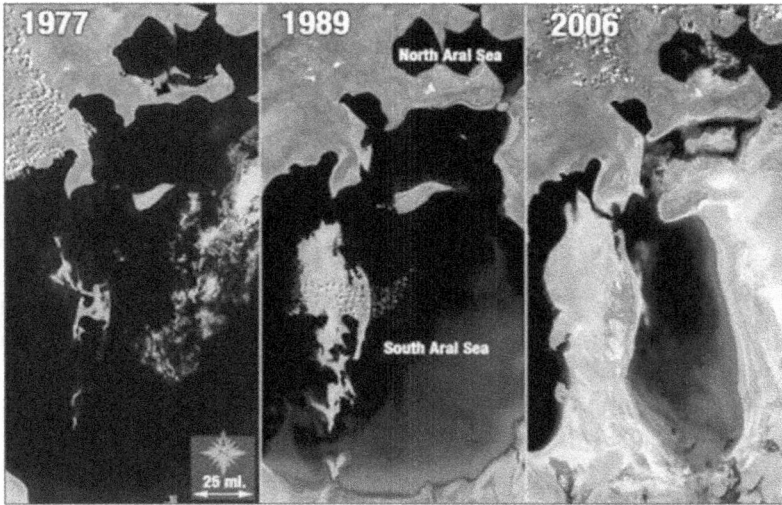

Fig-4.9: Aral Sea An Environment Disaster

Table-4.3: State Of Induced Salinity

Ser No	Country	State of Salinity
(a)	Turkmenistan	95%
(b)	Uzbekistan	50%
(c)	Kazakhstan	33%
(d)	Tajikistan	16%
(e)	Kyrgyz Republic	11.5%

Sources: Ministerstvo okhrany prirody Turkmenistana for UNEP, 2000, Doklad po osushchestvleniiu Natsional'noi programmy deistvii po bor'be s opustynivaniem v Turkmenistane, p. 24; FAO, 2002, Aquastat (figures are for 1993-94); TACIS, 2000, Kyrgyz Republic National Irrigation Strategy and Action Plan. Supporting Document, pp. 2-13.

Note: The salinization statistics for Kazakhstan are based upon 1989 land surveys, because the present reported figures are too low to be credible. The present dimension of land salinization is probably greater than that shown above.

The state of salinity in the region is as tabulated below:-

Despite above state of salinization of soil, the water consumption goes at the same pace as before. The most populated nation in the region (25 million in 2002), Uzbekistan, alone uses three-fifths of regional water supplies.[cxxx] In fact, industrial consumption of water in Uzbekistan and Turkmenistan is twice than in Kyrgyzstan and Tajikistan.[cxxxi] Wasteful use of water on Uzbekistan's very large irrigated area has contributed to a dramatic decline of the combined flow of the Amu Darya and Syr Darya and acted as a major factor in the Aral Sea Crisis. Consequently, water over exploitation is the major reason for downstream riparian states' water scarcity. Uzbekistan and Turkmenistan use their water inefficiently and hence they experience water scarcity in a time of water abundance. [cxxxii] The quality of water in the major Central Asian Rivers has declined dramatically over a period of time due to large-scale irrigation required for cotton harvesting. Huge amounts of salt, fertiliser, herbicides, and pesticides found their way to the rivers as the return flow from the fields. The groundwater table has risen and has got contaminated with high levels of salts and other minerals. Groundwater quality ranges from a maximum of 0.5 g/L of total dissolved salts to 6 g/L, which is 20 times more than the levels in North America (about 300 mg/L). Within the Soviet Union, inter-republican water resources were managed on the basis of water utilization plans. These plans were developed by local Ministries of Land Reclamation and Water Management and then sent to Moscow to the Ministry of Land Reclamation and Water Management of the Soviet Union for approval. These plans and schemes provided for annual water withdrawal limits with respect to each tributary, reservoir or canal and the limits were calculated against annual crop requirements. Under the Soviet system of water allocation, water quotas imposed by Moscow favoured downstream countries at the expense of the upstream riparian states: water-abundant Kyrgyzstan and Tajikistan were supposed to supply irrigated agriculture economies of Uzbekistan and Turkmenistan with water in spring and summer when water should be available for cotton fields. In autumn and winter, when Kyrgyzstan and Tajikistan experienced peaks in electricity demand, they were supplied with Turkmen and Uzbek gas and Kazakh coal to satisfy energy consumption. They also received electricity from downstream countries during winter to be compensated for the hydropower produced in summer. Maintenance and operating costs of dams and reservoirs were covered by Moscow. Since the collapse of the Soviet Union, Central Asia has become a tangle of unresolved Trans Boundary water disputes. Water is the most critical resource in Central Asia and it "has more often been the source of competition rather than the focus of conservation".[cxxxiii] Absence of mechanisms to handle the water problems has already resulted in various accusations of improper water utilization. Consequently, the whole region becomes the site of potential conflict that requires a framework which should incorporate a great many variables to identify the proneness to water conflict and to allow for the possibility of preventive diplomacy. Such method which has never been used towards the specific problems of Central Asian water disputes can provide solutions based on a more holistic approach to natural resources, while recognising the historical, geopolitical and natural characteristics of the region.

Current Water Disputes. Central Asia's two major rivers, as well as their tributaries, have become a focus for growing competition among the riparian states, with Syr Darya being a particular point of tension. Amu Darya is also rapidly becoming a focus of disputes as the governments of Turkmenistan and Uzbekistan are increasingly becoming more hostile towards each other. Afghanistan is also becoming a party to the simmering water dispute and likely to put forth its demand for its share of water being a riparian of these Trans boundary rivers.[cxxxiv] These tensions have so far been contained without conflict, but all parties have shown a willingness to put their interests first at any cost, including military intervention. Due to their reliance on agriculture, Uzbekistan and Turkmenistan view irrigation as a key security issue. [cxxxv]

Fig-4.10: River Basins Of Syr Darya And Amu Darya

The Syr Darya Basin. The Syr Darya is shared by Kazakhstan, Uzbekistan, Tajikistan and Kyrgyzstan, and in case of Uzbekistan, it enters twice, first time; from Kyrgyzstan into Ferghana Valley, from where it enters Tajik territory and again enters into Uzbekistan.

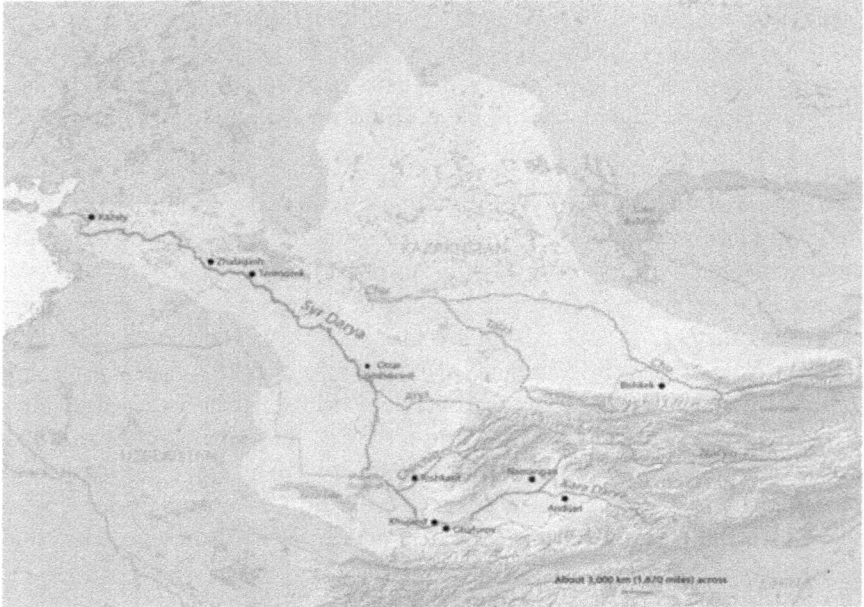

Fig-4.11: Syr Darya Alignment

▶ **Syr Darya-** After crossing the Hunger Steppe, the Syr Darya runs into Kazakhstan. Kyrgyzstan and Uzbekistan have had particularly discordant history over the use of water from the Syr Darya. Since independence, Kyrgyzstan faces serious economic problems, mainly because of a shortage of energy supply from Russia, Kazakhstan and Uzbekistan. The primacy of energy production over the irrigation needs downstream has already created a major discord between Uzbekistan and Kyrgyzstan.[cxxxvi] The 1998 Syr-Darya Framework Agreement between the two has been broken by both sides. The implementation of such barter agreement runs across one major problem – all barter agreements are delayed until the late spring when the downstream countries urgently need water for irrigation. As this might be the case, Kyrgyzstan would have had an incentive to produce less electricity. However, due to Kyrgyzstan's uncertainty whether enough gas would be provided, it produces electricity to protect itself giving rise to a vicious circle.[cxxxvii] Uzbekistan intensified the tension more than once by acting in a unilateral manner. In July 1997, it cut off 70 percent of the downstream flow, which caused a riot among the Kazakh farmers whose 100,000 hectares were threatened.[cxxxviii] Practice of altering water flow by upstream riparian states is no more acceptable to lower riparian states. In summer 1999, Tajikistan released 700 MCM of water from its Kairakum reservoir without warning its downstream neighbours. As a result, cotton crops in southern Kazakhstan, which had received less water than was agreed, were devastated. The situation was seriously aggravated by Kyrgyzstan's concurrent move to reduce the flow to southern Kazakhstan in retaliation for Kazakhstan's failure to supply coal under the barter agreements. After months of talks, the incident was finally settled.[cxxxix] There is also an issue of Naryn-Syr Darya cascade of dams in Kyrgyzstan. Every year Uzbekistan insists on releasing water from it to improve downstream agriculture. Many a times, the conflict in recent past had reached on the verge of war. In 1997, Uzbekistan deployed 130,000 troops on the Kyrgyz-Uzbek border, near the Toktogul reservoir, to conduct military exercises aimed at seizure of a 'well guarded object', using the armour and helicopters. Meanwhile, Kyrgyzstan, through media leak, hinted that in case the reservoir would be blown up, the resulting flood would sweep away Uzbekistan's Ferghana and Zeravshan Valleys[cxl] Kyrgyzstan has tried to persuade Uzbekistan and Kazakhstan to share the maintenance and operating costs of the Toktogul reservoir but these attempts were turned down by the downstream countries. Kazakhstan claimed that it would not be able to pay the costs – between US$ 15 and 27 million per annum. Thus, the opportunity for the downstream riparian states to settle the dispute was missed. However, by adopting Law on the Interstate Use of Water Objects, Water Resources and Water Management Installations on 29 June 2001, the Kyrgyz parliament left the door open to push the downstream countries into negotiations regarding the maintenance costs of the Toktogul reservoir as later Kyrgyzstan stated that in fact it demanded to pay only for the water passing through Kyrgyz reservoirs, i.e. share maintenance costs. This was welcomed by Kazakhstan who agreed to pay for the maintenance of the Kyrgyz water installations, but initially was opposed by Uzbeks. However, in March 2002 Uzbekistan reached the agreement with Kyrgyzstan that it would share certain cost in return for the guarantee that it would receive water for irrigation. It is felt that if a better barter agreement had been worked out the dispute between Kyrgyzstan and Uzbekistan could have been resolved.[cxli] Shared water storage facilities, like the Andijan reservoir located in the Uzbek part of the Ferghana Valley also represent an inter-state problem.[cxlii]

The Amu Darya Basin- The Amu Darya is shared by four countries, namely; Tajikistan as the upstream riparian, Afghanistan, Uzbekistan and Turkmenistan and forms the border in some stretches between Tajikistan, Uzbekistan and Afghanistan, and between Turkmenistan and Uzbekistan.

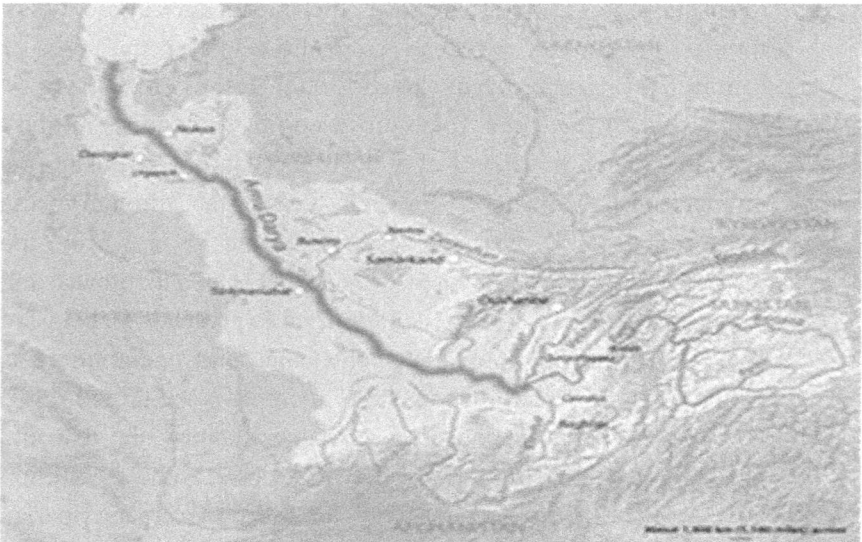

Fig-4.12: Amu Darya Alignment

> **Amu Darya-** The Amu Darya is much less regulated and has fewer dams and reservoirs thus a source of potential problems. There are serious tensions along the flow of the river not only

between the upstream and downstream riparian states, as, for example, between Tajikistan and Uzbekistan, but also between the middle and lower riparian states, for example, Uzbekistan and Turkmenistan. According to the 1992 water quota agreement, Tajikistan is entitled to 9 CUM of about 75 CUM of annual flow of the Amu Darya, or 12 percent. This is considered low by Tajikistan who needs to expand its agricultural output to supply the growing population with food. Tajikistan's agriculture is underdeveloped since the Soviet times, and the irrigation system is derelict and in need of urgent repairs. Tajikistan sees the only way out as using more water either by increasing its water quota from the Amu Darya or by diverting the Zeravhsan River. As 95 percent of the water of latter is used by Uzbekistan, this would cause serious tensions with Tajikistan's much powerful neighbour. In contrast, increasing the Amu Darya quota seems to be quite easy, since Tajikistan has an upper hand in distributing water resources of the Amu Darya. In principle, nobody could prevent Tajikistan from taking more water than was allocated by the water quota agreement. It is very hard to monitor Tajikistan's performance, as most equipment needed has been destroyed during the civil war in 1992-1997. In this connection it needs to be appreciated that if Tajikistan were to increase its water quota moderately, this would have an immediate impact downstream. The same water/energy complex as with Kyrgyzstan has developed between Tajikistan and Uzbekistan. Tajikistan's central and southern parts are well provided by electricity from the Nurek hydro plant, and northern Tajikistan having no grid lines with the rest of the country relies on Uzbekistan's intermittent supplies of electricity and gas in winter. In return, Tajikistan provides power to southern Uzbek provinces and often requests that Uzbekistan switched off electricity to northern Tajikistan to keep imports within the agreed limit not to pay higher price. This causes serious discontent as Tajikistan is forced to have electricity rationed in many provinces due to poor state of Tajikistan's grid lines. The country desires to develop its hydropower resources to break dependence on Uzbekistan. But increasing hydro consumption would seriously affect the downstream access to seasonal water supplies and to create further discord along the Amu Darya course. The most dramatic conflict over the Amu Darya water resources is between downstream nations of Uzbekistan and Turkmenistan. Both equally depend on their cotton production and irrigation agriculture and both claim that each of them exceed their water quotas. Due to a very poor state of Turkmenistan's water infrastructure, most of the water received by Turkmenistan, is wasted. The country does not want to spend huge funds for the expensive rehabilitation of crippling Turkmen canals and draws off more water from the Amu Darya instead. The relations between two countries dramatically worsened in the late 2002 when the Uzbek ambassador has been declared persona non grata in Turkmenistan on accusation of participating in the conspiracy to oust and kill President Niyazov. Uzbek-Turkmen relations over water can grow even worse, given Turkmenistan's ambitious plan to complete a huge reservoir in the Karakum desert, called the Golden Century Lake. Another point of contention is the Tyuyamuyun reservoir in the delta of the Amu Darya divided between Uzbekistan and Turkmenistan. Both sides feel displeased with the wasteful use of water, and this led to an outbreak of violence in 1992 over the re-direction of drainage waters and raids by both sides to cut off pipes and irrigation canals (Smith, 1995). Today, the Tyuyamuyun remains one of the several disputed areas in continuing water dispute with Uzbekistan. Throughout the independence period, rumours have circulated of a small-scale secret war between the two states over the river resources, Uzbekistan troops taking control of water installations on the Turkmen bank of the Amu Darya, and even of a massacre of a large number of Uzbekistan troops in Turkmenistan in 2001. While these reports seem to be unsubstantiated, they are very indicative of simmering tensions between the two.[cxliii]

Major Reasons for Tensions and Potential Conflicts. Thus probability for growing tension on account of sharing water and resultant conflicts, in Central Asia post break down of the Soviet Union in 1990, cannot be ruled out. the reasons for tensions can be summarised as; population explosion; leading to demand supply gap widening and hence attempts to over exploit the ground water further without any kind of formal arrangement for equitable distribution of available resources; unplanned growth and finally damage to the canal system created by the Soviet Union. Some of the other contours of the problems are as follows:-

► Central Asia's water fault-lines include the division of the Caspian Sea between the five littoral states (Azerbaijan, Iran, Kazakhstan, Russia, and Turkmenistan) and a dispute over access to water from the Syr Darya and Amu Darya rivers between upstream states (Kyrgyzstan and Tajikistan) and downstream states (Kazakhstan, Turkmenistan, and Uzbekistan). While Central Asia is rich in water resources, more than 90% of it is concentrated in Kyrgyzstan and Tajikistan[5] where the region's two main rivers, the Syr Darya and Amu Darya, originate. Meanwhile, Uzbekistan and Kazakhstan are the region's main water consumers with Uzbekistan alone consuming more than half of the region's water resources[6]. As such, Kyrgyzstan and Tajikistan control the water needed by the other Central Asian states. The upstream states, however, view water as a strategic commodity as they are poorly endowed with other resources and use water to generate much of their own power needs. With the independence of the Central Asian republics, frictions have arisen over the breakdown of the Soviet system. Water flow to downstream states has fallen, significantly affecting cotton production and cooling needs during the summer, while downstream states have not met the gas and coal needs of upstream states, especially during the harsh winters.

► The region's growing water consumption has also reduced water levels in the Aral Sea, which is fed by the Syr Darya and Amu Darya river systems. The drying of the Aral Sea is an ecological disaster whose full dimensions are difficult to fathom. Suffice to summarise that not only water table is going down but the resultant desertification coupled with other adverse parameters is hurtling the region to a state of unimaginable intensity of conflicts. Although the states established the Interstate Commission for

---

[5] Ibid24.
[6] Ibid24.

Water Coordination in 1992, they have failed to implement an effective water management mechanism. Combined with inter-state tensions over disputed borders, great power competition over the region's energy resources and internal instabilities emanating from rising poverty, authoritarian rule and religious extremism, water disputes have the potential to tip the region into conflict.

Fig-4.13: Water Sources In Central Asia

► A further source of instability emanates from the lack of agreement on the legal status of the Caspian Sea between the five littoral states (Azerbaijan, Iran, Kazakhstan, Russia and Turkmenistan). The Caspian Sea is the world's largest inland body of water. It is rich in hydrocarbon reserves and sturgeon, which is harvested for the production of caviar. Prior to the collapse of the Soviet Union, the Caspian Sea was divided between Iran and the Soviet Union on the basis of the Friendship Treaty of 1921 and the Treaty of Commerce and Navigation of 1940, although some issues continue to remain unresolved such as the protection of the local environment and development of resources on the seabed. It also failed to distinguish whether the Caspian was a "sea" or a "lake," the former of which would lead to an equidistant division of the body of water under the United Nations Convention on the Law of the Sea while the latter would lead to joint development, characterized as the condominium approach. The six littoral states have adopted differing positions on the status of the Caspian, which have shifted with the growing importance of resources that Caspian Sea offers. Russia, Kazakhstan and Azerbaijan want sharing the surface waters and dividing the seabed based on the principle of the median line but Iran and Turkmenistan prefer a multilateral condominium approach whereby all five littoral states collectively agree on developing the resources on the seabed, with either joint development or equal division of the sea. By dividing the sea using the median line approach, the seabed would be divided between Kazakhstan, Azerbaijan, Russia, Turkmenistan and Iran as 28.4%, 21%, 19%, 18% and 13.6% respectively; under the condominium approach favoured by Iran, each state would receive 20% of the seabed.[7]

East and South East Asia

Mekong Region. In East and South East Asia, water-related tensions arise from attempts by the six riparian states of River Mekong namely; China, Myanmar, Thailand, Laos PDR, Cambodia and Vietnam to construct dams in order to reroute the Mekong River system.

---

[7] Ibid24.

Mekong Region

Fig-4.14: Mekong Region

The Mekong region covers over 2.3 million square miles and is home to 240 million people. The 4,880 kilometres long Mekong River begins her journey from the Tibetan plateau[8] , and makes its way through China's Yunnan province, Myanmar, Laos PDR, Thailand, Cambodia, Vietnam and discharges out into the South China Sea. Close to 70 million people depend on the river for food, water and transport and the region accounts for 20% of all fish caught from the inland waters of the world. Also the Mekong Basin is the major rice bowl of the world. The Asian Development Bank launched the Mekong Sub-region project in 1992 as an initiative aimed at promoting development, trade and integration through enhancing transportation, communication, and power networks between the six countries in the region.[9]

---

[8] Ibid24
[9] Ibid24.

Impact Of Chinese Efforts To Dam The River. In the Upper Mekong Basin in Yunnan Province, China has planned to construct eight cascade hydropower dams[10], the first of which, the Manwan Dam, has already been completed in 1996. This has diverted water from downstream countries in the Mekong River Delta, resulting in irregular fluctuations in water levels, which has harmed local industries in the region, including farming and fishing in Cambodia and Thailand, and the tourism industry in Laos. China is planning to construct 15 more dams along Mekong River.

Fig-4.15: Location And Design Of Manwan Dam

---

[10] Ibid24.

Environmental Impact of Dam Construction by the Riparian States in Mekong Basin. A study co authored by Stuart Orr and published in the October 2012 issue of "Global Environmental Change" flags the ongoing debate over the environmental and social implications of construction of the Xayaburi Dam on the Lower Mekong in Laos PDR.[cxliv] The US $ 3.5 billion funded dam is expected to be completed by 2019, and will export 95 per cent of its electricity to Thailand, which is funding its construction. It may be noted that while there are four dams in the Upper Mekong basin in China, Xayaburi is the first of 11 planned dam projects on the main stem of the river (downstream river segment), and there are plans to construct another 77 dams in the basin by 2030.[cxlv] According to a study, the planned construction of hydro powered dams on the Mekong River in South-East Asia could jeopardise livelihoods, water access and food security for 60 million people, across Cambodia, Laos PDR, Thailand and Vietnam. The study reports that dams will block fish migration routes and decimate fish supplies in the lower Mekong region.[cxlvi] Following in the footsteps of China, other countries in the delta have also pursued a unilateral approach toward projects along the river system. Vietnam has engaged in several dam construction projects without consulting with Cambodia, as has Laos PDR. Coupled with long-standing historical animosities between states in the region such as between China and Vietnam and Thailand and Myanmar, as well as internal frictions caused by poverty and a number of long-standing insurgencies, water disputes may act as a potential catalyst for regional conflict.

Impact of Unregulated Efforts to Exploit River Mekong. A major impact of the unregulated construction of dams on the river is likely to result into an economic down turn of the lower riparian states in long run with consequent tensions amongst them and also between them and the upper riparian China as a natural corollary. [cxlvii] The exploitation of the Mekong River — the world's 12th longest river, has loomed as an increasingly divisive issue among nations through which it flows — Myanmar, Laos PDR, Thailand, Cambodia, Vietnam, and its source country China.

Fig-4.16: Mekong River Through Riparian States

Impact of Kra of Isthmus in Southern Thailand. The environmental impact of China's Mekong River policy is being further felt by its US$20 billion proposal to build a canal across Thailand's Kra Isthmus to transport petroleum from Thailand to southern China.[11] This initiative is being encouraged by China's desire to bypass the narrow Strait of Malacca, through which 80% of China's oil imports currently transit, which Beijing views as a strategic vulnerability given that the waters are a hub for piracy and potential terrorist attacks and patrolled by the U.S. Navy and the coordinated patrolling by Indonesia and Malaysia. However, an oil spill along this waterway would devastate the ecosystem of the Mekong River as well as the economies of the region that depend on the river for their livelihood.

Salween River. The Salween River (known as the Nu in Chinese) originates in the Tibetan plateau and drains an area of 320,000 km2 in China, Myanmar, and Thailand before it flows into the Gulf of Martaban. Totalling 2,413 kilometres, it is the longest undammed river in mainland

---

[11] Ibid24.

South East Asia. More than 10 million people from at least 13 different ethnic groups depend on the Salween watershed for their livelihoods: fisheries are a major source of dietary protein, and the river's nutrients nourish vegetable gardens in the dry season and fertilize farmland. The Nujiang, the section of the Salween that flows through China, is found in the Three Parallel Rivers area, a rich centre of biodiversity recognized by; the UNESCO as a World Heritage Site. Despite the fact that studies since the 1950s have identified tremendous hydropower potential, the Salween is a relatively undeveloped basin-with only one major hydro-electric project at Baluchaung. However, it is likely that with economic development and more political integration in the region, development pressure in the river basin will increase, and there will be more demands to use the waters for irrigation, urban and industrial uses, and navigation. The three riparian states, namely; China, Myanmar, and Thailand do not yet have an agreement on the use of the Salween, thus allowing each of them free use of the river. Each of these countries has unilateral plans to construct dams and development projects along the Salween, but these sets of plans are not compatible. Tensions are created when a country within a basin acts unilaterally without consulting other nations. Though Thailand and Myanmar have been working together for some time on the development of the Salween River basin, but China has been acting unilaterally, potentially constructing up to 13 dams on the upper stem of the river. Without working with the two downstream nations, China risks creating conflict with Thailand and Myanmar. China, with far more military might and economic power than both Thailand and Myanmar combined, has little incentive to work jointly with them in the management of the Salween River. Thailand and Myanmar's water resources from the Salween may be at great risk depending on what China decides to do on the upper part of the river. It is indeed an emerging flash point for a conflict in future.[cxlviii]

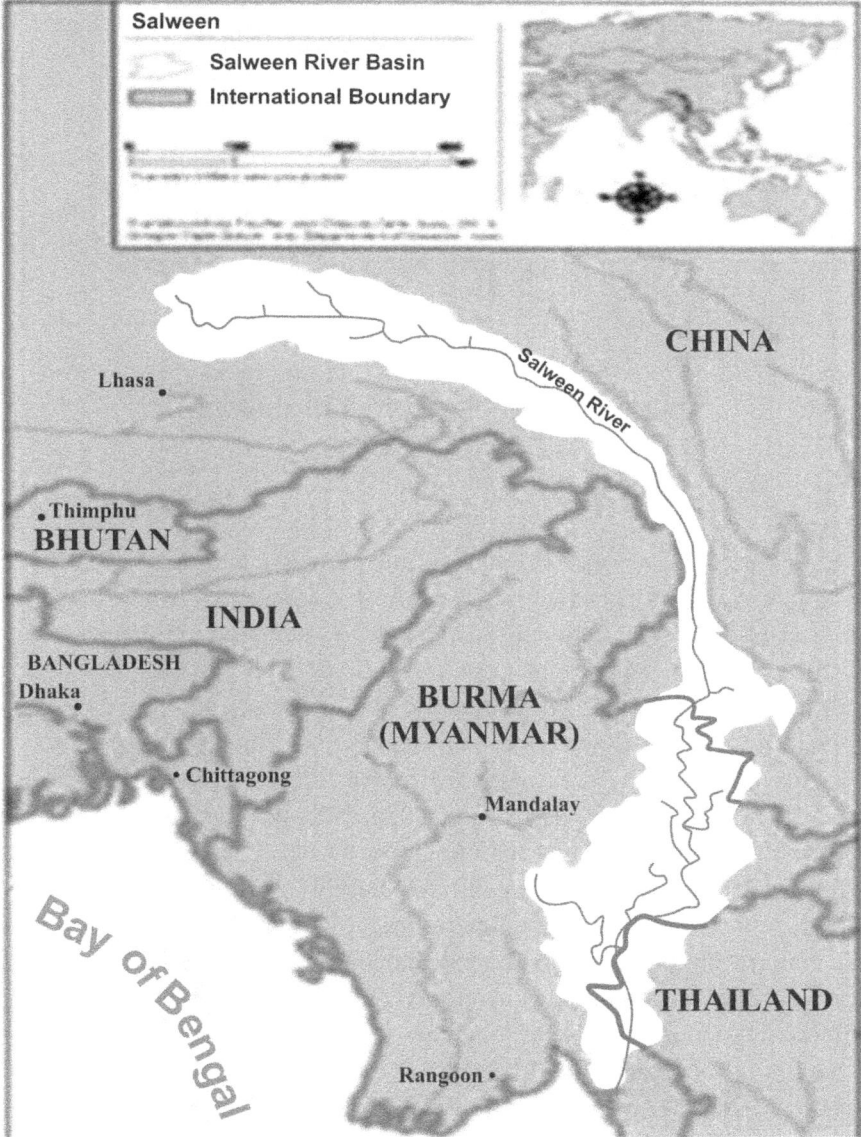

Salween

Salween River Basin
International Boundary

Chapter-5
Water Issues of South Asia

When the well is dry, we know the worth of water."

-Benjamin Franklin (1706-1790),
Poor Richard's Almanac, 1746

Water is a renewable resource, but a finite one. As mentioned earlier about 3% of the world's total water resource is fresh (not saline) of which one third is inaccessible for various reasons. Whatever is available; it is unevenly distributed, particularly in South Asia. Other major reason for water shortage in this region is contamination with wastes and pollution of both; ground as well a surface water. On demand side increasing population, industrialisation and water intensive newer agricultural techniques are adding to the yawning gap of the demand supply. South Asia is one of the most densely populated regions of the world. It houses roughly one fifth of the world's population and this share is likely to increase to one fourth of the total world's population by the year 2025.[cxlix] Economies of the countries of the region are highly depended on agriculture, hence need for more quantum of water, which is less than the required. This deficiency affects the food production which directly impinges on security issue. Area wise South Asia has almost the same amount of land area which Central Asia has. Central Asia is a water stressed region, however compared with Central Asia; South Asia has 18 times more population but water resources are just six times.[cl] This is the crux of the problem and it is likely to further get aggravated due to the rate of the growth of the population which is much higher in the case of the South Asia.

Nature of International Rivers in South Asia. Indian Sub continent has been a geographical entity which was partitioned on political considerations and the common resources of the region were artificially divided between the new states which came about post partition. As such apart from the crisis in the Himalayan River basins in India, there is a parallel threat in the countries of China, Nepal, Bangladesh and even Pakistan. Lack of water will mean food shortages in these countries, which India will have to contend with on a regional level. Workers who have lost their farmland in Bangladesh or Nepal are likely to migrate to India, causing a serious security threat to the country. Any instability in these countries will lead to further instability in the region, of which India is the most prominent entity. Most importantly, since all the Indian Himalayan Rivers are trans-boundary in nature, the problem will not be fully solved unless the solution is also trans-boundary. Long term solutions will have to be found only through joint action and collaboration. Even if the water crisis is somehow staved off in India, unless it is resolved in Nepal or Bangladesh as well, it is not likely to reach to a logical conclusion.. In this connection Indus Water Treaty of 1960 between India and Pakistan and Indo Bangladesh Ganges accord of 1996 are good examples of regional cooperation. Water shortages in the region need to be addressed with due sagacity by the leaders of all the countries of the region collectively. In this connection China's interest and impact is of a great concern to all the countries which are lower riparian with India as middle riparian and China as the upper riparian. In this Chapter inter-state water dynamics in the over arching influence of China is being examined.

Fig- 5.1A: International Rivers In South/ South East/ East Asia

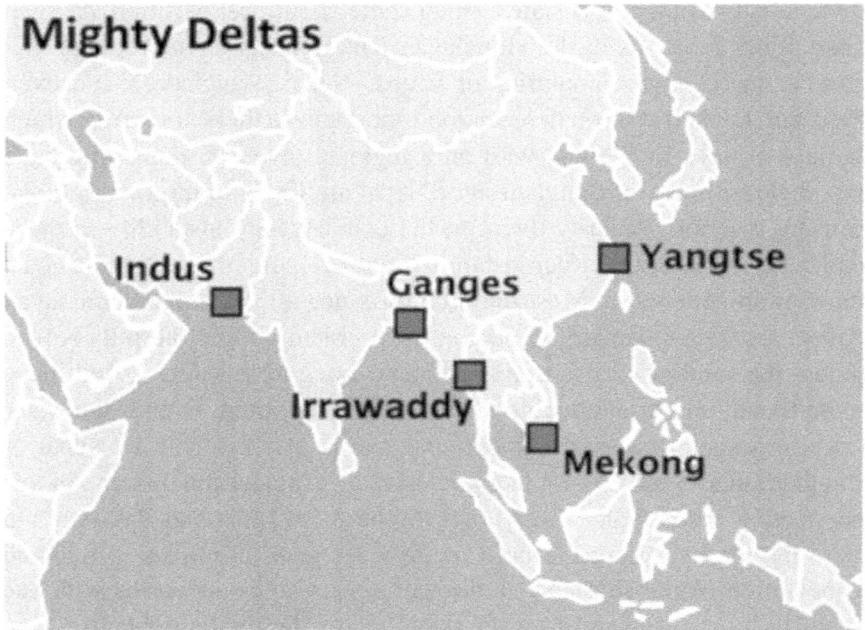

Fig-5.1B: Deltas of International Rivers In South/South East/ East Asia

History Of Human Migration to South Asia. Indian Subcontinent from time memorial has been well endowed by nature and has always been an attractive destination for foreigners to come for plunder, but invariably they settled here only, consequent to their arrival. The settlements had invariably been in various river vales. There is an evidence of dry river beds overlapping with the Hakra channel in Pakistan with the seasonal Ghagghar River in India. Many Indus Valley (or Harappa) sites have been discovered along the Ghagghar-Hakra beds.[1] New immigrants kept pushing forward resulting into a number of conflicts and coming up of new settlements.

---

[1] Possehi, GL (oct 1990), Revolution in the Urban Revolution: The Emergence of Indus Civilisation, Annual Review of Anthropology19:261-282.

Fig-5.2: Ghaggar/Hakra Alignment

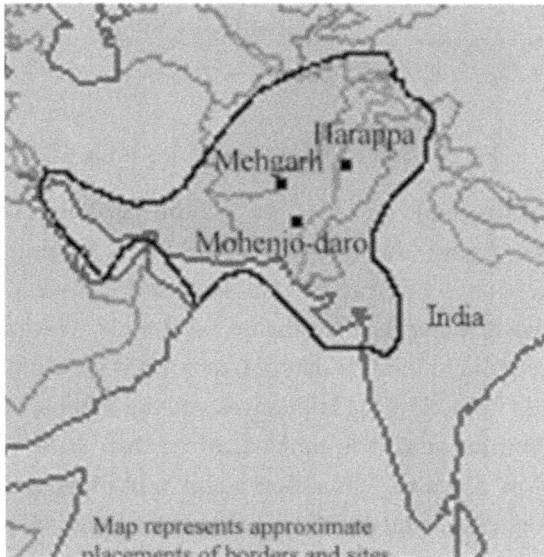

Fig-5.3: Indus Valley Civilization

Importance of Tibet. Tibetan Plateau is called the "Third Pole" because it has the largest perennial ice mass on the planet after the Arctic and Antarctica.

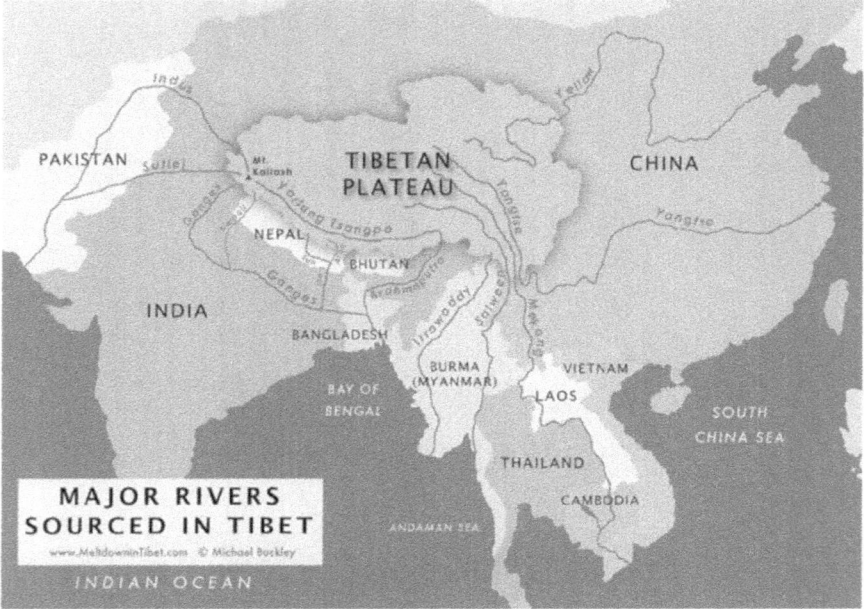

Fig-5.4: Major Rivers Emanating From Tibet

With its snowfields and glaciers feeding virtually every major river system of Asia; from Indus in the West to Yellow (Huang He) in the east the Plateau holds more ice and by implication fresh water than any other place in the World, other than North and South Pole. The importance of the Tibetan resource lie in the fact that unlike poles it is readily available. Ten key watersheds formed by the Himalayas and the Tibetan highlands spread out river waters far and wide in Asia. More than 90% of the runoff, of these rivers flow down to China, South and South East Asia.[cli] In addition as the Inter Governmental panel on Climate Change has pointed out that the rivers originating on the Tibetan plateau forms 11 Asian mega deltas, which are home to cities like Tianjin, Shanghai, Guangzhou, Bangkok, Kolkata, Dhaka and Karachi.[clii] Indeed 47% of the world's population is dependent on water rising in the Tibetan plateau.[2] Tibet Plateau plays a triple role: It is Asia's main fresh water repository, largest water supplier and principal rainmaker. Stretching 2,400 kilometres from East to West and 1,448 kilometres from North to South. Average elevation in Tibet is 4900 meters above the sea level. With its height the Tibetan Plateau literally towers over the rest of Asia. It actually rises up to the middle of the troposphere and helps deflect wind outward during winter and inward during summer. As such it influences Asian Climatic, weather and pattern of Monsoon. The rivers flowing out of Tibetan Plateau include the main rivers of China, South East Asia and South Asia; Yangtze, Yellow, Mekong, Salween, Irrawaddy, Arun (Kosi), Brahmaputra, Karnali and Indus with River Ganges, although rises on the Indian side of the plateau's rim, however many of its main tributaries flow in from Chinese controlled areas of Tibet. These include; Karnali; Gandak and Kosi (which is known as Arun in upper reaches). But it needs to be remembered that while rivers with sources in the icy Tibetan plateau are rich in water, but their sources are not inexhaustible, as Chinese officials claim. Scientists say glaciers on the Tibetan Plateau are receding faster than in any other part of the world. If the present rate of melting continues, most of these glaciers would have gone by 2035.[cliii] Almost half of the world's population lives in the watersheds of the rivers whose sources lie on the Tibetan Plateau. There are more than 1000 lakes on the Tibetan Plateau, including the world's highest salt lake — Namtso (Nam Co). Both sourced in the Tibetan Plateau, Yangtze (Chang Jiang) River and Yellow River serve roughly 520 million people in China.[cliv] The lakes include Mansarovar. According to an assessment by the Qinghai-Tibet Plateau Study Institute of the Chinese Academy of Sciences, these lakes, spread over 45,000 Sq Kms of area, hold 608 BCM of water, which constitutes 70% of China's total lake water reserves.[clv] The Tibetan plateau is ice-covered but it is an arid desert with very little rainfall. The source of much of its water bodies and rivers is glaciers. There are more than 18000 high altitude glaciers in the great Himalayas, where a zone of permanent rock and ice begins at about 5,500-6,000 meters. The glacier spread over 42,946 Sq Kms, cover 17% of the

---

[2] "India Quakes Over China's Water Plan" by Sudha Ramachandran pub in Asia Times 09 Dec 2008

Himalayas.[clvi] The portion of Himalayas which is there in Tibet has at least three times more glacier area than the portion of Himalayas which is there with India.

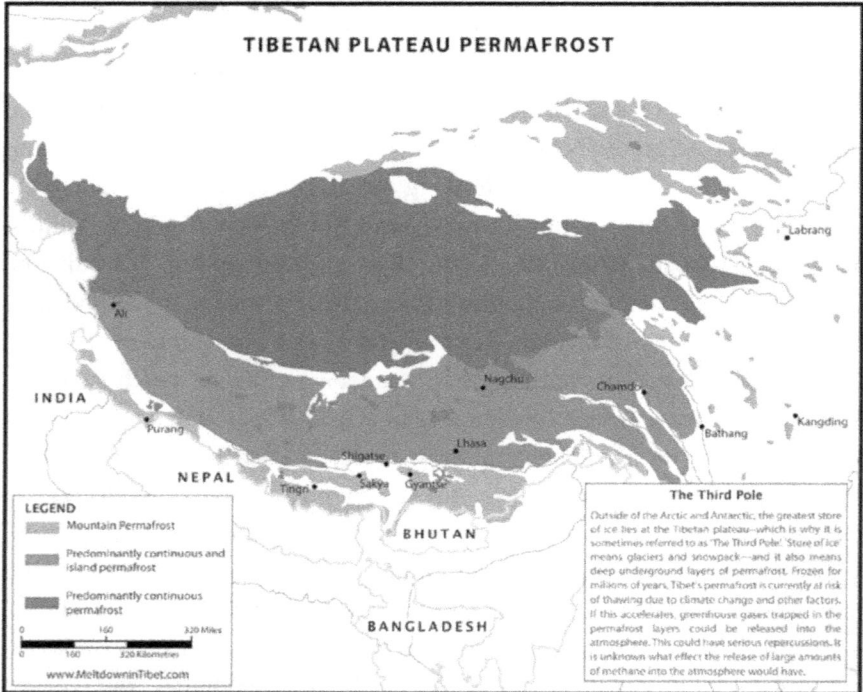

Fig 5.5: Glacier Wealth Of Tibet

About 10,000 Sq Kms of the Himalayan Glacier area is in India, compared with more than 30,000 Sq Kms under Chinese portion of Tibet. In fact but for few glaciers in Xinjiang, Chinese glaciers are mainly located on Tibetan Plateau (besides TAR these are also located in those areas which have either been merged with Sichuan, Gansu and Yunnan or have been organised into a separate province Qinghai.). As per China there are about 15,000 large glaciers in the Himalayan region of Tibet with a volume of locked water estimated to be 12,000 Cubic Kms.[clvii] These glaciers are melting due to global warming. If, alongside the impact of rising temperatures on glaciers, China diverts water from its natural course, Tibet will be a water-scarce region in a few decades. Critics also point to the environmental and ecological destruction it is likely to cause.

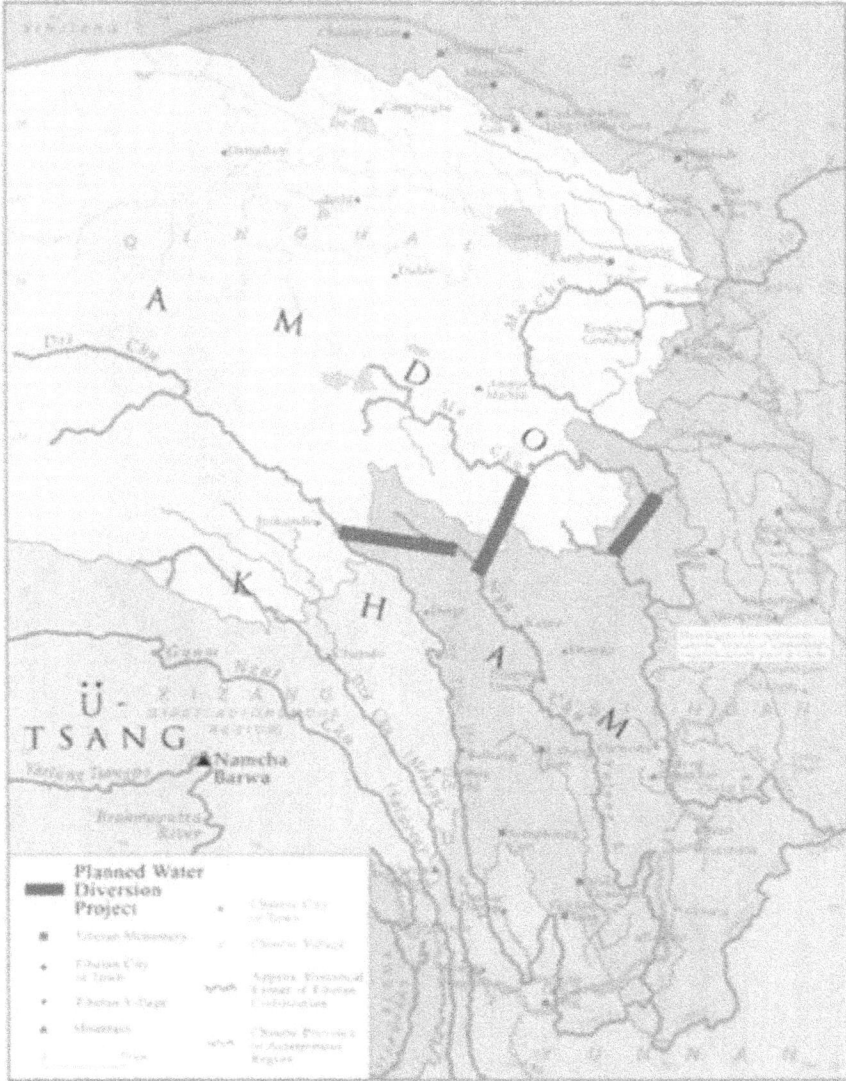

TIBET WATER DIVERSION SKETCH-MAP
This map shows the Western Route of the South-to-North Water Diversion Plan. The aim of the Western Route is to divert water from the Dri Chu (Yangtse) via the Nga Chu (Yalong) to the Ma Chu (Yellow River). Another branch would divert water from the Dadu River to the Yellow River. The data for this map is as yet unconfirmed and is thus subject to revision.

Fig-5.6: Water Diversion Project

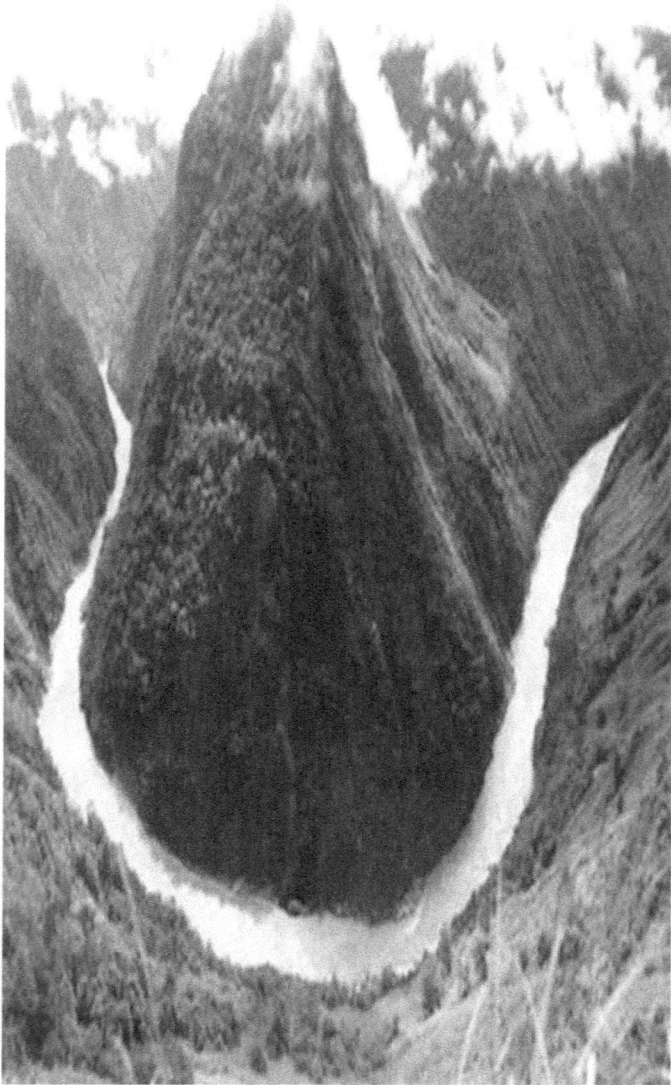

Fig-5.7: Great Bend In Brahmaputra

Just before going into India, River Brahmaputra makes a U shaped turn, (refer Fig-5.7) to form the so called Great bend in the Nyangtri Prefecture of the Tibet Autonomous Region (TAR) (China calls it Yarlung Tsangpo Great Canyon). It is 504.6 Kilometres long, 21 kilometres wide (on an average) and spread over an area of 64,300 Sq Kms . The average depth of its core section is 2673 metres. The deepest point recorded is 7,057 metres.[clviii] The Brahmaputra's Great bend Canyon indeed has the largest slope gradient of 75.34%, of any river surface in the world. The massive hydro power potential at the Great bend arise from the fact that the Brahmaputra at that stretch plunges several thousand metres by cutting through the high mountains, with the consequent rapids creating a source of immense energy. However the water diversion project at the Great Bend spells disaster not only for the Tibetan plateau but also for the lower riparian countries - India and Bangladesh. These countries view the project with some concern as it represents a direct threat to the lives and livelihood of millions of people living downstream. With the Yarlung Tsangpo's waters being diverted, the amount of water in the Brahmaputra will fall significantly, affecting India's North East and Bangladesh. It will severely impact agriculture and fishing there as the salinity of water will increase, as will silting in the downstream area.[3] Besides reducing the availability of water to lower riparian states (in this case India and subsequently Bangladesh), such a project also gives a handle to China to use thus regulated water supply for political purposes. Recent fast pace of melting and warmer temperatures due to global warming, though will be good for agriculture and tourism in the shorter term but may also result into floods and mudflows. However, in long term, availability of water is likely to reduce. Worst affected river systems are Indus and Brahmaputra. Massive reduction in availability of water in these river basins is going to affect adversely the production of food grains and thus by implication a source of conflict on account of serious threat to food security of lower riparian state silt may reduce as much as 50%. Today, five rivers originating in the Himalayas and the Tibetan Highlands rank among the world's top ten endangered rivers and these are: the Yangtze, the Indus; the Mekong; the Salween and the Ganges. In addition, over stressed Yellow River is widely seen as having been ecologically damaged by over damming; pollution and untreated sewage still finding its way into the river, including its upstream portions.[clix]

---

[3] Ibid73.

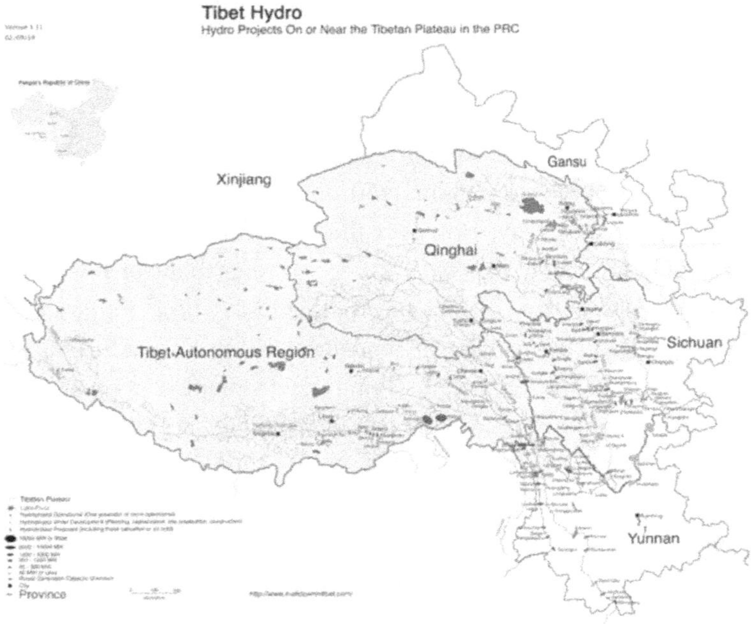

Fig-5.8: Hydro Projects In Tibet

Thus there is also a need to explain to China that Tibet's Water sources are a common heritage and not the sole preserve of China. Tibet besides being a water tower is also a rain maker for the South Eastern, Southern and Central Asia, China and Japan as it happens to be a heat sink during winters and a heat source during summer months.

Table-5.1: Volume Of Water Flowing Out Of Tibetan Plateau To Countries Other Than China

Ser. No	River system	Direct Destination	Mean annual Runoff Volume Flowing Out (Cubic Kms)
1.	Brahmaputra and Tributaries	India	165,400

2.	Rivers from South Western and Western Tibet	India	181,620
3.	Rivers from Southern Tibet	Nepal	12,000
4.	Salween	Myanmar	68,740
5.	Mekong	Laos PDR and Myanmar	73,630
6.	Tibetan rivers flowing out from Western Yunnan	Myanmar	31,290

Source: AQUASTAT online Data, Food and Agriculture Organisation on the United Nations, 2011.

Sources of Water Within Indian Subcontinent. The three river systems of the Northern Indian Subcontinent, namely; the Ganges, the Indus and the Brahmaputra, alone support half a billion people, who are dependent on the waters for agricultural and other economic practices as well as daily personal needs.[clx] Half of South Asia's 1.3 billion depend on river systems for water needs. Some of the world's largest rivers are located in this part of the world. Provincial boundaries within the countries of the South Asia and the national boundaries are frequently a source of tension within the region.[clxi] Problem gets further compounded during lean season as water availability reduces which results into intense competition among the upper and lower riparian states. All major rivers of Indian Subcontinent originate from one of the three watersheds, namely; Himalayas & Karakoram Ranges, Vindhya & Satpura Ranges & Chota Nagpur Plateau and Sahyadri or Western Ghats. Except those originating in Himalayas and Karakoram Ranges others originate within India and as such are sources of a number of inter-state water disputes. Case of rivers originating in Himalayas and Karakoram Ranges is different because many of them are trans-border Rivers and as such are root cause of water disputes between India and her neighbours. There are 16 major rivers, which have their origins in Himalayas. Some of the important river systems from this group are as follows:-

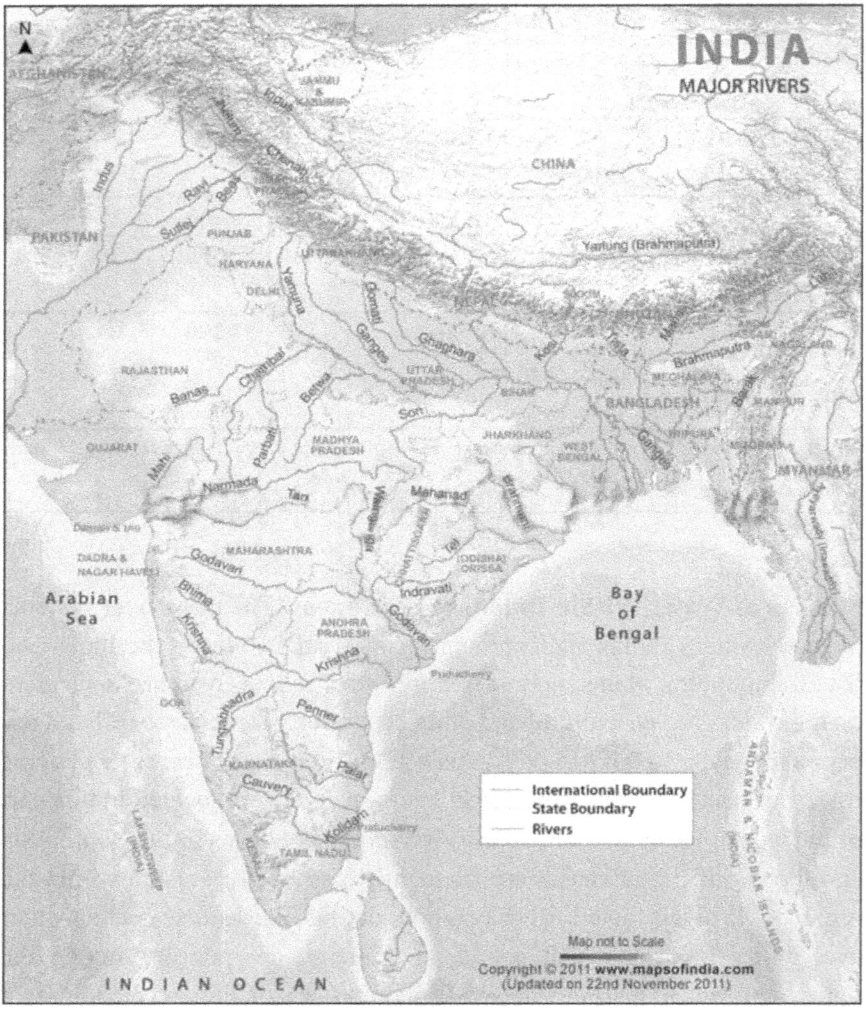

Fig-5.9: River Systems In Indian Subcontinent

▶ **Ganges River System-** River Ganges originates at Gomukh and after running a course of 1600 kms drains into Bay of Bengal. It is known as Padma in Bangladesh. Some of its tributaries originate in Nepal, like Kosi & Gandak and some in China like Mahakali. River Ganges along with Brahmaputra forms the largest river delta in the world covering an area of 59,570 Sq Kms and is known as Sunder bans. Most of area of Sunder bans is located in Bangladesh.[4] Peculiarity of the Ganges is that it has the largest sediment discharge in the world due to its relatively short upstream area and the high elevation from which it rapidly plunges into the plains. Its implication is that all along its course technical solutions need to be found to ensure that the sedimentation does not affect the flow of water, otherwise chances of regular flood and problems on account of shallow depth like stagnation of running water and impediment navigation among other effects remain quite certain.

► **Indus River System-** Indus originates in the Northern slopes of the Kailash Ranges near Lake Mansarovar in Tibet. In her journey, she traverses through Tibet (China), India, Pakistan Occupied Kashmir (POK) & Pakistan, over a distance of 3180 kms and finally drains into Arabian Sea. River Indus is joined by Sutlej, Ravi, Beas, Jhelum and Chenab from Eastern side and Shyok, Shingo, Shigar and Kabul amongst many others from Western / North- North Western side en-route. The total drainage area of the Indus river Basin is 11,65,000 Sq Kms. Indus River system supports one of the largest Irrigation Network in the World. However the problem with this river System is that there is wide difference between the basic precipitation and the net irrigation demand. It needs to be noted that the flow in Indus River System is mainly generated on account of snow and the glacier melt and therefore highly vulnerable to global warming.[clxii] It is appreciated that between 2046 and 2065 due to accelerated melting of snow availability of water for irrigation will become scarcer.

---

[4] Singh Vijay P; Sharma, Nayar; C. ShekharPogha, " The Brahmaputra Basin Water Resources", springer, pp-113.

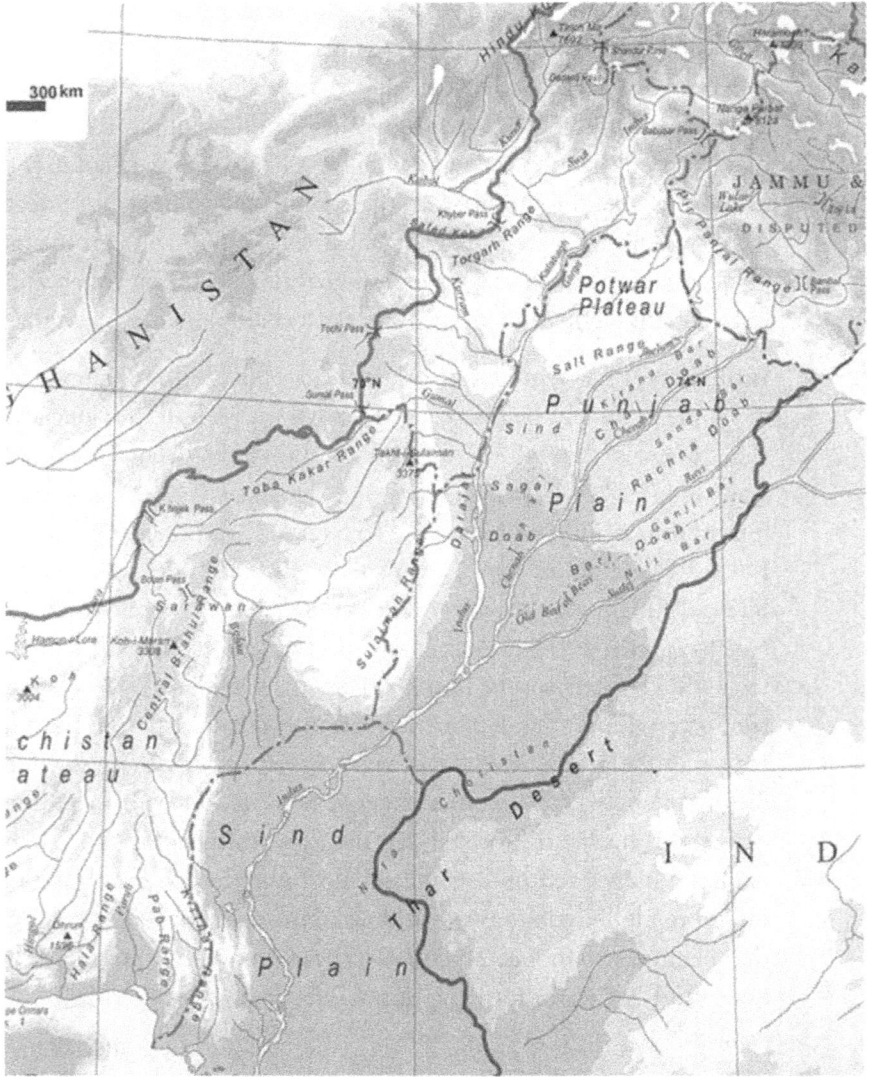

Fig-5.10: Indus Basin Rivers

► **Brahmaputra System**

Yamdrok Lake, located approximately 90 kilometers southwest of Lhasa, is the largest freshwater lake in southern Tibet and, through man-made tunnels, feeds the Tsangpo River. Photo: Kate Lord | katelordphoto.com

Fig-5.11: Yamdrok Lake Origin Of Brahmaputra

► River Brahmaputra originates from Yamdrok (TalungTso) Lake in South Western Tibet, gets most of her volume in Arunachal Pradesh and is 2900 Kms long. In Tibet it is known as Yarlung Zangbo River or Tsangpo, in Arunachal it is known as Siang, in plains as Dibang and flows southwest through the Assam Valley as Brahmaputra and South through Bangladesh as River Jamuna (not to be mistaken with Yamuna of India). In the vast Ganges Delta it merges with River Padma, the main distributary of the Ganges, then with River Meghna, before emptying into the Bay of Bengal. A major tributary of Brahmaputra is Kameng (Jia Bhareli). Only 30% of water in the river is generated in North and balance of it is generated once it comes down therefore possibility of her drying up due to construction of one or more dams in Tibet is quite remote.[5] However this river is also affected like Indus due to melting of glaciers as major source of feed into this river is on account of snow load and situation is likely to assume criticality between 2045 and 2065.[clxiii] Before entering into Bangladesh it splits into two tributaries and the bigger one is known as Jamuna in Bangladesh where it joins Ganges and forms Meghna and finally drains into Bay of Bengal. River Teesta is another river which joins it in Bangladesh.[6]

---

[5] Part of Report of the Symposium at Chinese Academy of Social Sciences, in chair Dr Rita Padwanginad panellists Dr UttamkumarSinha of IDSA and Dr Xiao Ping Yang of Institute of Asia Pacific Studies.
[6] Ibid 21.

Fig-5.12: Ganga, Brahmaputra And Meghna Basin

► **Peninsular River systems-** Mahanadi, Godavari, Krishna and Cauvery flow eastward and drain into Bay of Bengal. Narmada and Tapti are the only two major rivers which flow westward and drain into Arabian Sea.

The National Commission for Integrated water Resource Development (NCIWRD)

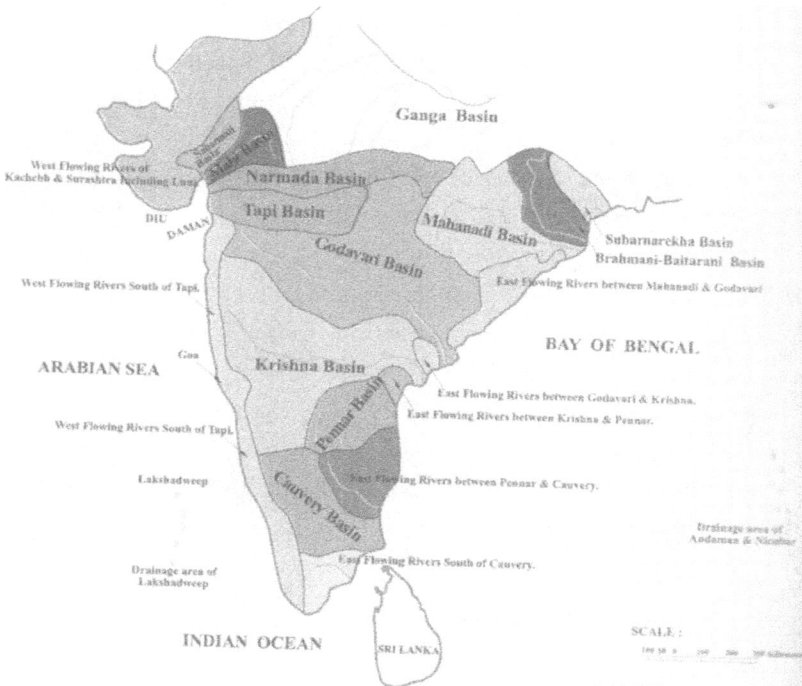

Fig-5.13: River Basins of peninsular India.

Total Water Resources Available in the South Asia.

The details are as tabulated below:-

Table-5.2: Water Availability In South Asia

Ser No	Data	Bangla desh	India	Nepal	Pakistan	Total (%of the World)	World
1.	Area (million HA)	14.8	329.0	14.7	88.2	446.7 (3.32)	13,422.3
2.	Population	126	980	23	132	1,261 (21)	6,005
3.	Average Annual Precipitation (MM)	2,360	1,170	1,530	238	1,117@	820
4.	Average Annual Water Potential(Internal Renewable Resource in BCM)	373#	1,870	237	236	2,716 (6.8)	40,000
5.	Average Annual utilizable Surface Water Potential BCM	1160$	690	225	180	2,255	
6.	Total Ground Water resource Potential BCM	23	432	6-12	56		
7.	Total Utilizable Ground Water Resource Potential-BCM	23	396	6-12	56		
8.	Total Utilizable Surface and Ground Water Potential-BCM	1183$	1,086	237	236	2,742	
9.	Per Capita Availability of Fresh Water Resources-BCM	10,714 (1998)	1879 (2000)	10,304 (2000)	1685 (2000)		

Note: @- Weighted average of WASSA region.

#- 340 BCM Generated by local flows and 23 BCM by ground water flows.

$- Includes cross border flows.

Source: GWP-SASTAC Vision Documents;FAO Country Papers; NCIWRDP Report of India.

It can be seen that as early as 2000 India and Pakistan (Pakistan a little more than India) were being threatened of becoming water scarce. Presently Pakistan has already slipped to the status of becoming water scarce country India is barely away from that state.

Common Problems of the Countries of South Asia

The present shortage and the future scarcity of water is a major source of tension amongst the countries of the Indian Subcontinent. Some of the common problems are as follows:-

- ► **Lack of an Institutional Structure-** for sharing of information with respect to flow in the common rivers which normally is denied under the garb of classification of confidentiality. Presently it is more of individual cases rather than an all-encompassing formal arrangement.

- ► **Pollution of Water Bodies-** due to a host of reasons which is further affecting the availability of potable water.

- ► **Global Warming-**most of the rivers which are originating in Himalayas are glacier fed. Due to global warming, the feed in these rivers has already started getting affected, and likely to be a major source of reduction in the availability of water in these rivers in future.

- ► **Uneven Distribution of The Available Water Within The Country-** Bangladesh, though a water surplus country has areas which are draught prone. Similar is the case with India and that is one of the reason that the inter basin transfer of the water is the way ahead. However in case of rivers which are common; it needs to be done in a manner that the lower riparian states are not denied their rights.

Water Resources of India

The country can be divided into 24 river basins comprising 12 major and 12 medium and small river basins. The 12 major rivers have a total catchment area of 252.8 Mha. Of the major rivers, the Ganga-Brahmaputra-Meghna (GBM) system is the biggest, with a catchment area of 110 Mha. Other basins greater than 10 Mha are the Indus (32.1 Mha), Godavari (31.3Mha), Krishna (25.9Mha) and Mahanadi (14.2 Mha). As can be seen from above Map at Fig-5.9, India shares GBM basin with Bangladesh, Nepal and Bhutan and the Indus Basin with Pakistan.[clxiv]

In India, the availability of water is highly uneven, spatially as well as temporally. The variation in rainfall could be attributed to the varied climates of the country, ranging from arid to tropical wet climatic zones. The prime source of water in the country is rainfall, which is confined to only three to four months in a year. The annual rainfall also shows significant spatial and temporal variations. It varies from 10 cm in the Western parts of Rajasthan to about 1100 cm at Cherrapunji in Meghalaya (GOI, NCIWRDP,1999). The average precipitation including snowfall is estimated (GOI, NCIWRDP,1999) to be of the order of 4,000 BCM of which the monsoon rainfall during June to September is around 3000 BCM and the net annual inflow in the rivers in India is 1,869 BCM.[clxv]

Table-5.3: Water Resources Potential In India

Name of the River Basin	Avg Annual Surface Water Potential (BCM)	Estimated Utilizable Flow excluding Ground Water (BCM)	Total replenishable Ground Water Resources (BCM)	Population -in 1991	Per capita available Surface Water CUM	Per capita available Surface and Ground Water CUM
Indus (up to border)*.	73.31@	46.00	26.49	41.90	1,750	2,382
Ganga*	525.02	250.00	170.99	356.80	1,471	1,951
B'putra*	585.60	24.00	53.91	35.24	16,617	18,147
Barak*	-	-				
Godavari*	110.54	76.30	40.65	53.98	2,048	2,801
Krishna*	78.12	58.00	26.41	60.78	1,285	1,720
Cauvery*	21.36	19.00	12.30	29.33	728	1,148
Pennar*	6.32	6.86	4.93	9.70	652	1,160
East Flowing Rivers between Mahanadi and Pennar	22.52	13.11	18.22	23.60	954	831
East Flowing Rivers between Pennar and Kanyakumari	16.46	16.73	5.5.1		45.20	364

River Basin							
Mahanadi*	66.88	49.99	16.46	26.60	2,514	3,133	
Brahmini & Baitarini*	28.48	18.30	4.05	9.77	2,915	3,329	
Subernrekha*	12.37	6.81	1.82	5.5.1	9.46	1,308	1,500
Sabarmati *	3.81	1.93	18.42	5.5.1	10.58	360	1,120
Mahi*	11.02	3.10	5.5.1		10.48	1,052	
West Flowing Rivers of Kutch, Saurashtra, including Luni	15.10	14.98	5.5.1		22.10	683	
Narmada*	45.64	34.50	10.83	14.70	3,105	3,842	
Tapi*	14.88	14.50	8.27	14.80	1,005	1,564	
West Flowing Rivers from Tapi to Tadri	87.41	11.94	17.69	25.80	3,388	3,744	
West Flowing Rivers from Tadri to Kanyakumari	113.53	24.27	5.5.1		32.60	3,483	
Area of Inland Drainage in Rajasthan desert	NEG			7.10			
Minor River Basins draining into Bangladesh & Myanmar	31.00			2.10	14,762	14,762	
Total	1869.35	690.31	431.44	842.62		2,731	

Note: @-Refers to only three Eastern Rivers; Ravi, Sutlej and Beas.

* - Indicates Inter State River Basins.

Source: Water Vision 2050, Indian Water Resources Society (IWRS), 1999.

The above table clearly brings out that the utilizable flow in Indian basins is cumulatively is 690.31 BCM as against the average natural flow of 1869.35 BCM because of large number of constraints and limitations. Another disturbing observation is the declining availability of water per capita in India over the years. There is a steady decline in the volume of water which is available every year per person. This trend is quite clear from following table:-

Table-5.4: Declining Availability Of Water Per Capita In India

Ser No	Year	Average Water Availability (m3 /person/ year)
1.	1947	6,000
2.	1957	5,300
3.	1967	4,200
4.	1977	3,500
5.	1987	3,000
6.	1997	2,246
7.	2007	2,100
8.	2017	2,000
9.	2027	1,800
Source: Engleman and Roy (1993)		

As can be seen the per capita availability is on the decline. There could be many reasons for that. First and foremost is the population explosion which has resulted into per capita share from a constant resource getting reduced. Simultaneously the size of pie itself is getting reduced due to a number of reasons which have already been covered in detail in Chapter-3. Another issue which merits consideration is the uneven distribution of population. As has been explained at the beginning of the chapter that the human settlements had come up where the water was available and as such the population density has always been maximum in the Gangetic Basin. Also for various reasons upper riparian, in case of most of the rivers, is China, whose own requirements are insatiable due to a number of reasons which have been addressed in this chapter earlier. All this paints a very grim future where Countries in South Asia will have many conflicts coming up for water.

Bangladesh: An Appraisal Of Her Water Resources

Bangladesh, located in the delta of two the world's largest rivers, ie, the Ganges and the Brahmaputra, is the lower riparian state of the three river basins, namely; the Ganges; the Brahmaputra and the Meghna. About 93 % of the catchment area of the country's river system lies outside the country.[clxvi] The catchment area is as tabulated below:-

Table-5.5: Catchment Area Of Major River Basins Of Bangladesh

Ser No	River	Total Catchment Area (Sq Kms)	Catchment area in Bangladesh (Sq Kms)	Percentage of Catchment Area in Bangladesh
1.	Ganges	949,667	34,188	3.6
2.	Brahmaputra	582,750	50,505	8.7
3.	Meghna	78,405	29,785	38.0

Source: Bangladesh water Development Board (BWDB), 1998.

Status of Ground Water. As far as ground water is concerned, 80% of it is contaminated with Arsenic; as such Bangladesh depends essentially on surface water (that is why Bangladesh is so vocal about her water needs vis-a-vis India). Bangladesh gets 85% of her surface water from Ganges and Brahmaputra. Bangladesh's problems are on account of her being lower riparian and she depends substantially on India; the upper riparian. [7]

The natural surface water resources in Bangladesh are mainly obtainable from the country's dense network of river systems, which include a combination of upstream inflows and runoff generated from rainfall within the country. Preliminary estimates at the inception phase of the National Water Management Plan (NWMP) indicate the cross-border flows into the country amount to around 1010 BCM and an additional amount of 340 BCM is generated from local rainfall, averaging 236 Centimetres. The Ground Water is 10%, Standing Surface Water is 1%

---

[7] TauhidulAnwer Khan, Secretary General Bangladesh,"Water Partnership", paper presented at Symposium of IDSS.

and surface water is 89%.[cxlvii] Of this total amount of available water (1350 BCM), about 190 BCM of water is lost in the atmosphere through evaporation transpiration, while the balance of 1160 BCM is available for use of flows into the Bay of Bengal. 80 % of this huge flow of water is concentrated in the five month monsoon period of June to October.

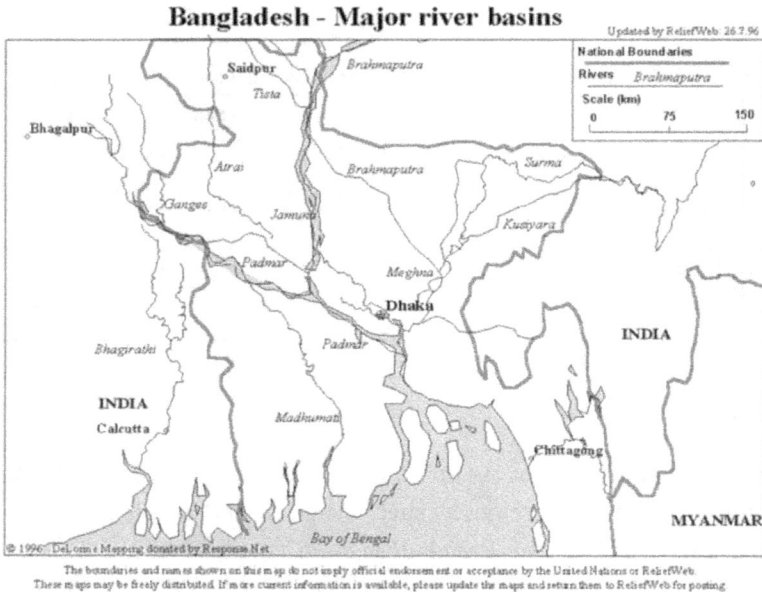

Fig-5.14: River Basins Of Bangladesh

Water Resources of Nepal

Nepal has a major bearing on the availability of water within India, and as such it is important to analyse the water resources and their pattern of flow which contributes to availability of water within the Gangetic plains. Nepal is endowed with 6000 rivers and rivulets that carry a substantial amount of water flow. 80% of the flow is received during South West monsoon (June to September). About 64% of the precipitation directly contributes to the flows as surface run-off, and the rest is utilized as snow, recharge of ground storage, or lost as evaporation and transpiration. The snow and the ground water later appear as base flow during the lean periods in the rivers. Most of the country receives rainfall in the range of 1,500 to 2,500 millimetres per annum and the average precipitation is in the range of 1,770 millimetres.[cxlviii]

There are nine major and medium river basins in the Nepalese river systems, covering a total drainage area of 194,500 km2, of which 47,290 km2 is in Tibet, China or India.[clxix] The rivers can be classified into three categories;-

▸ **Major Rivers-**Some of these are; Kosi, Gandak, Karnali and Mahakali. These originate in the Himalayas and the high mountains and are snow fed. After flowing through the Terai region of Nepal, they merge with Ganges in India. These rivers are perennial and carry sufficient flow even during the dry season.

▸ **Medium Rivers-** Some of these are; the Kankai, Kamala, Bagmati, West Rapti and Babai. Most of these originate from the middle mountains below the snow line and are rain fed. These are also perennial rivers with contributions from ground water and springs during the dry season.

▸ **The Minor Rivers-** originating from the Shivalik Range or in the Terai, these are much smaller in size and carry very little flow during the dry season.

Kosi is the largest river basin with a drainage area of around 60,400 Sq Kms . On the other hand, the Gandak Basin with a drainage area of 34,960 Sq Kms, has the highest surface water availability. The Gandak and Kosi Basins account for 24.6% and 23.3% of the total water availability respectively in Nepal.[clxx] About 74% of the total annual surface flow occurs in the period June to September. This kind of peak around July to September causes havoc in the downstream area and therefore it is important that a framework be evolved under the aegis of SAARC to address the peak water load.

In Nepal good potential for ground water exists only in Terai region (The Southern plains bordering Uttar Pradesh and Bihar), the inner valleys and the mountainous regions. The annual ground water recharge available for extraction is estimated to range from 6-12 BCM/ year.[clxxi] It may however be noted that the ground water availability is not uniform but is concentrated in certain specific areas. It can further be seen that the magnitude of the average availability of surface and ground water resources of the whole country can be misleading when it comes to actual utilisation. The variations of water resources availability in terms of time and space are considerable. Thus while in some area water may be surplus but there may be certain other areas which could be categorised as water stressed/ scarce.

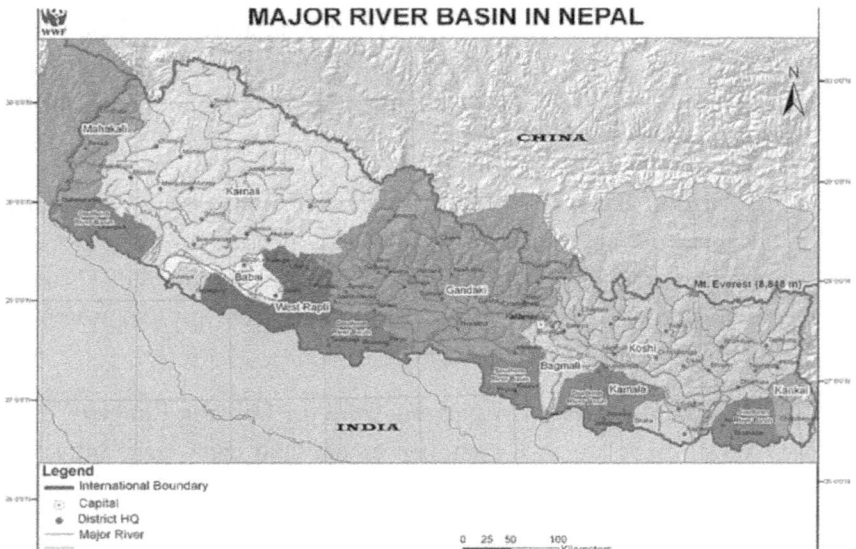

Fig-5.15: Major River Basins In Nepal

Water Resources of Pakistan

The rivers in Pakistan originate in the higher reaches of Himalayas and derive their water; primarily from snowmelt and monsoon rains. The Indus River Basin is as shown in the Fig- 5.15. The rivers of the Indus system can be classified into Western Rivers (Indus, Jhelum and Chenab) and the Eastern Rivers (Ravi, Beas and Sutlej). River Indus is the main river of Pakistan and the North West India and in terms of the extent of dependent agriculture and population, this river system can be ranked as one of the most important river in the world. It is important to note that post partition of India in 1947, the Indus River basin, which hither to fore was monolithic in nature and the development of which was planned accordingly, was subjected to a viva-section with attended issues. The water availability in rivers of Pakistan is highly erratic and unreliable. The highest annual water availability in the recorded history from 1922 to date; was 186.79 MAF (million acre feet) in the year 1959-60, as against the minimum of 95.99 MAF, in the year 2001-2002. 140 MAF of water annually available in Pakistan in a normal year, some 40 MAF reach the Indus delta (though it has been much less in recent years).[cxxlii] The resultant tension and its resolution is being discussed in sections appearing later in this chapter.

INDUS BASIN IRRIGATION SYSTEM IN PAKISTAN

Fig-5.16: River Basins In Pakistan

Pakistan has one of the world's largest gravity-flow irrigation systems, with three reservoirs, 19 barrages, 12 river interlinking canals, and 59,200 kilometres of distribution canals. More than 160,000 watercourses comprise the distribution network that takes water directly to the farms.[clxxiii] The irrigation distribution in Pakistan dates back to colonial period when the population was smaller and future partition was nowhere in sight and as such it was planned with the aim that was for the overall development of the irrigation system in the erstwhile United Punjab which came in conflict of purpose post partition. Originally the irrigation system was planned for a much larger area. Many of those canals became redundant post partition and important ones like Dipalpur and Central Doab Canal were realigned.

An Analysis 0f the Water Resources. Some the relevant aspects are as follows:-

- ▶   Primary Source of Water- Surface water is the primary source of water in the country. Pakistan's problem is that out of 180 BCM, which Pakistan gets every year, though almost 75% of the surface runoff is diverted to canal head, only 30% reaches the crop for reasons like seepage and evaporation.[clxxiv] This quantity is barely sufficient to meet their requirement.

- ▶   Ground Water- Infiltration from rivers, canals, watercourses and fields is the main source of ground water. Around 51.3 BCM of the ground water is pumped for irrigation use. The province wise ground water recharge and the current use is as tabulated below:-

Table-5.6: Ground Water Recharge And Current Use

Ser No	Province	Recharge (BCM)	Current Use (BCM)
1.	Punjab	49.3	41.9
2.	Sindh	12.3	4.3
3.	Khyber Pakhtunkhwa	3.0	2.5
4.	Baluchistan	1.1	0.6
5.	Total	65.7	49.3
Source: ACE/ Halcrow, "Exploitation and Regulation of Ground Water", June 2001.[clxxv]			

- ▶   **Uneven Distribution of Ground Water-** The ground water use is nearing the upper limit in most parts of Pakistan. The rate of extraction of ground water is much more than the recharge. Virtually there is no planned recharge mechanism in place, therefore, the aquifer depletion rate is about 10 feet/ year.[clxxvi] Hence, due to this phenomenon, there could be a big environmental disaster in making in Pakistan. Over extraction of ground water has caused fast depletion of aquifer which has raised alarming levels of bacterial contamination. It is estimated that to recharge aquifer/ Depleted Water table in the provinces of Punjab, Baluchistan and North West Frontier, Pakistan needs to spend at least 1 percent of the GDP on water resources to avert crisis like situation in future. The World Bank has lamented that the military spending in Pakistan is 47 times higher than the spending in water sector, which is currently only 0.25 percent of the GDP, which in real terms is likely to be in the range of $10 billion/year. [clxxvii] The ground water table is falling in most fresh ground water areas. Most of the unutilised discharge is in areas of saline ground water and cannot be used. As has been estimated that probably a maximum of 1.2 to 2.4 BCM, can be extracted additionally. Another issue in this regard is the uneven spread of deficiency of the ground water. This state does not auger well for the availability of water for the thirsty Pakistan. In fact it is assessed that Pakistan has reached a stage where further increase in extraction could lead to serious problems of ground water degradation from salt- water percolation and encroachment.[clxxviii] It is estimated that only 79% of the area of Punjab and 28% of the area of Sind is suitable for irrigation with the ground water.[clxxix]

▶ **Salinization of Ground water-** Another serious long-term problem is salination. When irrigation water soaks down into the soil, it absorbs mineral salts from the earth, flushing them to the surface. As the water evaporates, these salts dry out on the fields, gradually destroying their fertility. According to one estimate, some 25 per cent of Pakistan's cultivated land has already been damaged in this way.[clxxx] Recovering poisoned fields is vastly expensive. The environmental damage done by ill-managed irrigation schemes is a time bomb that threatens to reverse the progress in food production made by past schemes. Pakistan is currently using half its available run-off, that is, the water that falls on the country and is collected in rivers, lakes and streams, and is drawing half as much again from underground springs and aquifers.

▶ **Pollution of Ground Water-** Both state and non-state actors
have overwhelmingly contributed towards deteriorating the water
quality due to indiscriminate over extraction of ground water
complemented with polluted recharge sources. At the moment
the Northern part of Pakistan has microbial contamination of
64 % (Diagnostic Survey, 2007).[clxxxi] Central part of the country
has both chemical and microbial contamination. Rivers Ravi and
Chenab receive industrial waste water of textile, leather and light
engineering industries amounting to more than 1700 MGD, from
both India and Pakistan. This phenomenon is not only polluting
surface water but also contaminating ground water aquifer, which
is flowing towards southern areas during recharge process. The
most prominent contaminants comprises of 50,000 thousands
dyes (heavy metals and trace elements), chromium, fluorides,
iron which have not only polluted the surface water but has also
contaminated potential ground water resources (Major source of
drinking water in Pakistan). In addition to the above mentioned
contaminants, the Central and Southern part of the country is
also experiencing prevalence of heavy concentration of arsenic
ground water contamination ranging up to 1100 Particles Parts
per Billion (ppb). Comparatively higher nitrate levels of <70 %
in the groundwater sources like hand pumps and wells support
the possibilities of increased contamination in the areas cultivated
using heavy doses of fertilizers. Worst affected provinces are
Punjab and Baluchistan.[clxxii]

Water Problem Outside Indus River Basin. Outside the Indus Basin and
outside the canal command area in the Indus Basin, water is even more
limited. Ground water depletion is a major issue. In parts of Baluchistan,
where, geological fossil water is being mined. For example; in the Quetta
Valley, the water table is falling by up to two meters every year, primarily
due to competing demands for water from concentrations of orchards and
human settlements. Also five fold increase in goats and a four fold growth
in the sheep population since independence has led to overgrazing and
reduced the productivity of grazing ground to as little as 15-20 % of their
potential.[clxxxiii]

Demand-Supply Gap in South Asia

Analysis of the resources of the countries of South Asia brings out clearly that the availability of water is steadily reducing due to global warming, deforestation, pollution and above all China's excessive efforts to use water resources of Tibet which contributes substantially to meet the water needs of the South Asia. The demand is steadily increasing because of the additional requirement of water to meet the requirement on account of rising population, water intensive crop pattern and industrial requirement. Therefore in the analysis of water based tensions/ conflicts and its probability, the next logical step would be to analyse the forecasted water requirement and the availability some time in future. A reasonable date would be 2025. The likely status in 2025 would be as tabulated below :.-clxxxiv

Table-5.7: Demand- Supply Gap In 2025

Ser No	Country	Total Water Requirement (BCM)	Projected water Availability (BCM)	Projected Water Surplus/ Deficit Gap (BCM)
1.	India	1060	1086	(+)26
2.	Pakistan	335	236	(-)102
3.	Bangladesh	48	1,181	(+)1,133
4.	Nepal	60	237	(+)177

Note: the above figures exclude non- consumptive uses and rain–fed agriculture use for the sake of maintaining uniformity for all the countries of the region.

As can be seen, that although South Asia as a whole will have water problems due to declining availability and increasing requirement but the worst affected country would be Pakistan. Pakistan will further be getting affected by the Chinese efforts of constructing a dam on River Indus near Nagri prefecture opposite Eastern Ladakh before it enters India. Situation will further worsen as far as water availability in Pakistan is concerned if India decides to make use of full quantity of water as provided by the Indus Water Treaty-1960 and also dams planned on Kabul River by Afghanistan (a feeder of River Indus) come through. Shortage of water in Pakistan is likely to result into internal tensions among the provinces (A little more about it in subsequent sections) and tensions between India and Pakistan.

Water Problems of Various Countries of South Asia

Northern and Eastern part of the Indian Subcontinent is watered by mainly two water drainage systems, namely; Indus Basin and Ganges-Brahmaputra-Meghna Basin. All the countries of South Asia suffer from a number of water problems on account of a gap between demand and supply which is also growing due to population explosion in the region, inter-state disputes due to real or perceived disparity in fair & just division of water and pollutions of water sources .[8]

India. India is having enormous water problems. The Union Ministry of Water Resources has estimated the country's water requirements to be around 1093 BCM for the year 2025 and 1447 BCM for the year 2050. With projected population growth of 1.4 billion by 2050, the total available water resources would barely match the total water requirement of the country. In 1951, the annual per capita availability of water was 5177 meters, which got reduced to 1342 meters by 2000. The facts indicate that India is expected to become 'water stressed' by 2025 and 'water scarce' by 2050. Some of the relevant issues are as discussed below:-

> ▸ **Availability-** The National Commission for Integrated water Resource Development (NCIWRD) has estimated that against a total annual availability of 1953 BCM (inclusive of 432 BCM of ground water and 1521BCM of surface water) only 1123 BCM (433 BCM ground water and 690 BCM surface water) can be put to use, i.e., only 55.6 per cent. The high-level of pollution further restricts the utilisable water thus posing a serious threat to its availability and use.

> ▸ **Water Security for India is Emerging as an Issue of Extreme Urgency-** Broadly defined, water concerns are multi-dimensional in nature combining the sufficient need of quality water for socio-economic uses as well as adequate water to sustain ecosystem functions. Water security for India implies effective responses to changing water conditions in terms of quality, quantity and uneven

---

[8] Dr Rita Padwangi and ArpitaMathur, " Inter State water Conflicts".

distribution. Unheeded it can impact relationships, tensions at the inter-provincial level & political expediency and finally the compulsions of the coalition politics in the country is likely to erode the overall capacity of the Indian Nation to deal with such complexities.

▶ **Uneven Rainfall Pattern-** India is a having a very diverse pattern of the rainfall; from highest to almost scarce. It is a reality in the country which affects the water availability substantially. The rainy days on an average are about five in the desert areas and about 150 in the North East. In Andaman and Nicobar Islands these (rainy days) are even more. Due to this peculiar rainfall pattern, about 40 Mha of agricultural area is flood-prone, and about 108 Mha is drought-prone. 80 per cent of the run-off in the Himalayan rivers and 90 per cent of run-off in the peninsular rivers occurs during the period; June to September. Excessive deforestation has further aggravated the problem due to degraded soil's reduced capacity to absorb the water. The attended effect is that the dry weather flows reduce substantially and massive floods on account of surface run off running away to the sea results in heavy silt concentration accumulated during flood time. Such an accumulation of silt results in creating obstacles for unimpeded flow of water otherwise, thus shrinking, not only the size of the river channels but also causes erosion in the self cleansing capacity of the river. The reduced size of the water channels reduces the valley storage capacity resulting in higher flood peaks. The inhabitation of floodplains and increased development and cultivation has augmented flood damage. The impact of droughts is even more severe than that of floods and leaves a permanent mark on the economy.[clxxxv]

▶ **Problems on Account of Internal and Externally Triggered Migration-** The water availability has reduced by 60% in last century. Per capita water availability having dropped from 5,177 cum per year in 1947 to 1,342 cum in 2000 and is, expected to drop further due to burgeoning population. In fact by an assessment, by 2050 India's requirement is likely to go up to 1447 BCM and the availability is likely to plateau at 1123 BCM resulting into a shortfall of 29 %. In India, in addition to slowly eroding water availability, issues like burgeoning population and lack of pollution control is further affecting the availability of water. A shortage of water in the Ganges has already affected the lives and livelihoods of millions in Bangladesh, pushing them to migrate to India, especially to the North Eastern part of India. This migration of Bangladeshis has changed the demographic composition of vast tracts in the North-East (especially in Assam) and triggered serious ethnic conflicts there.[9] A shortage of water in River Brahmaputra is likely to emerge in not too far distant future (due to Chinese efforts to dam Brahmaputra in TAR), and that will further accentuate these problems to dangerous levels. There is another concern that with the water diversion project on Brahmaputra taking off in Tibet to feed Yellow River, China will acquire great power and leverage over India and by implication on Bangladesh also , worsening tensions between these two countries.[10]

However shortage of water is adversely impacting the basic integrity of the nation. To understand this issue in correct perspective a typical geographical fact about India needs to be understood. In India there are pockets which are water surplus and some other places which are water deficient. This is resulting into internal migration also. That is how population in Mumbai and Delhi is on the rise causing conflicts between the earlier inhabitants and the new arrivals.

Uneven Distribution of Water through the Country-   There is a wide variation in the availability of water within the country. If there are places where water availability far exceeds the national average then there are places which are water scarce.   Therefore there is a need to think in terms of an infrastructure for inter river/ river basin transfer. However such a solution is easier said than done because water in India is a state subject (List II, entry 17 to Indian constitution) but for Interstate relations it is covered in concurrent list also (List I, entry 56) , specially with respect to management of rivers which are interstate in nature. Such a contradiction

---

[9] Ibid73.
[10] Ibid73.

leads to interpretations by various stake holders as convenient to them. However in the national interest it needs to be addressed with certain give and take by the concerned States. Such a sagacious response can be possible as finally India Parliament has full jurisdiction for dispute resolution under Article 262, Article 246 which gives powers to Indian Parliament to deal with Laws made by the Legislatures of the States and finally under List III, Entry 20 which deals with planning under Concurrent List.[11] In addition to these constitutional provisions, The River Board Act 1956 which came into effect on 12 September 1956 provides for the establishment of River Boards for the Regulation and Development of Inter-state rivers and river valleys. The scope of these boards is envisaged to be advisory in nature. It, however, is of interest that the Central Government has not constituted any River Board under this Act, though some boards outside the provisions of the River Board Act 1956, with specific purpose, like Yamuna Board, Brahmaputra Board among many others, have been constituted. This Act has been getting amended from time to time to meet the newer challenges which have been coming up from time to time. It was amended last on 18 March 1986. Under the provisions of the amended Act a Tribunal can be constituted by the Central government on the complaint of a State for the conflict resolution. A Standing Committee on Inter-State Issues in Water Resources in 1990 by the Ministry of Water Resources in April 1990 to assist the National Water Resources Council (NWRC) has also been constituted. The Committee renders advice on modifications to specific elements of Water Plans and on such other issues that may arise during the planning or implementation of projects. In this connection Sarkaria Commission formed in June 1983 to examine Centre State Relationship also examined the constitutional provisions related to water in respect of Inter-State Water disputes. The Commission was of the opinion that there is need for Union control over waters of Inter State rivers and river valleys. The National Commission has recommended to the Government of India to enact a new Act called, "Integrated and Participatory Management Act" in place of the existing River Board Act, 1956. Thus in the present circumstances, it calls for a will power on the part of the law makers and

---

[11] "Inter State Water Disputes in India : Institutions and Policies" by Allan Richards and Nirvikar Singh Oct 2001

a deliberate effort to build the consensus on the subject. The formation of National Water Development Agency is step in the direction developing infrastructure for the transfer of water from water surplus areas to water deficient areas. For this two links have been planned one for Himalayan Rivers and another for the Peninsular rivers.

Fig-5.17: Proposed River Linking Of Peninsular Rivers

Current Internal Water Disputes- There are in all 19 Water disputes which are still unresolved and the number is likely to further go up as the water shortage increases and assumes the form of existential crisis for various states. As far as national security issues are concerned, it has been seen in past that the issues being highly emotive, may degenerate into major law and order problems in the affected states and also may stoke the fire of disturbance beyond law and order. Cases in point are; water dispute between Haryana and Punjab and Tamil Nadu and Karnataka among others. The important water based disputes within India, which are like festering wounds are as follows:-

▶ **Cauvery Dispute-** An Inter-state River basin in the Southern peninsula is spread across the States of Karnataka, Kerala, Tamil Nadu and Pondicherry. During the 200 years of British rule, substantial development of irrigation took place in the deltaic plains of Tamil Nadu and only partly in the then princely State of Mysore, now Karnataka. Since independence the pace of development has been remarkable and almost 95% of the surface water is reported to be utilized, which is the highest for any basin in the country. The earliest agreements that governed the use and development of the Cauvery waters are the 1892 and 1924 Agreements between erstwhile princely State of Mysore and the province of Madras. The State Kerala which came up much later was not party to these agreements. These are the agreements on which the case of the Cauvery Water Dispute hinges, with Karnataka calling it unjust while Tamil Nadu swears by its validity considering their established prescriptive rights. The 1924 Agreement, a water sharing agreement, came up for review at the end of its 50 years of validity, and since then the sharing of the waters of the Cauvery has remained under discussion between Karnataka and Tamil Nadu with the Government of India acting as a mediator. The case has gone to the Supreme Court for issuing direction to the GOI to refer the dispute to the Tribunal. Kerala has also filed suits to refer the dispute to the tribunal. The Cauvery Waters Tribunal was accordingly set up in June 1990 for adjudication of the dispute. However the dispute is still not resolved and has become quite an emotive issue which has potential to degenerate into a serious law and order problem between Tamil Nadu and Karnataka. A little detailed look at the water availability and its utilisation clearly brings out that it is about sharing of waters which are already fully utilized and hardly any scope for further resolution, because any further change in status will be at the cost of other party and both the warring parties are refusing to relent. In fact it keeps erupting from time to time. Recent Hogenakkal Falls water dispute between Tamil Nadu and Karnataka is a manifestation of this unresolved issue. [12]

► **Ravi- Beas Dispute-** The dispute is between Punjab and Haryana and is a legacy of pre-partition water sharing between various stake holders in Undivided Punjab. In 1955 an agreement was reached between various districts of Indian Punjab. Situation changed post state reorganisation of 1966 when Haryana was carved out of Punjab. Both states have agriculture as the main source of livelihood. Also change in the cropping pattern which is dependent on greater quantity of water and finally increase in the cultivated land area have generated a need of water which is far greater than what was needed till now. Next agreement was in 1976 and thereafter another agreement in 1981 (by now Rajasthan had also become a stake holder). Finally in 1986 a Tribunal was formed. The Tribunal gave its report in January 1987,[clxxxvi] but the issue is far from resolved and erupts from time to time, not on the merits/ de-merits of the award but mainly due to electoral politics where water is treated as an emotional issue rather than an existential problem which can be solved if the solution recommended is a win-win formula for all stake holders.[13]

► **Krishna-** Godavari Dispute- It is a dispute between Maharashtra, Karnataka, Odisha, Andhra Pradesh and Madhya Pradesh. It is about the tapping of surplus water of the river system. The Krishna Tribunal is in existence since 1973 and Godavari Tribunal since 1974. Krishna Tribunal has given its Award three times and Godavari Tribunal once but issues are far from resolved and erupt from time to time, case in point is recent Babhali Barrage issue[14] between Maharashtra and Andhra Pradesh. The work of the barrage is nearly complete. The Andhra Pradesh government complained to the Central government in 2005 that Maharashtra had violated the Godavari Water Dispute Agreement of 1975 by undertaking the construction of the barrage in the backwaters of Pochampad dam (Sriram Sagar Project). It (Andhra Pradesh government) feels that the barrage will reduce the flow of water to the Sriram Sagar

---

[12] http://en.wikipedia.org/wiki/category:inter-state_disputes_in_india
[13] Ibid29.
[14] "Babhali Barrage Issue" mentioned at the site of Ministry of Water Resources. http://www.mowr.gov.in/index3.aswp/

Project (SSP). It was also decided that status quo be maintained on the Babhali project. The Andhra Pradesh government filed a suit in the Supreme Court in July 2006 under Article 131 of the Constitution against the Maharashtra government. The apex court issued an interim order on April 26, 2007, saying that Maharashtra could go ahead with the construction of the Babhali barrage but should not install its gates.[clxxxvii]

Fig-5.18: Location Of Babhali Barrage

► **Mullaperiyar Dam Issue-** The Mullaperiyar Dam is a masonry gravity dam on the Periyar River in the Kerala state of India. [clxxxviii] It is located 881 m (2,890 ft) above mean sea level, on the Cardamom Hills of the Western Ghats in Thekkady, Idukki District of Kerala, South India. It was constructed between 1887 and 1895 by the British Government to divert water eastwards to the Madras Presidency area (present-day Tamil Nadu). It has a height of 53.6 m (176 ft) from the foundation, and a length of 365.7 m (1,200 ft).[clxxxix] *The control and safety of the dam and the validity and fairness of the lease agreement have been points of dispute between Kerala and Tamil Nadu states.*[cxc] Supreme court judgment came on 27 February 2006, allowing Tamil Nadu to raise the level of the dam to 152 ft (46 m) after strengthening it. Responding to it, Mulla periyar dam was declared an 'endangered' scheduled dam by the Kerala Government under the disputed Kerala Irrigation and Water Conservation (Amendment) Act, 2006.[cxci] For Tamil Nadu, the Mulla periyar dam and the diverted

Periyar waters act as a lifeline for Theni, Madurai, Sivaganga and Ramnad districts, providing water for irrigation and drinking, and also for generation of power in Lower Periyar Power Station. Tamil Nadu has insisted on exercising its unfettered rights to control the dam and its waters, based on the 1886 lease agreement. Kerala has pointed out the unfairness in the 1886 lease agreement and has challenged its validity. However, safety concerns posed by the 116-year old dam to the safety of the people of Kerala in the event of a dam collapse has been the focus of disputes from 2009 onwards. Kerala's proposal for decommissioning the dam and constructing a new one has been challenged by Tamil Nadu. On 8 March 2010, Tamil Nadu told the Supreme Court that it was not interested in adjudicating the dispute with Kerala before the special "empowered" committee appointed by the apex court for settling the inter-State issue.[cxcii] However, Supreme Court refused to accept Tamil Nadu's request to scrap the decision to form the empowered committee. The Supreme Court also criticized the Union Government on its reluctance to fund the empowered committee.[cxciii] Setting at rest the controversy over the safety of the 116-year-old Mullaperiyar dam, the Empowered Committee, headed by the former Chief Justice of India A.S. Anand, has said it is "structurally and hydrologically safe and Tamil Nadu can raise the water level from 136 to 142 feet after carrying out certain repairs."In its report submitted to the Supreme Court on 25 April 2012, the committee is understood to have said: "The dam is seismically safe." Last year's earth tremors in that region "did not have any impact on the Mullaperiyar dam and the Idukki reservoir and there was no danger to the safety of the two dams." [cxciv] Independent scientists are divided on Kerala's claims that the dam is in mortal danger, but they are no more convinced by Tamil Nadu's assertions that it is completely safe after 116 years of use. The Indian Institute of Technology Roorkee, one of the country's leading institution, has concluded that the dam will collapse if the area is struck by an earthquake of magnitude 7 or more. The Mullaperiyar Dam dispute between Kerala and Tamil Nadu is unnecessary[cxcv] However the dispute is far from resolved and comes up again and again.

Fig-5.19: Mullaperiyar Dam

▸ **Narmada Basin Issue-** Narmada basin states are Madhya Pradesh, Maharashtra and Gujarat. The State of Rajasthan though not a riparian state was later included as a beneficiary on the grounds of social justice. The water dispute between the basin states had retarded the progress of water resources development in the basin until in 1969 when a tribunal was formed (Narmada water and development tribunal) to adjudicate the disputes. The Tribunal gave its award in 1979 and laid down the basic framework for water resources development in the basin. A total of 29 major dams on the river and its tributaries, 135 medium reservoirs and 3000 small size storages were proposed. The apportionment of the share of each of the state   was to be reviewed after 45 years. A Narmada control Authority (NCA) was established to implement the decisions of the Tribunal. One of the recommendations of the award was about the rehabilitation of the displaced persons. People affected by the Sardar Sarovar project (one of the two major dams being constructed in Gujarat with a large area of Madhya Pradesh getting submerged) protested strongly, with the help of a dedicated and strong NGO groups. The protest is still going on. In the mean time Madhya Pradesh also went to Supreme court aginst the height of the Sardar Sarovar project. In October 2000 the Supreme Court gave its Judgement restricting the height to what was initially given in the NWDT award and NCA to monitor rehabilitation and resettlement of the displaced persons. However the issue is far from over.

Fig-5.20: Partially Completed Indira Sagar Dam In Madhya Pradesh

Fig-5.21: Sardar Sarovar Dam

Pakistan. The gap between water supply and demand is widening. In 2004, Pakistan's water shortfall was 11 MAF which is expected to go up to 31 MAF by 2025.[cxcvi] Pakistan's agricultural performance is closely linked with the supply of water for irrigation which uses 93 per cent of its rivers' water. The agricultural sector plays a key role in Pakistan's economy. It is the largest sector, accounting for over 21 per cent of the gross domestic product (GDP), and remains by far the largest employee of the farm labour, absorbing 45 per cent of the country's labour force. Nearly 62% of the country's population resides in rural areas, and is directly or indirectly linked with agriculture for their livelihood.[cxcvii] Further, Pakistan has very little water storage capacity, barely storing 30 days of water in the Indus basin, while India can store for 120-220 days, Egypt up to 700 days and the US for 900 days. About 80% of Pakistan's cultivated lands are irrigated by water from the Indus River system, the lion's share being governed by the Indus Water Treaty-1960 (IWT) between India and Pakistan, signed in 1960. Of the IWT water, more than 70% of water flows from the Indian state of Jammu & Kashmir. As it is, by 2005, per capita water availability in the case of Pakistan had already reduced by nearly 80% as compared to 1947 figures; plunging from 5,600 CUM to 1,200 CUM, which is likely to plunge further, dangerously close to the 1,000-CUM-per-person-per-year, which is considered as the "water scarcity" threshold. Pakistan's rainfall exceeds 500 mm per annum, only over 7% of its area. Hence, dependence on rivers and ground water is there, to irrigate around 18 Mha, by other sources.[cxcviii] The mathematics of water gets worsened for Pakistan because; the country's population is projected to increase by 82% from 184 million in 2010 to 335 million in 2050. Successive governments in Pakistan have neglected its water and irrigation sectors, which has resulted in the unfortunate state that the country finds itself in. Pakistan spends only about 0.25% of its Gross Domestic Product (GDP) on the water sector. To make matters worse, according to a 2003 survey by Transparency International, Pak's Water and Power Development Agency (WAPDA) is perceived to be the second most corrupt institution in the country. Close to half of more than 31,000 complaints received by Pakistan's Anti–corruption Board in 2002 were related to this one institution. The failure of institutions like the Indus River System Authority (IRSA) in dealing with the water issues has added to Pak's water woes further[15] . Indus River Basin which is the main source of water in the country is also getting affected by the following issues:-

▶ Climatic Change Leading to Reduced Flows in River Indus per se. The Inter Government Panel for Climate Change (IPCC) has predicted that the Western Himalayan glaciers will retreat for the next 50 years which will result into increase in the flow in the River Indus. Then the glaciers reservoir will be empty, resulting in decrease of flow by up to 30-40% over the subsequent 50 years. After three decades, Indus River is likely to become a seasonal river which will be fed only from the glacial melt and thus will affect agricultural sector and hence the food security of the country.[16]

▶ Silting of Water Channels- most of the feeder glaciers feeding into the River Indus, are Sun facing and at great heights, as such when they slide they carry a heavy quantity of silt with them; especially during summer and rainy season. Such heavy quantity of silt accumulation, raises the bottom of the water channels, which in turn leads to shifting of the river course & silting of dams and barrages. The three largest dams in Pakistan, Tarbela, Mangla and Chashma have already lost 25% of their capacity due to silting. This is a serious problem in a country wherein 74% of its total cultivated land depends on supply from rivers for irrigation purposes rather than the monsoon rains.[17]

▶ Afghanistan's Efforts to Exploit Kabul River[18] - According to Arshad Abbasi, a water and energy expert from, the Sustainable Development Policy Institute, in Islamabad; Afghanistan, with the assistance from India and the World Bank, has plans to construct 12 dams on the Kabul River with a combined storage capacity of 4.7 MAF. Pakistan feels that these dams will further reduce the

---

[15] Indus Waters Governance-I: Crisis of Institutions by D SubaChandran, 15 Jul 2010

[16] AwaisPiracha&ZahidMajeed, Water Use in Pakistan's Agricultural Sector : Water Conservation Under the ChangedClimatic Condition, pub in International Journal of Water Resources and Arid Environment page-175-176

[17] http://www.pakistanpaedia.com/mega/tarbela_dam.html

[18] Proposed Dams on Kabul River : Pakistan to suffer Drop in Water Supply, http://www.dawn.com

supply into Indus River which is, as it is having increasingly lesser supply due to a large number of reasons. Pakistan's hypothesis is based on the fact that India is one of the largest donor to the Afghanistan's reconstruction ($1.3 billion). It is indeed a strange arguemeent, probably a deliberate attempt to distort the facts of the case or not being able to see the facts of the case in the correct perspective. According to Pakistani media reports, Afghanistan (with assistance from India and the World Bank) has plans to build 12 dams on the Kabul River (a tributary of the Indus which runs through Afghanistan and Pakistan), with a combined storage capacity of 4.7 MAF. Pakistan is concerned that these dams will stop crucial water supply from flowing to the Indus River. It is also concerned that Indian support for these dams will increase India's sphere of influence over water issues in the region. India has not confirmed its support to build all 12 Afghan dams on the Kabul River, though it is currently one of Afghanistan's largest assistance donors. Afghan media reports that India has $1.3 billion invested in infrastructure projects. Water infrastructure, including dam building, is an integral part of Afghanistan's 2008 Development Agenda.[cxcix] Issues that need to be seen in the correct perspective are as follows:-

▸ Firstly, due to successive wars in Afghanistan, water infrastructure in the country is incredibly underdeveloped. The existing 12 water reservoirs in the country were built between 1920 and 1940. Afghanistan has sufficient water to meet its needs. Overall, around 2,775 CUM of water is currently available per capita[cc] (an all-inclusive figure accounting for consumption and agricultural needs), which is well above the water threshold of 1,800 cubic meters per capita. However, the country has not been able to harness this water adequately because of an inadequate infrastructure and lack of funds to construct new infrastructure.

▸ Secondly, even though the Kabul River Basin (KRB) is the most important river basin in Afghanistan - containing half the country's urban population, including the city of Kabul. It is one of the most under utilized basins in Afghanistan in terms of overall surface water availability. The proportion of water utilization in the KRB is 25 percent. In contrast, in the Northern and Helmand basins, water use is 100 percent and 58 percent, respectively, of the available surface water. Such figures refer to the amount of renewable freshwater reserves; any use beyond this will be overutilization as it might not be replenished.

▸ Thirdly, Disaster Management Information systems have revealed that the mountainous North Eastern region of the country where the Kabul River is situated is one of the most flood- and drought-prone areas in Afghanistan. Annual flow is extremely erratic, dropping as low as 11.2 MAF and rising as high as 34.8 MAF. This makes storage all the more essential in order to provide water in lean periods, and to avoid disasters like flash floods during sudden flow outbursts. (Afghanistan currently has one of the lowest storage capacities in the world.) However it needs to be appreciated by Pakistan and Afghanistan that the Kabul River, in ultimate analysis, is a tributary of the Indus, and as such needs to be a shared river between Pakistan and Afghanistan. Therefore, this challenge of the 12 dams is essentially an Afghanistan-Pakistan issue, rather than an Indo-Pak one. The issue of the 12 Kabul River dams, rather than simply being a reference point for India's development assistance program in Afghanistan, should be the spark for a water agreement between Afghanistan and Pakistan. Afghanistan and Pakistan came close to drafting a water treaty in 2003 and 2006, but these attempts failed on both occasions. Now probably time is ripe for Pakistan to once again take up the issue rather than continue levelling baseless allegations against India. From a strategic standpoint, It is felt that the timing could not have been better for a water treaty between the two countries. Recent months have seen an increase in tensions between them, reaching an apex with the assassination of former Afghan President Burhanuddin Rabbani. A comprehensive water accord; one that addresses both the Afghan need for water development and Pakistan's apprehensions about a reduction in water flows could do wonders not only for water security, but also for mutual confidence building.

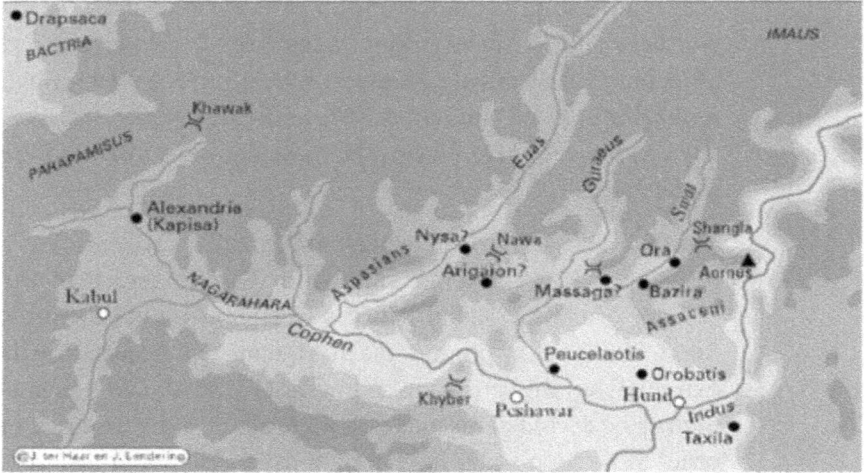

Fig-5.22: Kabul River And Its Impact On Water In Indus

Perceived/ Actual Uneven Distribution Of Water Amongst Various Provinces Of Pakistan- One of the report says that in 2004-05, Sindh's share in irrigation water was cut by 25-40%. Also insufficient flow in Indus in the lower reaches is unable to prevent sea intrusion in the Indus estuary.[19] In Sindh, sea water has intruded upstream, as much as 87 km into the estuary of the Indus River due to low or no flow in the river in the lower reaches. Across the country people are suffering from contaminated water, lack of electricity and lack of sanitation arrangement.[20] There have been widespread protests in Sindh, Pakistan Occupied Kashmir (POK) and Khyber Pakhtunkhwa against the proposed dams at Kalabagh, Bhasha, Chilas and in Gilgit area. In fact Sindh is of the view that Mangla be filled only once the needs of Sindh have been met. Out of the four provinces of Pakistan; Sindh, Baluchistan and Khyber Pakhtunkhwa are against these dams. Even people of Gilgit Baltistan are opposing the dam projects of Diamer Bhasha. People of POK are also protesting against the raising the height of the Mangla dam by 40 feet in Mirpur, as it would submerge a very large fertile tract in the enhanced reservoir created on account of additionally accumulated water. Besides loss of livelihood for the affected people, it will also result into a large number of 'Internally

---

[19] AditiPhadnis, Water Conflict in Kashmir, Business Standard, 16 May 2005.
[20] Trans Boundry Wter Politics and Conflicts in South asia: Towards 'Water for Peace' by Richasingh.

Displaced Persons' and other environment and human problems. Ironically the beneficiaries are going to be only from Punjab. POK has another issue with the Government of Pakistan. To their demand of water for drinking IRSA refuses as POK is neither a signatory to the IWT nor to the Pakistan's Water Apportionment Accord (WWA) of 1991 (Indeed a very insensitive approach!).[cci]

Effect on Power Generation- The reduced flow in water channels has led to their reduced capacity to produce power. There is a distinct possibility, not too far in future of shutting down the power generation arrangement permanently at Tarbela due to reduced availability of water and leaving it for irrigation purposes only.

Wasteful Use of Water which is already Short- A number of canals in border areas have been made by Pakistan which have defence orientation. Filling of these "defence oriented canals" at strategic locations is achieved by the diverted waters, with a view to either create water obstacle in case of hostilities with India or to use the water of these canals for flooding the area, once again to enhance the degree of difficulty for the advancing columns of Indian Army during operations. This approach accentuates the already severe water shortage of 50% to over 70%.

Losses on Account of Seepage- Pak loses nearly 40 % of the total available irrigation water to seepage from the unlined or poorly lined water conveyance channels. A World Bank evaluation found in 1996 that effective water conservation measures could save more water than building a new dam having the largest water storage capacity and that too at 1/5th the cost .[21]

Water Related Issues- It needs to be appreciated that despite political partition in 1947, the Indian Subcontinent continues to remain a single geographic entity, and as such dividing the natural resources equitably was and continues to remain a major challenge for the countries of the subcontinent. Water availability in India was 1902 metres3 in 2001 and is likely to get reduced to 1401 CUM in 2025.[22] In Pakistan; it has dropped

---

[21] Simulating Seepage from Branch Canal under Crop,Land and Water Relationship by Mohammad Arshd,Niyaz Ahmad and MUsman

[22] "Water Use Efficiency Measurement in the Manjira Sub Basin, Andhra Pradesh, India", Report No &, Jan 2011 by Rajesh KV Raietal.

down to 1200 CUM in 2005 and likely to plunge further to 1000 CUM in near future.[23]

While there is a wide spread concern in Pakistan regarding water availability in future but other than labelling India as the root cause of their water problem, there is hardly a consensus on the approach which should be taken to deal with the situation.

Increased Salinity and Desertification. The dams, barrages and canals built on the upper reaches of River Indus have reduced the availability of the fresh water in the estuary of River Indus causing the sea to push in and increase the salinity in 1.2 million acres of farmlands. In some areas the water table has gone up to one metre. This has resulted in more than 5.7 million hectare of land becoming salt affected and 2.4 million hectares becoming highly saline. Worst affected area is Sindh which has almost 23% area affected by salinity.[24]   The discharge of freshwater from the Indus into the Arabian Sea has declined steadily from 85 MAF in the 1940s to about 10 MAF in the 90s and even lesser today. 38% of Pakistan's irrigated land is generally water logged and 14% has turned saline.[25] Owing to leakage in canals and inappropriate irrigation practices there is a heavy loss of water available through Indus Basin Irrigation System. The change in grazing practices has virtually reduced some areas in the Cholistan desert to sand dunes. It is estimated that more than 60% of the natural grazing areas of the country have production levels lower than one third of their biological potential. More than one third of the country has been classified as under risk of desertification (45 Mha)[26]

Effect of Chinese Water Needs- No discussion on water management within Indian Sub-Continent will, however, be complete without taking into account the Chinese water needs, because a number of rivers have their origin in China/ Tibet Autonomous Region (TAR). China has a far greater problem at hand. With 20 % of the world's population she has just 7% of the global water. As on date, over 660 cities of China covering a

---

[23] An IDSA report reported by X News during Mar 2012

[24] Envirnment and Biodiversity of Pakistan, Learning to live on Planet Earth, Environment Issues of Pakistan, edu.iucnp.org

[25] Simi Kanwal, Chair of Hissar Foundation Karachi and a member of Global Water Partnership, Bharat Rakshak, dated13 Mar2012.

[26] Environment and Biodiversity of Pakistan, Learning to Live on Planet earth, Environment Issues of Pakistan, edu.iucnp.org

population of 160 million suffer from water shortage. Presently per capita water availability in China is one fourth of the global average. 2/3rd of China's hydropower potential is located on the Tibetan Plateau or that the present dam building activities of China, Myanmar, India, Bhutan, Nepal and Pakistan are concentrated in the extended Himalayan Range. As per one of the study excessive exploitation coupled with receding glaciers will negatively affect water supply in the next few decades in China and parts of Asia, including India because of burgeoning population.[ccii]

Water Issues Between Bangladesh and India. South Asia is having a large number of conflicts on account of issues other than resources but the water issue has the potential to degenerate into a major conflict. Especially between India and Bangladesh, which is the lower riparian and what India does with the common water resources has a direct bearing on the water interests of Bangladesh. Even the discussion on other political issues with Bangladesh like; illegal migration, Chakma Refugees, sanctuary to insurgents by Bangladesh, Border demarcation (both land as well as maritime boundary) and Trade imbalance gets affected by the Water issue.[27] The illegal migrants issue has assumed the alarming dimension because presently over two million Bangladeshis are there in India and in many a places their presence is resulting into change of demographic pattern. As explained in earlier sections of the chapter even illegal migration is also a function of declining water availability in Bangladesh from where affected people are migrating, many a times illegally to India. Some of the other water related issues are as follows:-

▶ **Lack of Framework Treaty-** India and Bangladesh share 54 rivers but water treaty exists only for Ganges. Lack of a policy framework leads to a Laissez fair state and it becomes a matter of interpretation based on the perceptions and requirements of each of the stake holder with respect to usage of common water resources. Thus there is a requirement to go in for treaties for sharing of waters of Teesta, Muhuri, Maur, Gumti, Khowai, Brahmaputra, Dharla and Dudh Kumar.

▶ **Sharing of Ganges' Water-** River Ganges rises from a Glacier at Gangotri. However all tributaries do not originate in India.

---

[27] Iyer Rama Swamy

Some of the important tributaries not originating within India are; Mahakali, Gandak, Kosi and Karnali which actually originate in Nepal and Tibet. Total length of the River Ganges is 2600 kms and has a drainage area of 10,80,000 Sq Kms shared by China, Nepal, India and Bangladesh. Average annual volume of flow in the river is 12,105 CUM, however during lean period, ie, January to May, it is lower than the average and as such the down-stream side area in Bangladesh becomes water stressed during the period of January to May. The genesis of the problem is the incongruence of perception between India and Bangladesh. India considers Ganges as the Indian River whereas Bangladesh considers that not only they, who are the lower riparian, but even Nepal and China who are upper riparian states for many of the tributaries that contribute to the water in Ganges are also the stake holders and as such be involved in any discussion which is for the augmentation of water availability in Ganges. The problem was first highlighted in 1951; when India decided to construct a 2246 metres long Farakka Barrage 17 Kms from the border, at Manoharpur on Bhagirathi river, in order to divert water from Ganges to Hoogly by a 42 kilometres long feeder canal with the capacity of 1136 CUM/second to 1236 CUM/second. The Barrage finally got completed and started operations in 1975. The barrage was constructed without the consent of Bangladesh. Bangladesh feels; firstly that this barrage has resulted into greater control going to India on what they consider is a common resource, secondly; as per them the water flow measured at the Hardinge Bridge in Bangladesh has reduced substantially from 2340 CUM/ second. They feel that while threats of floods have not diminished during Monsoons but availability of water during lean season has definitely reduced due to Barrage. There have been two treaties and two MOUs between the two countries on sharing of water, namely; 1977 Treaty and 1996 Treaty and 1983 and 1985 MOUs. 1996 Treaty is based on the principle of reasonable and equitable sharing of water and the river basin approach. Non-Navigational Laws and the Helsinki Rules of 1966 are followed accordingly to formulate the treaty. The treaty has adopted Article IV of the Helsinki Rules: "Each Basin State is entitled, within its territory, to a reasonable and equitable share in the beneficial uses of the waters of an international drainage basin." According to the treaty, the total availability of water will be measured and shared at Farakka (India) on the basis of the previous 40 years of historical 10-day average flows. There are also some provisions in the treaty for both parties to discuss options for the augmentation of the Ganges flow during the dry period and the way in which optimum allocation of waters of other common rivers between Bangladesh and India is possible. These are guided by the principles of equity, fairness, and no harm to either party.[cciii]

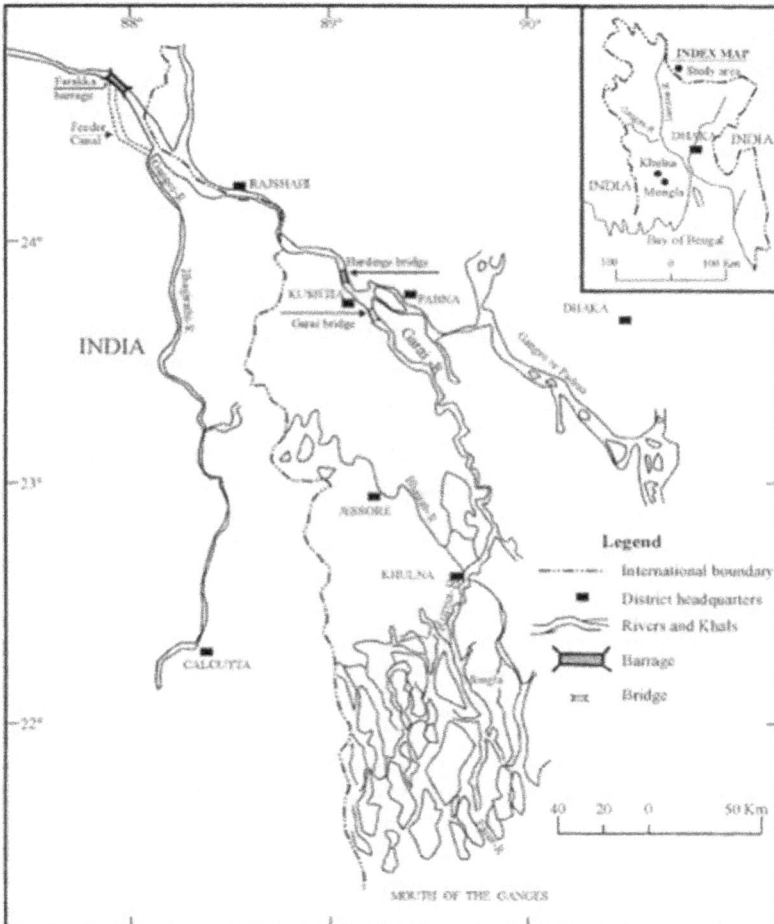

Fig-5.23: Farakka Barrage Location

The treaty will come for review after 30 years ie,2026. Some of the analysts in Bangladesh think that 1996 treaty does not address the draught situation in Bangladesh during the lean season and has a very limited scope for improvement.[28] Another problem is about the dispute resolution mechanism. Article VII of the 1977 Treaty provided a mechanism for the dispute resolution; however with the treaty having expired in 1982 it was felt that subsequent treaties did not have adequate teeth for the same. Bangladesh, in addition to loss of discharge during lean season due to Farakka Barrage, also claims that the barrage has resulted into massive environment degradation. As per their claim, the diversion of Ganges water has affected fishing and navigation in Bangladesh portion of the river and has brought unwanted salt deposit in the farm land. Another consequence is further drying up of Sunder bans, a world heritage site, due to non-availability of the fresh water.[29] Finally Bangladesh feels that to augment lean period flow, cooperation of other riparian states; Nepal and China is essential. There is another side of the issue. Investigation by some of the analysts of Bangladesh themselves have admitted that reduction in the discharge below Farakka was also on account of excessive extraction of the Ground Water in the Rajshahi district of Bangladesh. The criticism of the Treaty is also a manifestation of the political rivalry between Awami League and the Bangladesh Nationalist Party (BNP). The deal was signed by Begum Sheikh Hasina Wajed on 12 Dec 1996 as the Prime Minister of Bangladesh and as such Begum Khaleda Zia criticised the Treaty but once she took the office in October 2001 she did not abrogate the Treaty. That shows that the opposition by the BNP was for the sake of it.

---

[28] Ibid21
[29] MuhammedMizarurRahman,"The Ganges Water Conflict", Asteriskos (2006) 1/2: 195-208, ISBN 1886-5860

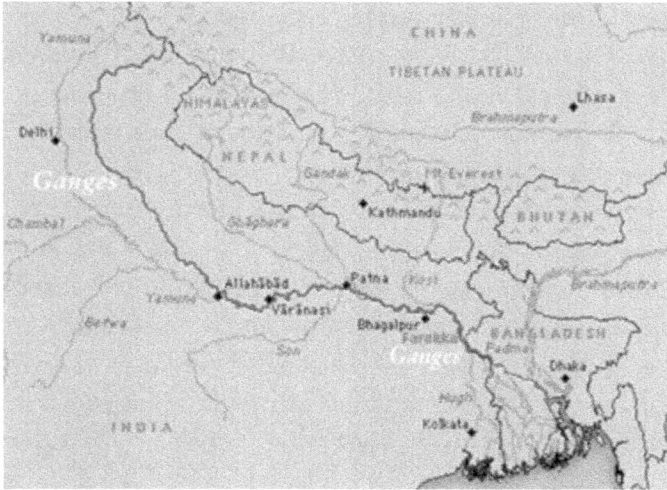

FARAKKA BARRAGE

A project of internal and importance, being the terminal barrage on the river Ganga, located in the state of West Bengal, completed in 1974, serves the purpose of flushing the channels of Calcutta Port, as well as to augment water supply to Calcutta city.

Fig-5.24: Farakka Barrage And Feeder Canal Connecting River Ganges And River Hoogly

Tipaimukh Dam- India is planning a 390 metres long, 162 metres high dam across Barak River in the state of Manipur, approximately 100 Kms from the Bangladesh Border near Sylhet on Bangladesh side, by state owned North East Electric Power Corporation Limited to improve water availability in the Barak Valley and produce 1500 MW power[30] but Bangladesh considers that this project will affect the quantity of water which is coming to Bangladesh.[31] By an estimate it will impound 15 BCM of water at peak level which is about 31% of the water that enters Bangladesh and thus will reduce the flow into downstream rivers Surma-Kushiyara- Meghna, wherein this water finally drains.[32] There is another view in Bangladesh which was articulated by State Minister of environment of Bangladesh on 27 January 2010 while talking to the United States Principal deputy assistant secretary for South and Central Asian affairs, Patrick Moon and as reported by Wikileaks, is that since Bangladesh could not prevent India from developing water and hydroelectric projects, as such it had decided to demand India to address Bangladeshi concerns. He further added that the hydroelectric projects such as the controversial Tipaimukh Dam could actually benefit Bangladesh by regulating water flow. Although this project now has become controversial, Dr Mahmud pointed out that originally Bangladesh had asked India to build this project in 1988. Apart from Bangladeshi concerns, the Indian people in Manipur have also expressed concerns as well, most notably the Sinlung Indigenous People Human Rights Organisation of India (SIPHRO). SIPHRO is quoted as saying according to the International Rivers Website, the process of choosing the project site should be with the consent of the locals. In addition Manipur claims that the project will inundate 26000 hectare of forest land and uproot 78 lacs of trees.[33]

---

[30] NHPC.retrieved 06 Aug 2011.
[31] http://www.thedailystar.net/magazine/2009/07/04/followup.htm
[32] MdKhalequzzaman, "Impact of Tipaimukh Dam on Haor Region
[33] Ibid 30.

Fig-5.25: Tipaimukh Dam On Barak River

Sharing of Teesta Water- Teesta River was the principal tributary of the Karatoya-Atrai-Jamunaswari river system in the eastern part of India until late eighteenth century (BWDB 1999). The 414 Kms long Teesta River originates from Kangse Glacier in Sikkim, travels through Sikkim for 151 Kms 123 Kms through West Bengal and then enters Bangladesh near Tin Bigha of Lalmonirhat district, travels for 124 Kms and then joins Brahmaputra River. Its summer flow, according to one estimate, is reportedly about 280,000 cusecs and minimum flow is about 10,000 cusecs. In 1983 an arrangement was worked out for sharing the Teesta waters in the ratio of 36% for Bangladesh, 39% for India and 25% unallocated for later decision.[34] It needs to be noted that Bangladesh occupies about 2071 Sq Kms or 17% of the total Teesta catchment area[cciv] and the Teesta River supports 8.5% of the population and 14% of the crop in Bangladesh.[35] Bangladesh wants a minimum of 3000 cusecs of water per day (10, 95,000 cusecs per year) which is almost 50%. But India wanted 55%. Furthermore, India wanted a 15-year agreement on water-sharing of the Teesta River. It was reported in the media in June 2011 that the two sides agreed that India would get 42.5% and Bangladesh 37.5%. However West Bengal is not in agreement with this proposal. Articulating the views of the government of the day, one of the Lawmakers of the West Bengal, Shri Anwarul Chowdhury told the BBC in early September that India would retain 75% of Teesta river water while Bangladesh would receive 25%.[ccv] Besides rhetoric the underlying reason is that Bangladesh has constructed a barrage in 1990 on the Teesta River at Dalia in Lalmonirhat district to provide irrigation water for her three crop seasons from the river through canal networks in the Teesta Barrage Project area. But this arrangement is workable only if India releases water as demanded by Bangladesh.[36] Bangladesh's arguement is that as a lower riparian country Bangladesh is largely dependent on trans-boundary rivers for the supply and management of its water resources. Bangladesh shares these rivers basins with India. The non-navigation treaties between these two countries for international water courses remain weak during the past 50 years for lack of water allocation; poor water quality provision; lack of monitoring, enforcement and conflict resolution mechanisms and failure to include all upper riparian countries.[ccvi] While Government of India is willing to resolve the issue but West Bengal is not willing to shed more than 25,000 cusecs per year.[37] Thus Teesta water is becoming a major stumbling block in the way of improving Indo-Bangladesh relations.

---

[34] Ibid33.

[35] http://www.rsinsight.com/index.php/home/58-river-teesta-issue-port-i.html

[36] "India and Bangldesh: Teesta River agreement", by SoumyaSuryanarayanan, pub in Strategic Foresight, May 2010.

[37] "Teesta water Hits Chopping waters", Indo Asian News Service, 05 Sep 2011.

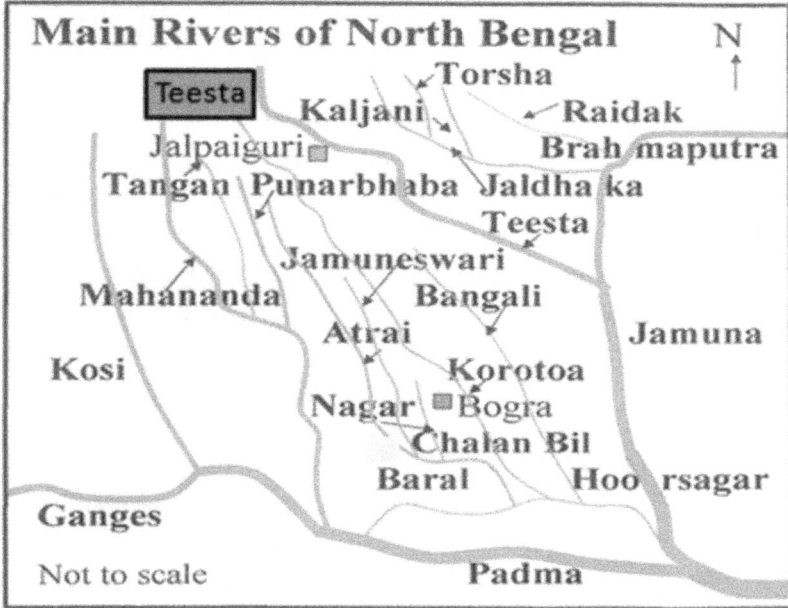

Fig-5.26: Alignment of Teesta River

Water Issues Between India And Nepal. Water issues have affected the bilateral relations between the two neighbours. Basically it is a case of lack of understanding on the part of both the neighbours of each other's view point. Various issues are as follows:-

▶ **Kosi agreement**- it was signed on 25 April 1954. It was meant for the water management and the flood control and prevent free oscillation of the Kosi River over time. Project also entailed power generation. It was revised on 19 December 1966 in response to the dissatisfaction and protest of the Nepalese people. The construction of the embankment and the barrage got completed in 1959 and 1963 respectively.[ccviii] The Kosi Barrage also provides water for irrigation to Bihar in India through Eastern and Western canals. In treaty it is also enshrined that Nepal has every right to withdraw water from the Kosi River and its tributaries for irrigation and other purposes in Nepal as may be required from time to time. For all these years the agreement held very well and served its purpose but post floods of 2008 certain discord has emerged. During the floods almost 30 lacs in India and 50,000 in Nepal got displaced. Nepal blamed India for neglecting to maintain the assets of the project which caused disaster. Other point of dispute was compensation which India was required to pay for construction of the dam. Nepal feels that though the barrage has submerged their territory, only 29,000 people in Nepal benefitted whereas its capacity for irrigation is 1.5 million acre. Also it has resulted into massive internal displacement of local population. Another point of incongruence is that while India wants to develop the Kosi multipurpose project, being planned to augment water supply for irrigation and control floods, with a concept of providing a flood cushion in the Kosi high dam to provide flood relief to the State of Bihar, Nepal, besides having certain difference of opinion about the scope of the projectalso wants to maximize its benefits from the project Finally it appears that the control of the Kosi Barrage by India is being resented by Nepal and she considers it as an infringement of her sovereignty.[38]

Fig-5.27: Rivers From Nepal Which Contribute Water To Ganges

---

[38] Ibid23.

► **Nepal's View Point-** According to South Asian Journal, Nepal being an upper riparian has different relationship with India, the lower riparian and faces problem in construction of dams over the common rivers. Nepal mistrust gets reinforced because of various unequal treaties from Sharda Dam Construction (1920), 1950 Treaty, Kosi Agreement (1954), Gandak Agreement (1959), Tanakpur Agreement(1991) and Mahakali Treaty (1996). One of the major reasons for the distrust is the interpretation of the Sugauli Treaty signed in 1816 between British East India Company and Nepal which delimited the boundary along Mahakali (known as Sarada in India) River. In 1997 Nepal wanted to construct a hydroelectric project on the river. The point of dispute was the origin of the river; Nepal claimed that it was Limiyadhura and India was of the view that it was Lipulekh.[39] The Mahakali Treaty is also considered flawed by Nepal, on account of the fact that

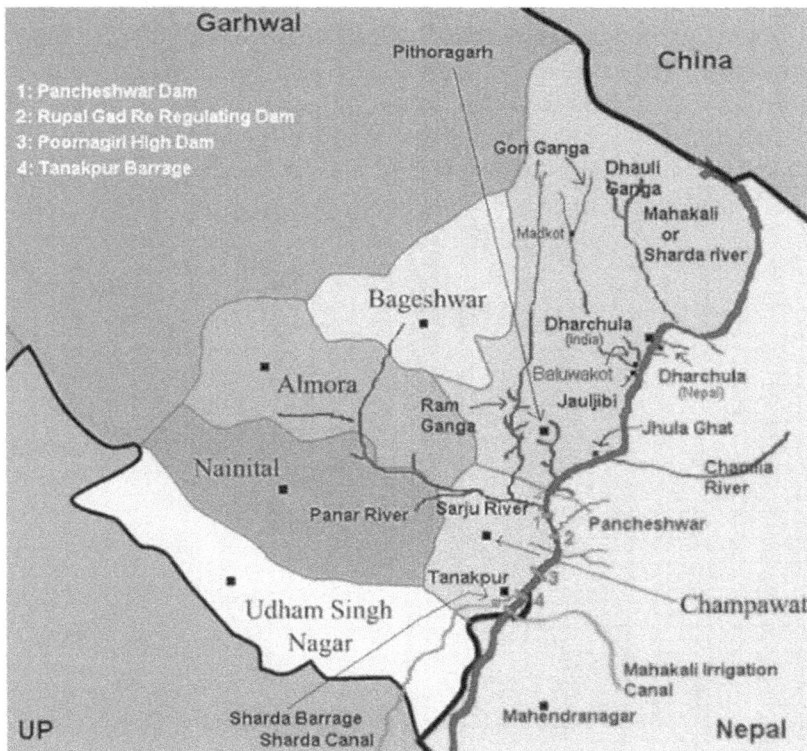

Fig-5.28: River Mahakali And Projects On This River

---

[39] Ibid21.

the Pancheswar Project, which would produce 6000 MW when completed, will allocate only 4% of the power generated from the project to Nepal.[40]

▶ One of major issues which is bugging the Indo Nepal water relations is the weak institutional frame work for the implementation of various treaties, agreements and understandings. Although a total of 14 joint committees exist to manage, develop and implement cooperation between India and Nepal in the field of water resources.[ccix] .The performance of these committees has been far from satisfactory. Therefore it is absolutely essential that the institutional framework to oversee and monitor implementation be strengthened and given more teeth.

Issues between India and Pakistan. The dispute on account of sharing of water from Indus River Basin (IRB) is a historical legacy of the partition between India and Pakistan. The problem has its genesis in the nature of the irrigation system planned and thereafter developed during the pre-partition days. It was planned as an integrated system to store water from all the six rivers, namely; Indus, Jhelum, Chenab, Ravi, Sutlej and Beas and transfer the surplus/ impounded water to areas which were water deficient through a very well planned and well executed canal system which linked all the rivers.

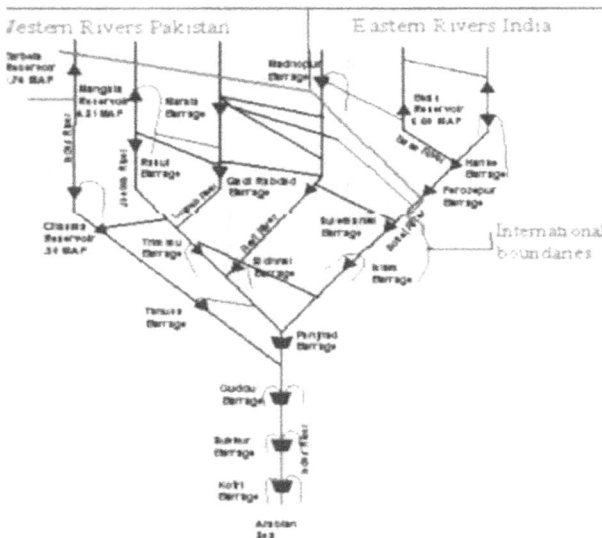

Fig-5.29: Integrated Canal System of Indus Basin

---

[40] Ibid23.

While drawing the Boundary Line between India and Pakistan probably no thought was given to the impact of this line on the integrated irrigation system on which both the countries depend. As a result, partition left two of the major regulating structures in the form of Madhopur HWs on Ravi River and Ferozepur HWs on Sutlej River in India while canals emanating from these HWs with Pakistan. It had a major impact on Pakistan's agriculture. In fact after partition in Dec 1947, both the newly liberated nations signed a standstill agreement which was valid till 31 Mar 1948, with a view that during the interim period a final agreement for sharing the water of the rivers of the Indus River Basin would be signed. However it did not happen and as such India stopped water on 01 Apr 1948 and Rabi crop in Punjab Province of Pakistan got destroyed and a demand to go for war was given by a large section of Pakistani society. Though an interim agreement was signed on the initiative of the then Prime Minister of India, Jawahar Lal Nehru, in May 1948 (Delhi Accord), but Issue could finally be addressed only in Sep 1960 when under a World Bank sponsored initiative, a treaty was signed between the two disputing countries. Though both the countries have their reservations on its fairness, but it is a tribute to the two countries that despite going to war three times and once almost to a war, since signing the Indus Water Treaty in 1960, the treaty has withstood the test of the time. As per the Treaty; India was awarded full waters (33 MAF) of the Eastern rivers namely; Ravi, Sutlej and Beas and 3.6 MAF of storage rights, 1.34 MAF for irrigation on the Western rivers and the non-consumptive use of the waters of Western rivers, namely; Indus, Jhelum and the Chenab. Balance of the water of these rivers was allocated to Pakistan. She also got the rights for some minor irrigation usage on four nullahs that join the River Ravi, downstream of Madhopur HWs. In quantified terms Pakistan got about 80% waters of the Indus River System and India got only 20%. In addition India agreed to pay a fixed sum of £ 62,060,000 to Pakistan to build regulating structures to compensate for the regulating structures left on Indian side, post partition. The treaty also has a dispute resolution mechanism built into it. This mechanism has already been exercised a number of times and has been honoured by both the countries. Though the treaty has its shortcomings but has withstood the test of time as Pakistan had hardly any choice and the terms offered were reasonably favourable to

Pakistan. Pakistan's vulnerability and their compulsion to sign can best be summed up by two statements; first by David Lilienthal, Chief Interlocuter of the Indus Water Treaty and second by Field marshal Ayub Khan the then President of Pakistan. These are as follows:-

" No armies with bombs and shellfire could devastate a land so thoroughly as Pakistan could be devastated by simple expedient of India's permanently shutting off the source of water that keeps the fields and people of Pakistan green. "

-David Lilienthal

"Every factor was against us. The only sensible thing to do was to try and get a settlement , even though it might be second best , because if we did not, we stood to loose everything. The very fact that Pak had to be content with waters of three western rivers underlined the importance of having physical control over the higher reaches for max utilization of the growing needs of West Pak. In my mind therefore the only solution of the Kashmir issue acquired a new sense of urgency on the conclusion of the treaty".

Field Marshal Mohammad Ayub Khan

An overall analysis of the IWT brings out following:-

▸ **Interests of Jammu & Kashmir-** The interests of the State of Jammu and Kashmir were not given due thought at the time of signing the Treaty, which Jammu & Kashmir has started questioning in recent times. In fact the treaty has virtually capped the economic development of Jammu and Kashmir, as India has been able to develop only 15% of the hydroelectric potential of the rivers in the state. On demand side for water sustenance for agriculture and horticulture, the population of the state has increased by three times from what it was in 1960; to 10 million, thereby increasing the mismatch. Thus, power shortage in a potentially power rich state coupled with acute water shortage, has led to a general unrest in the state, demanding a revision of the treaty. The State of J &K

has a grievance; that despite being a stake holder their legitimate water rights have simply been ignored and the treaty was unfairly saddled on them. The general perception amongst the masses is that the state has been denied the potential benefits that they could have received, specially the use of Chenab water for irrigation and power generation. Some elements are even suggesting, the abrogation of the IWT by India, being discriminatory in nature. As per some political parties and other opinion makers, ceding of exclusive rights over Indus, Jhelum and Chenab of Kashmir to Pakistan can at best be described as controversial and a "huge loss to Jammu & Kashmir economy". The people of J&K term the Treaty as the "biggest impediment in the economic self-reliance of the state of Jammu and Kashmir". By an assessment; estimated potential of the Indus River basin is 20,000 MW and out of that an identified potential is 16480 MW.

Table-5.8: Water Shares Of India And Pakistan As Per Indus Water Treaty Of 1960

Ser No	Western River	Eastern River	Total Indus System Flows
1.	167.2 BCM	40.4 BCM	207.6 BCM
2.	Pakistan's Share of Total Indus System Waters: 80.52%	India's Share of Total Indus system waters: 19.48%	100%
Source:	The Indus Water Treaty-1960		

► **Type of Regulating Structures Permitted on Western Rivers-** As per the provisions of the Indus water treaty only run of the river projects are permitted in J&K which can help the state to exploit only 1/3 of the identified potential of the power generation capacity of the three Western rivers. J&K State hydroelectric project development policy 2011 spells out plans for setting up of projects both in public and private sector. These projects when

completed will add 5756.5 MW to the State's capacity. The
State's power demand for the FY 2012-13 is 2600 MW which
is likely to grow to 5500 by 2025-26. It is anticipated that the
State will become power surplus by 2018. Under Prime Minister's
Reconstruction Programme; out of 24000 Crores, 18912.25
Crores have been earmarked for the development of the power
sector. Issues; that the State has with the Centre are ownership
of the integrated hydroelectric projects at; Salal, Dulhasti and
Uri-1. The State contributes 1680 MW of power to the National
Grid while they themselves suffer acute power shortages. This
contribution is therefore being objected to, by the locals as they
face acute shortage of power. [41] As on date a meagre 1400 MW
has been harnessed and projects having an installed capacity of
1300 MW are in various stages of completion. The State actually
meets only 0.9% of the nation's need. Another issue which
needs to be taken into account is that the efficiency of the run of
the river projects during winter goes down by more than 50%.
Because of acute power shortage J&K purchases power from the
National Grid at @ Rs 3.60 per unit. The discontent in the State
is on account of the fact that though the State has the potential
but because of the restrictions imposed on account of the treaty
they are forced to pay rather than earn money. In May 2002 the
J&K Assembly unanimously passed a resolution to review the
Treaty.[42] Their demand is based not only on historical data but
the new developmental needs of the population of J&K'. In fact,
if properly projected at appropriate levels, the protests of Pakistan
on newer projects in J&K can be utilized by the Indian decision
makers as an opportunity to highlight the duplicity of Pakistan's
commitment to J&K.

▶ Also, if India exercises its right to store 1.5 MAF on Jhelum as per
the provisions of the IWT, it is possible that the reservoir due to
raised Mangla dam on Jhelum River may not get filled up.[43] Such

---

[41] IDSA Comment, Feb2012 by ArpitaAnant
[42] The Tribune, 04 Apr 2002, Chandigarh Edition.
[43] The Indus Water Treaty by Subrahmanyam Sridhar pub in Security Research Review,
    http://www.bharat-rakshak.com srr/volume13/sridhar.html

a state, while makes Pakistan extremely nervous, it provides some sort of control to India on the water of Jhelum, without violating the provisions of the IWT.

▶ **Defence Oriented Canals-** Pak uses waters of the rivers of Indus River System (particularly overflow of eastern rivers and Chenab waters) for the fortification of her defences along Indian border. Tributaries of River Ravi, which join it down stream of Madhopur HWs before it goes into Pakistan namely Basantar, Bein, Tarnah and Ujh. Though as per the provisions of the IWT, Pakistan is permitted to draw a maximum of 45,500 acre of water from these four nullahs but the water which because of non-existence of regulating structure goes surplus to this quantity is being utilised by Pakistan to feed ditches in front of her defences. Similar underutilisation by India of 6000 acres of water of the Chenab in area west of Devak, under the provisions of the IWT, is being utilised by Pakistan to feed her defence oriented canals. Therefore, if India decides to degrade the efficacy of Pakistan's defences, she can do that by choking this supply which is well within her rights as per the provisions of the IWT.

▶ **Diamer-Bhasa Project-**This project to produce 4,500 MW of power is being planned to come up on River Indus 315 Kms up stream of Tarbela and 165 Kms down stream of Gilgit town. The propsed dam will have a reservoir of about 75,00,000 acre feet which will be 15% of the yearly flow of the Indus, with a gross water capacity of 1.8 MAF, will cover an area of approximately 200 Sq Kms. It will be partly located in Khyber Phaktunkhwa and partially in Gilgit Baltistan. The project is being executed by Chinese firms at the current assessed cost of US $ 8.5 billion with a Probable Date of Completion of eight years from October 2011, when its foundation stone was laid. When completed it is likely to mitigate the power shortage of Pakistan substantially. However, this project is a source of discontent; within Pakistan as well as internationally. Some of the relevant aspects are as follows:-

► The project will flood 100 Kms of the Karakoram Highway and villages & farm land of about 35,000 people will disappear besides rock carvings of thousands of years' vintage (local cultural heritage). Apprehension for situation to unfold that way, has resulted into differences between Gilgit Baltistan and Khyber Phaktunkhwa about the right on the dam. People of Kohistan who are going to be affected by the dam are against the construction.[44] Also as the power generated will essentially benefit Punjab others are not very happy about the project.

► Local people and political parties are objecting to the construction of the dam because of the high seismic sensitivity of the area.[45]

► **India has also objected to this project on two counts;** firstly, India says that this project is being planned in J&K which is an integral part of India. Secondly, as confirmed by the WAPDA, most probably China will fund the project and provide the working force consisting of 17,000 personnel.[ccx] Presence of Chinese so close to Line of Control is a matter of concern due to related national security issues. Pakistan does not agree to India's protests to the proposed construction of Diamer Bhasha Dam and the presence of Chinese engineers in the area for the construction of the dam. They consider it as the infringement of their rights under the provisions of the IWT.

► **Pak Objections to Projects in India.** In the past decade or so, India has started building a number of hydroelectric projects on the Western rivers that has set off alarm bells in the water-insecure Pakistan which strongly feels that the Indian projects do not follow the criteria specified in the IWT and that unlimited proliferation of dams and diversion of water would badly disturb flow of the Western rivers into Pakistan.

---

[44] Express Tribune of Pakistan 26 Oct 2011.
[45]http://futurechallenges.org/local/changing-climate-conditions-and-electricity-crisis dated 26 July 2011 by Maria Farooq

It is stated that about 27 Indian projects on the western rivers have been questioned by Pakistan[ccxi] Prolonged controversy over the construction of dams on the Chenab such as Salal, Dul Hasti and Baglihar hydel power projects has left a trail of bitterness and suspicions. India has constructed three big and eight small dams on Chenab river, in addition to 24 other projects that are in the pipeline.

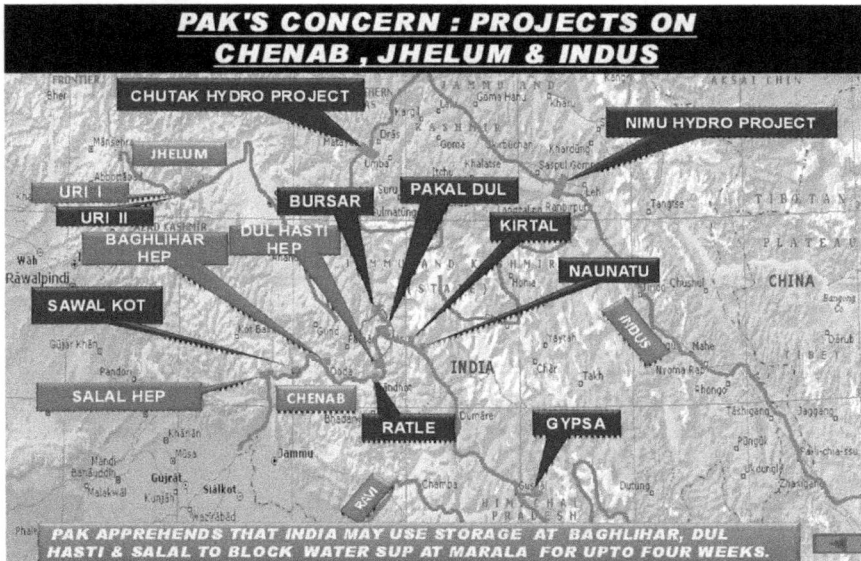

Fig-5.30: Projects On Western Rivers

Those constructed and in operation include Salal I&II with installed capacity of 690 MW, Baglihar I & II 450 MW each and Dul Hasti I & II, 780 MW. Besides, the major power projects planned on the Chenab are Sawalkot hydroelectric plant I&II, with installed capacity of 1,200 MW; Bursar I&II, 1,020 MW; Pakwal Dul I&IIm, 1,000 MW; Seli, 715 MW, Raltle I&II, 560 MW; Karwar, 520 MW, Kiru, 600 MW; Gypsa I&II, 395, Kirthi I&II, 300 each; Naunat, 400 MW; Shamnot, 370 MW; Barinium, 240 MW; Ans, 200 MW; Raoli, 150 MW, and Bichari, 104 MW. (100) According to district Doda website, eight hydropower projects with a total capacity of 5,320 MW have already been identified along Chenab's track.[ccxii]

Table-5. 9: India's Major Hydropower Projects On Chenab River

Ser No	Name of the project	Location	Installed Capacity	Status	Live pondage/af
1.	Salal I&II	45 miles u/s Marala Barrage in Riasi in Udhampur (Jammu)	690 MW	In operation	230,000 (full pondage level)
2.	Baglihar-I	On the Chenab main, 147 km u/s Marala headworks			
3.	Dul Hasti I & II	Near Kishtwar (Jammu) on the Chenab	780 MW	In operation	7,605.5
4.	Sawalkot I&II	Upstream Salal	1,200 MW	Under investigation	Not available
5.	Bursar I &II	Hanzal, Doda district (Jammu)	1,020 MW	Under investigation	Not available
6.	Pakwal Dul I&II	Doda district (Jammu)	1,000 MW	Under investigation	Not available
7.	Seli	Chenab river	715 MW	Under investigation	Not available
8.	Ratle I&II	Drabshalla, Kishtwar (Jammu) on the Chenab	560 MW	Under investigation	Not available
9.	Karwar	Kishtwar tehsil, Doda district (Jammu)	520 MW	Under investigation	Not available

10.	Kiru	Upstream Dul Hasti, Doda district (Jammu)	600 MW	proposed	Not available
11.	Kirthi I&II	The Chenab river	600 MW	Under investigation	Not available
12.	Gypsa I&II	On Bhaga river, a tributary of the Chenab	395 MW	Under investigation	Not available
13.	Naunat	Chenab river	400 MW	Under investigation	Not available
14.	Shamnot	On Bhut Nala, the Chenab	370 MW	Under investigation	Not available
15.	Barinium	Chenab river	240 MW	Under investigation	Not available
16.	Ans	Ans river, a tributary of the Chenab	200 MW	Under investigation	Not available
17.	Raoli	Chenab river	150 MW	Under investigation	Not available
18.	Bichari	On Mohu Mangat Nala, Chenab river	104 MW	Under investigation	Not available

Source: Based on data provided by Indus Water Commission.

On River Jhelum, India has constructed 13 hydel projects including Uri I &II with installed capacity of 480 MW, lower Jhelum 105 MW, and Upper Sind-phase II, 105 MW. It has identified another 74 such projects which include three major and 12 medium to small hydel projects, i.e., multipurpose Ujh storage with power generation capacity of 280 MW, Gangabal storage 100 MW, Sonamarg storage 165 MW and 330 MW Kishanganga hydropower project. The other 12 projects range in capacity between 15 MW to 84 MW.[ccxiii] On the Indus river itself India has so far identified nine hydel projects. The two major ones are the 44-MW Chutak and the 45-MW Nimoo Bazgo projects which are[ccxiv] under construction while a 130-MW plant at Dumkhar is in the pipeline. According to Pakistani

Indus Waters Commissioner Syed Jamaat Ali Shah, these projects would block 43 million cubic metres of water from flowing to Pakistan in the Indus.[ccxv] He maintained that Pakistan wanted nothing but honest and fair implementation of the IWT. If mechanisms and design parameters, defined in the treaty, are not adhered to, it will affect the flow of water to Pakistan. The provisions of the IWT have been scrupulously observed by India, despite the various conflicts that have taken place between the two countries. The Baglihar project, the Kishenganga project, as well as the Tulbul (Wullar) project, are all being opposed by Pakistan on the narrow definition of what it means by storage. The Indian argument rests on the premise that the pondage is within the limits set out by the IWT. The ambiguous clauses in the treaty legislate that all Indian projects on the Western Rivers be vetted by the Pakistani Indus Commission, which has consistently objected to these developmental activities. These interventions have caused substantial delays and losses to the Indian exchequer. In fact Pakistan is getting four to six MAF additional water due to not adequate storage available in the J&K, incomplete Indira Gandhi Nahar Pariyojna (IGNP), water going unchecked downstream of Madhopur HWs in the absence of any regulating structure and leakages from various regulating structure. Here; it is interesting to consider that a total average canal supply to Pakistan is 104 MAF and water available at farm gate is 70 MAF, therefore Pakistan needs to explain to her people as to where 34 MAF of water is being wasted.[ccxvi] Therefore Pakistan's objections, to say the least, are not based on facts. The Indian projects were/ being compromised on account of Pakistani interference are:-

> ▸ **Salal Hydroelectric Project.** Dispute had arisen over the construction of the Salal dam (1978) which was though settled amicably has resulted into a design which does not lent itself for better flushing. Pakistani objection was against construction of under sluices by India.[46] This has resulted in heavy siltation of the dam, which has considerably reduced the capacity of the dam (Out of 400 feet of height 300 feet is full of silt and as such power generation has gone down to half.[47]

> ▸ **Uri Hydroelectric Project**. Pakistan raised serious protests on the pondage of the project. This has resulted into design modification and as such the venture is producing only 35% of its capacity during the winter months.

---

[46] Poitical Fuss Over Indus I, by BG Verghese, pub in The Tribune 24 May 2005
[47] Dr DC Sharma in Daily Excelsior dated 28 Feb 2003

▶ **Tulbul Navigation Project / Wullar Barrage.** River Jhelum was traditionally being used for floating timber logs besides navigational purposes. Over the years the river has silted. India began constructing a barrage on the Wullar Lake in 1984 with a twofold objective of enhancing the hydroelectric power generation capacity and to create a 20 kms long navigation channel between Wullar and Baramulla. Incidentally this project will not only improve the navigability in the river but will also benefit both Uri and Mangla projects by reducing their siltation and thus enhancing their power production capability.[48] However, the project has been lying suspended since 1987, when India voluntarily stopped the work in response to Pakistan's objections, who alleged that the Indian Project was violative of the provisions of IWT with respect to the utilization of waters of Western Rivers. Since India wanted to settle the issue bilaterally they stopped the work on their own, instead of invoking Section IX of the IWT meant for Dispute Resolution . Regrettably India's magnanimity has not been able to elicit similar response from Pakistan. There have been nine rounds of Secretary Level talks but so far the issue remains unresolved. Probably the only solution is that India who voluntarily stopped the work resumes it unilaterally .

▶ **Kishenganga / Neelum Hydroelectric Project.** India began working on the 330 Mega Watt Kishenganga Hydroelectric Project, across the Kishenganga River, which is a major tributary of the Jhelum River. This project involves a 103 metre long and 34 metres high (concrete faced and rock filled) dam across the river, with a 24 kilometres long tunnel to divert the water to the Bunar Madmati Nullah. Pakistan also is going ahead with a hydroelectric project in POK down stream of the Kishenganga Project by the name Neelam Jhelam hydroelectric Project to produce 969 MW. As such Pakistan has three objections to India's Kishenganga Hydroelectric Project and these are; firstly;[49] as per provisions of the IWT, inter tributary diversions are barred and that water drawn from a given tributary must be returned to the same water channel; secondly the project will deprive river 27% of her natural flow and thus affect its existing irrigation capacity of 133,000 hectares in the Neelum Valley and will also have an

---

[48] Poitical Fuss Over Indus I,by BG Verghese, pub in The Tribune 24 May 2005
[49] Daily Times, 11 feb 2007

adverse impact on its envisaged 969-MW Neelum- Jhelum power project to be constructed with the Chinese assistance by almost 9%; [50] thirdly, the design parameters of the project. India has dropped the proposed dam and diversion of Kishenganga River by reconfiguring the design without compromising on the power output. [51] Now it will be a run of the river project. This project was initially planned for 1994-1997 but laid dormant because of lack of funds. The IWT allows India to store waters on Kisenganga for power generation and so Pakistan wants to finish its Neelam Jhelum Hydroelectric Project before India completes Kishenganga hydroelectric project, in order to deny waters to India, claiming the principle of "prior appropriation", as enunciated vide Paragraph 15(iii), Part-3, Annexure-D of the Indus Water Treaty, which states "Where a Plant is located on a Tributary of River Jhelum on which Pakistan has any agricultural use or hydroelectric use, the water released below the plant may be delivered, if necessary, into another tributary but only to the extent that existing agricultural use or hydroelectric use by Pakistan on the former tributary would not be adversely affected". Incidently International Court of Arbitration Hague in a recent judgement has upheld India's right to construct this project under the provisions of IWT. (Ref: A report of India Today dated 19 Feb 2013.)

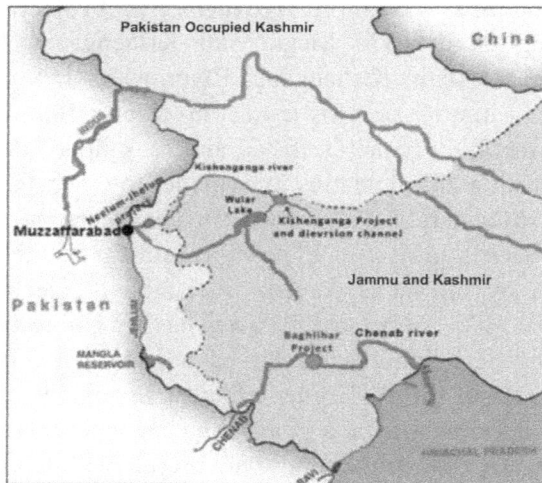

Fig-5.31: Kishenganga Hydroelectric Project

---

[50] ibid
[51] IftikarGilani, 'India Will Re-design Kishenganga Dam', pub in South Asian Kashmir Action Group New Delhi dated April 18

► **Baglihar Dam-** Baglihar Hydroelectric Power Project, is a run-of-the-river power project on the Chenab River in the southern Doda district of the Indian state of Jammu and Kashmir. This project was conceived in 1992, approved in 1996 and construction began in 1999. The project is estimated to cost US $1 billion. The first phase of the Baglihar Dam was completed in 2004. With the second phase completed on 10 October 2008, Prime Minister Manmohan Singh of India dedicated the 900-MW Baglihar hydroelectric power project to the nation.[ccxvii] After construction began in 1999, Pakistan claimed that design parameters of Baglihar project violated the Indus Water Treaty of 1960 provided India with excessive ability to accelerate, decelerate or block flow of the river, thus giving India a strategic leverage in times of political tension or war. In April 2005 the World Bank determined the Pakistani claim as a 'Difference', a classification between the less serious 'Question' and more serious 'Dispute', and in May 2005 appointed Professor Raymond Lafitte, a Swiss civil engineer, to adjudicate the difference. Lafitte declared his final verdict on February 12, 2007, in which he upheld some minor objections of Pakistan, declaring that pondage capacity be reduced by 13.5%, height of dam structure be reduced by 1.5 meter and power intake tunnels be raised by 3 meters, thereby limiting some flow control capabilities of the earlier design. However he rejected Pakistani objections on height and gated control of spillway declaring these conformed to engineering norms of the day. India had already offered Pakistan similar minor adjustments for it to drop its objection. The verdict acknowledged India's right to construct 'gated spillways' under Indus water treaty 1960. The report allowed pondage of 32,580,000 CUM as against India's demand for 37,500,000 CUM. The report also recommended to reduce the height of freeboard from 4.5 m to 3.0 m. On June 1, 2010 India and Pakistan resolved the issue relating to the initial filling of Baglihar dam in Jammu and Kashmir with the neighbouring country deciding not to raise the matter further. The decision was arrived at the talks of Permanent Indus Commissioners of the two countries who are meeting. "The two sides discussed the issue at length without any prejudice to each other's stand...Indian and Pakistani teams resolved the issue relating to initial filling of Baglihar dam after discussions," sources said. Pakistan also agreed not to raise the issue further On June 1, 2010.

Fig-5.32: Baglihar Hydroelectric Project

All these projects have increasingly made Pakistan nervous about the future prospects of the water situation in the country and as always India is being projected as the proverbial villain who is trying to steal their water. Though, the facts are quite far from the web of fiction, which, in a systematic manner, Pakistan Government and all her organs of governance including media, is trying to feed to their people, by selectively suppressing the facts about the effort which they were required to make post IWT. The debate on the issue was initiated by none other than their President Zardari. The main theme of the ongoing misinformation campaign in Pakistan is that India is "stealing" Pakistan's water, on the other hand the line of argument of the Indian media and officials is that India is not violating the IWT and only utilizing the amount of water allocated to it under the Treaty. The government and the political leadership in Pakistan have been quite vocal in expressing their concerns regarding Indian projects, especially on the Jhelum and Chenab rivers. In October 2008, shortly after filling of the Baglihar dam that caused reduction in Chenab's waters (it was delayed by five days: it was required to be filled between 21 June to 31 August but it got completed only on 05 September) into Pakistan, President Asif Ali Zardari asserted that "Pakistan would be paying a very high price for India's move to block Pakistan's water supply from Chenab River." He warned India "not to trade important regional objectives for short-term domestic goals."[ccxviii] On 28 January 2009, President Zardari in an article in the Washington Post warned that the water crisis in Pakistan was directly linked to relations with India. Resolution could prevent an environmental catastrophe in South Asia, but failure to do so could fuel the fires of discontent that might lead to extremism and terrorism.[ccxix] On 3 January, 2010, Sardar Assef Ahmad Ali, Deputy Chairman, The Palnning Commission of Pakistan while speaking at a seminar on the "Improvement on Energy Sector", organised by the Institute of Electrical and Electronics Engineers, Pakistan (IEEEP), stated that India would have to stop stealing Pakistan's water as the latter would not hesitate to wage war with New Delhi if it did not stop doing so.[ccxx] The Chairman, Indus Waters Treaty Council, Hafiz Zahoor-ul-Hassan Dahr, has warned that Pakistan could become another Somalia and Ethiopia.[ccxxi] He said the Indian projects aimed at controlling the waters of the Chenab, Jhelum and Indus rivers, were illegal and a clear violation of the IWT. He further stated that India had seized 70 per cent water of the Chenab and the Jhelum as a result of which over 0.9 million acres of land, being irrigated through the Marala HWs, was now presenting the view of Thar and Cholistan deserts.[ccxxii] The dominant perception in the mass media in Pakistan also shares the view that its rights to Western rivers are undermined by Indian violations of IWT. Majid Nizami, chief editor of a group of newspapers, observed that the water dispute with India could trigger a war. The Water dispute with India has also emerged on the radar of religious militants in Pakistan. Extremist organizations like Jamaat-ud-Dawa (JuD) have tried to use it to invoke anti-India emotions in general public. Pakistan's banned 'jihadi' publications like Jarrar (a publication of Jamaat-ud-Dawa), Zarb-e-Momin (a publication of Al-Rasheed Trust) and Al-Qalam (a publication of Jaish-e-Muhammad)have started highlighting this issue as "water terrorism." The main argument is that Pakistan's vulnerability to the trans-boundary impacts of India's ambitious hydro projects on the Western rivers goes unrecognized and underappreciated in India. It is not only violation of the spirit of the IWT but also ignoring the huge trans-boundary impacts on hydrology and ecology of the rivers assigned to Pakistan under the IWT. Given the growing water stress on the Indus water system, it is in the interest of both countries to observe the letter and spirit of the Treaty and take steps to ensure effective functioning of the Indus water regime.

Indian official sources and the media attribute Islamabad's water woes to "mismanagement of water resources", "less storage facilities" and a "huge 38 MAF of waters flowing every year un-utilised" into the Arabian Sea. They also argue that since rivers flowing in (Pakistani) Northern Punjab don't provide adequate waters to lower riparian, thereby, Pakistan "attempts to divert attention from growing discontent in Sindh and Balochistan over denial of their share of Indus waters." Also as the "population in Punjab increases, the demand for irrigation also increases."[ccxxiii] As a corollary, India wants Pakistan to look inwards to address its water issues and improve its water management. The Indian view was clearly made out by the High Commissioner Sharat Sabharwal in his speech at a function organized by the Karachi Council on Foreign Relations (KCFR) and Pakistan-India Citizens Friendship Forum (PICFF). He described allegations against India as "preposterous" as India, never hindered water flows into Pakistan even during the 1965 and 1971 wars. He contended that "apprehensions, misconceptions, misinformation and allegations pertaining to India ...characterize the debate on water scarcity in Pakistan."[ccxxiv] Sabharwal said, the Treaty permitted the limited use of water from the Western rivers of the Indus system by India and that this entitlement had not been fully used to date. As against the Storage entitlement of 3.6 MAF, India had built no storage so far. Of the 1.34 million acres permitted for irrigation, only 0.792 million acres was being utilized for irrigation purpose. "We have exploited only a fraction of the hydroelectric potential available to us on these rivers." Out of a total potential of 18,653 MW, projects worth 2,324 MW have been commissioned and those for 659 MW are under construction.[ccxxv] India also blames Pakistan for its water woes that India says are emanating from poor management of water resources The treaty has created a political and economic estrangement of the general populace of the state of J&K, who perceive themselves, to have been let down by the governments of both; India and Pakistan.

Impact of Chinese Interests

Ever Increasing Chinese Needs and Reduced Availability of water.

No discussion on water management within Indian Sub-Continent will, however, be complete without taking into account Chinese water needs, as a number of rivers have their origin in China/ Tibet Autonomous Region (TAR). China has a far greater problem at hand. In terms of a single basin, the Yangtze Basin supports the largest concentration of population in Asia. [ccxxvi] Another interesting fact is that while Brahmaputra Basin is the wettest major basin in Asia, the Yellow River Basin which has less than 2/5th precipitation of the Brahmaputra Basin, is the driest. With 20 % of the world's population she has just 7% of the global water. As on date, over 660 cities of China covering a population of 160 million suffer from water shortage. In the North, desertification is affecting agricultural production, and water scarcity is becoming more pronounced as demand and pollution increase. In the southern regions of China, the melt water of the Himalayan glaciers feeds Asia's most important rivers, but the quality and quantity of water from these rivers is increasingly getting threatened due to pollution, excess withdrawal, and climate change. Just over one-third of China lies in 19 different river basins shared with 14 countries. As the upstream source of the majority of these rivers, China's rivers outflow is nearly 40 times greater than its inflow. Yet internal river flow management and cross-border coordination have been minimal, presenting challenges to downstream communities/ countries.

Growth in China's Population. It is expected to grow from 1.33 billion in 2008 to 1.42 billion by 2050—produces significant water resource challenges, and the country's diverse landscape and large landmass make water problems distinct from the arid North to the more water-rich South. Northern China—which is characterized primarily by desert and grasslands—is experiencing drastic population growth that resulting into enhanced exploitation of scarce water resources at an accelerated pace. Resultant shortage of water is causing severe desertification which is further eating up land that once was used for agricultural production and "choking" heavily relied-upon rivers. Presently per capita water availability in China is one fourth of the global average.

Uneven Water Resources Distribution. The North China Plain, which is home to almost 40 percent of China's cultivated land area and 40 percent of the population, holds only 7.6 percent of the country's water resources. Yet agricultural and industrial water demands are growing by more than 10 percent a year and are expected to increase by 40 percent by 2020. Compounding scarcity issues in the North, a quarter of Yellow River is now piped to distant cities. At the same time, regional development may strain plateau communities' water supplies and raise equity and ethnic concerns. More than 25 percent of China's landmass currently consists of desert. Intended to halt the encroachment of the Gobi Desert with planted forest strips. While there is an abundance of water in Tibet but there is a scarcity in Northern and Western part of China. This is the defining factor in the water management and their (China) effort to transfer water from water surplus areas to water deficient areas is an important part of their strategy.

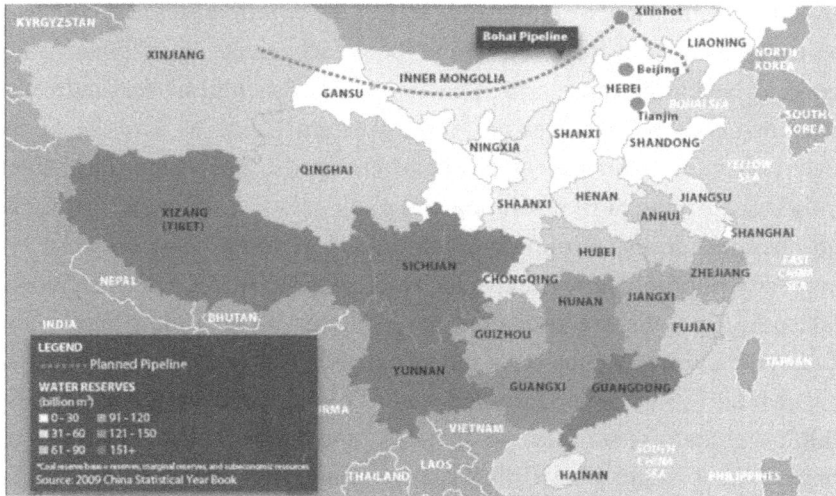

This map explains why China wants to divert water--from the water-rich Tibetan plateau to water-starved northern China. At the top of the map is another madcap diversion project: the Bohai Pipeline. This engineering scheme proposes dropping a pipe into the Bohai Sea in China's east, draw more than 340,000 cubic metres (90 million gallons) of seawater a day into a complex of coastal desalination plants, and then pump this water 1,400 meters uphill for more than 600 kilometers to Xilinhot, where it will be used for coal mining operations. And then continue pumping the water much further west, to Xinjiang.

Fig-5.33: Water Sources In China

Pollution of Water Channels. Officials have generally failed to curtail industrial dumping and sewage discharge into the plain's three major river basins—the Huai, Hai, and Huang He (Yellow) Rivers. South Eastern China is a major site of global manufacturing, resulting in agricultural and industrial pollution of its water. This pollution-driven loss of water access and the threats to human health and fisheries have provoked social unrest and resulted in bans on certain Chinese fish exports. Another factor which needs to be factored in while discussing China's water needs is the water pollution which makes water availability even further restricted. An estimated 70 percent of China's rivers are polluted, leaving an estimated 300 million people with limited access to clean water.

Global Warming. In Southern China, melt water from the Himalayan glaciers bordering the Tibetan Plateau feeds some of Asia's greatest water sources—including the Yangtze, Yellow, Ganges, Brahmaputra, and Mekong rivers. Rivers which have their origin in TAR depend on glacial feed which is getting further restricted due to receding glaciers. Climate change is projected to decrease China's glacial coverage by 27 percent by 2050, seriously diminishing water availability for communities throughout China and South East Asia. For the communities and countries living downstream from the trans boundary rivers of China, water access is becoming more critical as domestic, agricultural, and industrial water demands have surged in North Western China as a result of the development of water-usurping oil and gas fields; glacial melting, which could cause drying of rivers during non rainy seasons; and industrial waste and chemical spills. While increased glacial melting could cause severe short-term flooding, flow is expected to decrease as glaciers shrink. Winter and spring months are projected to be increasingly arid, which could exacerbate current strains on water resources. The resulting soil erosion, loss of biodiversity, and decreased water holding capacity could severely inhibit regional life sources, productivity, and stability. The dense coastal population of South East China is particularly vulnerable to forecasted sea-level rise. Of immediate concern, the rising sea level drives salinity changes in the freshwater rivers that feed the ocean, thus affecting water access and quality. If urban infrastructure proves incapable of handling the encroaching sea, the epicentre of China's manufacturing region could be destroyed.

China's Plans to Augment Water Availability. Some of the relevant aspects are as follows:-

> ▶ Case of Brahmaputra- The waters of River Brahmaputra are shared by China, India, and Bangladesh. The average annual trans-boundary flow into India from Brahmaputra is a maximum to any country (142,370 CUM). It may also be noted that although the mean trans-boundary runoff volume from Tibetan rivers aggregates; 185,660 Cubic Kms per year in the case of other riparian neighbours collectively, the figure totals 347,020 CUM in India's case. Thus all the hydro-engineering based projects have far greater implication for India than any other country, more so in the light of the fact that India is the only country among all the neighbours of China who has a potential to challenge China some time in future. This substantial dependency reveals India's vulnerability to China's capacity to use water as a political instrument. Another country which is likely to get environmentally affected badly due to diversion of the Brahmaputra waters, is Bangladesh, who

happens to be a lower riparian to India. Reduction in the volume of water coming to India is going to mean even lesser volume going to Bangladesh. This kind of reduction which will be in the range of 30% (It is based on the assumption that the diversion is going to reduce the water contributed by the River Siang, which is about 30%) will be devastating for Bangladesh, who is, as it is, having her own problems of water which have been on account of uneven distribution of the surface water within Bangladesh and the ground water being contaminated with Arsenic. It is worth considering that Bangladesh's reliance on trans-boundary water flow is one of the highest in the world; 91.33%[ccxxvii] (refer Table-4.1).

► **Water Diversion Project**

Fig-5.34 : Location Of Dam At Great Bend

► In the 1990s and 2000s, there were repeated speculations about China building a dam at the Great Bend, with a view to divert the waters to the North of the country. In early 2003 scientists from China's Water Conservancy and Hydropower Planning & Design Institute organised a feasibility study also for a major hydro project along the section of River Brahmaputra which flows through China. This section of the river, which later flows into India and Bangladesh has water energy reserve of 68 million KW. If successful it will divert 200 BCM of water annually to Yellow River and reduce the flow in the downstream side by 60%[52]. China is of the opinion that there is a scope for harnessing the potential for 40,000 MW by exploiting the drop of 6000-8000 feet at the Great Bend. However this was denied by the Chinese government for many years. In fact, at the Kathmandu Workshop of Strategic Foresight Group in August 2009 on Water Security in the Himalayan Region, which was a rare occasion that brought together leading hydrologists from the Basin countries, the Chinese scientists argued that it was not feasible for China to undertake such a diversion. However, just about eight months down the line, on 22 April 2010, China confirmed that it was indeed building the Zangmu Dam, a run of the river dam on the Yarlung Tsangpo (Brahmaputra).[53] This water diversion scheme will draw from the waters of the Yalong, Dadu and Jinsha rivers, which rise in the Tibetan plateau, and channel them to Yellow River. The aim of the project is to provide water for the human use, including farming and industry in China's water-scarce areas in the North and North West. The project options entail three diversion routes - the Eastern, the Central and the Western routes. The diversion of the YarlungTsangpo at the Great Bend is the Western route of the project - the most technologically challenging and controversial of the three routes. The proposed dams on the Yarlung, almost 28 in number, some of which are already underway, have the full support of the state-run hydro-power industry. It would have a capacity to produce 38 Giga Watts of power, almost twice the capacity of the Three Gorges Dam. Once completed, the water diversion scheme is expected to transfer over 40 BCM of water annually to China's water scarce areas, relieving China's thirst to a significant extent.[54] For Beijing, the argument in favour of the water diversion project is simple. More than a quarter of China

---

[52] http://indochina 102.blogspot.in/
[53] Macarthur Foundation, Asian security Initiative.
[54] Ibid73

is classified as desert. Its North and North West areas are water scarce. Increasing consumption of water, rapid industrialization and pollution have rendered the waters of many of China's rivers unusable. Also, a number of sections of Yellow River run dry. In contrast, rivers that rise in the Tibetan plateau's glaciers have much more water. In response to India's concerns about the reduction of the volume of water in Brahmaputra, downstream of the project site, China assured that the project would not have any significant effect on the downstream flow to India. However, notwithstanding the assurances by China, it would be naive to assume that this project will have no effect on the quantum of water downstream of the Diversion. There is a definite case for India to challenge, in consultation with the other affected nation; Bangladesh, this plan of China to transfer water in total disregard to the needs of lower riparian states. In this context, in a meeting of scientists at Dhaka at 2010, 25 leading experts from the Basin countries issued a Dhaka Declaration[55] on Water Security, calling for exchange of information in low flow period, and other means of collaboration. Even though the UN Convention on Trans-boundary Water of 1997 does not prevent any of the Basin countries from building a dam, Customary Law offers relief to the lower riparian countries. There is also another option, where instead of confrontation a cooperation can be thought between all the three riparian states, namely; China, India and Bangladesh to exploit the potential of the River Brahmaputra to undertake hydroelectricity projects and Trans-boundary water navigation projects as part of a collective basin development plan in a spirit of mutual cooperation.

---

[55] The New Nation, Bangladesh, 17 Jan2010

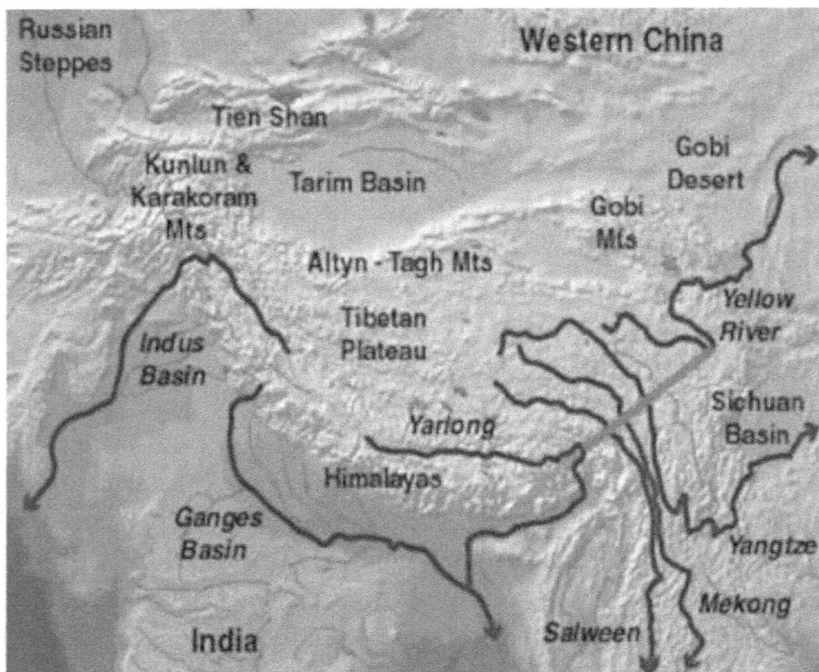

Fig-5.35: Diversion Plan- Brahmaputra Water Northwards

► **Chinese Efforts to Augment Storage Capacity**-Some of the reported dams which are being built/ already built are as tabulated below:-

Table- 5.10: Dams Being Built By China On Brahmaputra And Its Tributaries

Ser no	Project Name	Location	Intended Use	Generating / Storage Capacity	Construction Status
1.	Pangduo	Lhasa River On Brahmaputra, in Lhasa	Irrigation and Power	120 MW/687 million CUM	Completed or under construction
2.	Zangma	Prefecture	Power	510 MW	Under construction
3.	Yamdrok Tso	Lake Yamdrok On Nyang Chu	Power	90 MW 20 MW	Completed
4.	Manlha	Gyangtse	Irrigation and Power	157 million CUM	Completed
5.	Chonggye	Near Chonggye Township	Irrigation	11.58 million CUM	Completed
6.	Nyangtri-Payi	Nyangtri Chumo Gully in Sangri County	Power	84 MW	Completed
7.	Wolka	Lhoka	Power	20 MW 4.5 MW	Completed
8.	Yangjingshi	Lhasa River Basin	Mainly Irrigation	81 million CUM	Completed
9.	Tago (Tiger Head) Reservoir	Lhasa River basin	Irrigation	12 million CUM	Completed
10.	Suo Chang	Nye Chu, Panam County	Irrigation	18 million CUM	Completed

| 11. | Chun Sun | Naye Chu, Panam County | Irrigation | 24 million CUM | Completed |
| 12. | Darikong | Lhasa River | Power | 30 MW | Completed/ Under Construction |

Source: Environment and Development Desk of Central Tibetan Administration, internationalrivers.org; China Daily.

▶ **Other Planned Diversion/ Construction of Dams-** It has been reported that along with Brahmaputra, China is also trying to make use/ divert waters of Indus and Sutlej. In this direction a Dam at Nagri on Indus River and a barrage on River Sutlej at Zada in Western Tibet has already been constructed.[56] These dams built by the Chinese on the tributaries and upper reaches of the Indus[57] in the Ngari Prefecture of Tibet , the Senge – Tsangpo project, the Zada gorge on the Sutlej[58] are a cause of concern for both India and Pakistan. There is another fear that some volume of water of the Yarlung zangbo (the Brahmaputra) could be diverted into the Arun river of Nepal or the Gandaki in the same country. Both these rivers later flow into India, the former as part of the Sapta Kosi and the latter as the Gandak, Both rivers have been harnessed jointly by Nepal and India.[59]

---

[56] An IDSA report reported by X News during Mar 2012.
[57] China Builds Dam on Indus near Ladakh by Senge H Sering
[58] China Defends Dam on Sutlej pub in DNA Jul07, 2006
[59] "Eagle's Eye: Barrage across Parichu river"by ArabindaGhose   pub Central Chronicle[Friday, July 14, 2006 11:46]

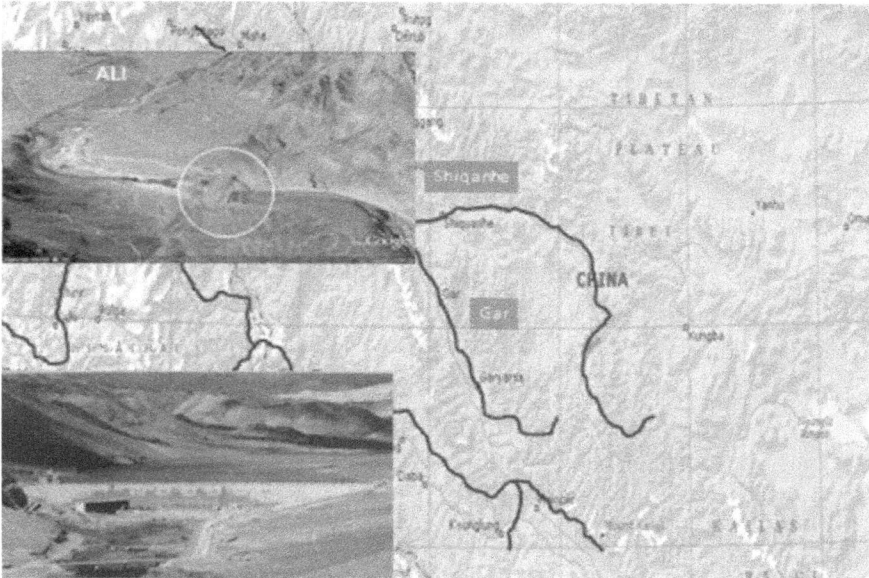

Fig-5.36: Dam On Indus At Nagri

▶ **Implications of China's Plans to Divert Sutlej Waters** [60]- the News from across the Tibetan border about the Chinese building a barrage on the Sutlej River portend strategic concerns to the country's border areas. According to media reports,[ccxxviii] the Chinese have constructed a diversion structure across the Zada Gorge in the river (locally known as Lang Chen Khambab) located in the Western part of Tibet and satellite imageries indicate the work as complete. China did not take India into confidence about this project which has the potential of controlling Sutlej flows into India. As of 2006 (at the time of reporting of this news), Indian authorities did not show much concern about the possible upstream uses in Tibet to cause reduction in Himalayan river flows on the presumption that such utilisation would be minimal due to the terrain conditions and sparse population there. But (as subsequent events have shown), if the Chinese plan is to divert the waters during lean periods in winter and release large flood flows during

---

[60] Ibid page 98

the glacier melting periods in summer, India will have to be bothered about it. India did have experience of such a happening twice. First time; a flash floods occurred in on the early hours of 01 August 2000, in the Parichu, which was carried into the Sutlej from a place called Khab on the border of Himachal Pradesh with Tibet, at about 0100 hours on August 1 and had reached the Nathpa Jhakri Project (NJP) at about 0515 hrs. Within a short span of time the level of the river Sutlej rose by 15 metres and the water discharge rose suddenly from 1480 CUMEC (cubic metre per second) at 0300 hours to 5100 CUMEC by 0530 hrs. It however came down to just 1416 CUMEC by 0900 hrs. It is interesting to note that there was no flood in the River Spiti which joins the Sutlej near Khab. The flash flood raised many intriguing issues, and left behind a trail of destruction in Himachal Pradesh. According to one report by a team of engineers connected with the Bhakra Nangal Project, "the devastating flood which gained momentum as it passed down the river from the heights of Kinnaur district, destroyed almost everything on its way including the costly infrastructures thus pushing back the clock of development by several decades. It resulted in a loss of lots of life and property, disrupting services such as power, water supply and telecommunication in the flood-affected areas of Kinnaur, Shimla and Mandi districts of Himachal Pradesh. More than 150 people were swept away, several were buried under the huge mass of rubble and the area had remained inaccessible for several days. About 50 bridges from Khab to Sunni and about 50 km of the Hindustan-Tibet Road. the lifeline of the Lahaul-Spiti district, were washed away The damages to the highway had a tremendous impact on the economy of the area with apple, peas and other cash crops getting stranded in the area, which otherwise would have been exported outside. The NJP, which was then under construction, was damaged by the backflow of the water in the tailrace tunnel. Tonnes of rubble and silt were deposited on the generating units. By an estimate the Project had suffered a loss of about Rs.700 crores.[ccxxix] The total loss because of the flood was estimated, at that point in time, was assessed to be Rs.2500 crores. Luckily the Bhakra Reservoir downstream could absorb the floods thereby containing the devastation in the lower reaches in Punjab. Earlier, it was also seen that there was reduced inflow in the summer months into the Bhakra reservoir, an unusual feature during the snow-melting season. The floods could have been caused due to heavy rainfall in Tibet, or breaches in lakes upstream or due to collapse of constructed structures or failure of temporary obstructions across the river channel upstream. Interestingly, rainfall in the area is a rare event as most of the precipitation in the upper Sutlej is in the form of snowfall. Hence the flood could not have been caused by rainfall. The pre and post flood event satellite data did not show any noticeable change in the water spread in the connecting channel of the upper lakes (the Mansarovar and Rakas Tal) and hence breaches of the lakes contributing to these floods could also be ruled out. Hence it has to be concluded that the floods were triggered by the failure of a blockage across the river channel caused either due to construction activities or landslips. The reduced inflow into the Bhakra in the previous months, the sudden rise and fall in water levels during August, all these strongly point to the failure of a dam on the river. Since Sino-Indian relationship was at a low ebb during that period, field verification could not be done to confirm the findings as China did not permit Indian team to visit the site. However an inquiry into the accident with the input and the logical extrapolations, had concluded, that the probable cause was "Glacial Lake Outburst Flow and a cloud burst at the same time in the catchment area of the Parichu in Tibet". The reason why the rest of India, particularly the Punjab cities and towns like Ludhiana did not feel the impact of this flash flood was that the Bhakra Dam's Gobindsagar reservoir with a capacity of 9868 million cubic foot absorbed all the flood waters. Second time flash floods in the Sutlej happened in 2005, reportedly due to landslips in Tibet. A lake was believed to have been formed in River Parichu due to landslides. Subsequently it is not certain whether due to water pressure the walls of the lake got collapsed and the water got released or the blasting of the walls of the lake were artificially triggered to release the water pressure, but the end result was that a major flash flood occurred in the Himachal Pradesh. It necessitated evacuation of people and even shutting down of the NJP power generation activities (this time an advanced warning was received) resulting in heavy losses. This incident resulted into a major devastation on the downstream side. A major damage occurred to the installations of the Sutlej Vidyut Board and as such its working was paralysed for 45 days. However as was the case in the year 2000, though generation of the power at the NJP (which by now had got completed) was stopped for a long time, the Bhakra Beas Management Board had welcomed the inflow into the reservoir which got much required quantity of water to fill it up. A debate ensued whether the formation of the lake was due to natural causes or was it an act of a deliberate effort on the part of the People's Liberation Army (PLA), to intimidate India. One school of thought was that it was done by the PLA by directional blasting. What gave credence to this theory was that China did not permit Indian 'Fact Finding Team' to visit the site. These instances highlight the need for India to be concerned about the Chinese activities in harnessing the rivers in the Tibetan region which influence the drought/flood conditions occurring in the border States. Interestingly, prior to 2000, floods of such intensity were not reported from the upper reaches of the Sutlej river whereas thereafter such floods have become frequent, probably due to construction activities in this reach. Although the Ministry of External Affairs did not comment on this development, water resources engineers of India did express concern over this development, particularly because of the fact that the huge Bhakra Dam and the reservoir formed by the dam across the Sutlej, is a virtual life line for North-Western India since it provides irrigation water, flood control and large hydro-electric power. Granted the fact that a barrage is actually a diversion structure and does not store water like dams do, any such structure upstream of a river that flows through strategic areas in India makes some people jittery, more so because the Parichu river has been a source of constant worry to engineers managing the 1500 MW power station of NJP across the Sutlej near Rampur in Himachal Pradesh, which had cost the exchequer more than Rs. 8600 crores to build and had started generating power only since the year 2002. In view of the increased interest China is showing to divert flows of some of the

Himalayan rivers such as the Sutlej and the possible repercussions there of, India has to take steps to minimise the impacts such as reduction of flows caused by upstream diversions or flash floods resulting from breaches, sudden gate openings or even dam failures. Possibility of such an occurrence in future cannot be discounted and that is why there is a need to evolve a strategy to pro-actively deal with it, both in terms of diplomatic measures to avoid its occurrence and preventive measures to deal with it on occurrence. Before we go into other aspects of this piece of information, it is relevant here to discuss whether India would at all be justified in raising the issue with the Chinese authorities formally on a legal basis. In other words, is China legally bound to inform and consult India before undertaking the construction of barrage or even a dam? In view of the existing state of rules with respect to non navigational use of the water of the rivers which are across more than one country, Upper Riparian states are not bound to inform their lower riparian neighbours, unless they have a treaty among themselves. China, therefore legally is not bound to inform other countries when it undertakes development of water courses for non-navigational purposes in her Thus there is a need to go in for a formal agreement between India and China with respect to usage of waters of the common rivers. Therefore in the present circumstances, the answer to above question would be a resounding NO. Hence it would be in fitness of things that the construction of a storage project near the border is considered on priority (may be as an interim measure) so that in an eventuality of a flash flood, as and when China informs of the situation or even otherwise, necessity to press the panic button is avoided. It is of importance to note, that at present, except for a memorandum of understanding (MoU) for sharing the hydrological information of the Tibetan rivers concerned during flood season, there are no subsisting agreements between India and China on water related issues even though Indian rivers such as the Brahmaputra, Indus, Sutlej, Kosi, etc., originate from Tibet.

While, presently China presently does not have adequate water storage capacity but they are steadily trying to build such a capacity. The issue that needs to be taken note of is; that to create necessary water storage capacity

China is not averse to environmental degradation. China's aggressive South-to-North water diversion projects on the rivers that originate from the Tibet region, particularly on the Yarlung-Tsangpo, is opening up a new front of uncertainty in Sino-Indian relations as well as the overall hydrological dynamics in South Asia. But for the implementation of such a plan China who is the upper riparian will have to show certain large heartedness and a spirit of accommodation. However past experiences on water cooperation with China, be it Parichu incident or even accommodation of the needs of lower riparian states in Mekong Region, do not inspire much of confidence and the very absence of any such cooperation, is opening up a new front of uncertainty in the Sino-Indian relations as well as the overall hydrological dynamics in South Asia.

Need for a Formal Arrangement to Deal with the Water Related Issues Between China and India and other Lower Riparians. China is upper riparian; in case of most of important rivers which pass through countries of Indian Sub-continent like Brahmaputra or rivers like Mahakali and Kosi which are feeder to the important rivers like Ganges. Presently there is no legally binding agreement in place to govern the water relations between China- Nepal or China-India or China and South Asian Countries as a whole. It has been the past experience that China does not hesitate to use, from time to time, water and rivers as instruments of political expediency to deal with the lower riparian states and also as a resource to meet her own domestic demands in total disregard of the needs of the lower riparian states. China is conscious of the possibility of lower riparian states ganging up and not allowing her to go ahead with her plans to use the water resources of Tibet unchecked. To ward off such an eventuality, China appears to be working consciously to ensure that such a possibility is nipped in the bud itself, by trying hard to have collaboration with; Pakistan, Myanmar and Bangladesh individually within the Indian Sub-continent.[61] Thus there is a need to engage China in the water needs of South Asia through a collective response from the affected countries, namely India, Bangladesh, Pakistan, Nepal and Myanmar. These engagements could be basin by basin say China –India –Pakistan for Indus River Basin, India-China for Sutlej Basin and China-Nepal-India- Bangladesh for Ganges Brahmaputra Basin. Only a formal arrangement will be able to probably pin down China to become sensitive to the needs of the lower riparian nations for a equitable sharing of the common resources.

---

[61] Ibid22.

Chapter-6
Way Ahead

"The wars of the twenty-first century will be fought over water."

- Ismail Serageldin,
World Bank Vice President for Environmental Affairs,
quoted in Marq de Villiers' Water, 2000

General

Conflict Resolution: Conceptual Framework. Before we arrive at the way ahead, it would be in order understand the underlying conceptual framework for the conflict resolution. It can be represented as follows:-

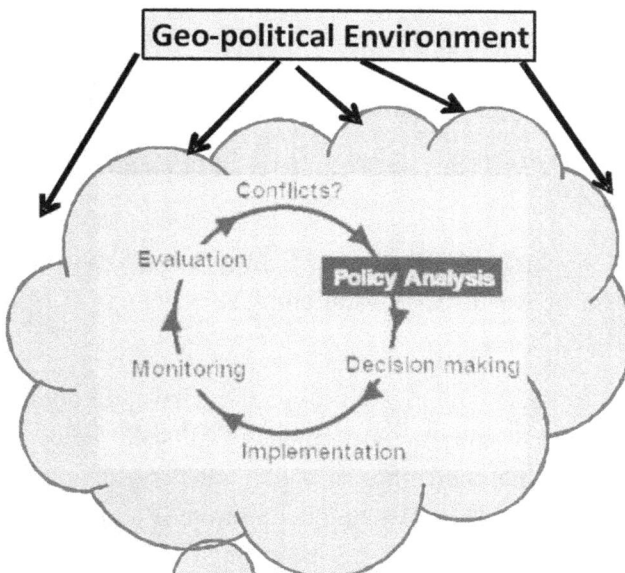

Fig-6.1 : Conflict Resolution Cycle

As can be seen the conflict resolution mechanism is a continuous process and is highly influenced by the geo-political environment which is dynamic. Therefore it is essential that all stake holders from time to time revisit the policy framework and continue to evolve /modify the existing framework to respond to new emerging geo-political challenges. In fact there is need to evolve a formal mechanism to continuously update policy issues to be able to respond to ever changing environmental challenges. In the above conceptual conflict resolution cycle the resource for the potential conflict is water sharing.

Attempts have continuously been made by all the stake holder countries from time to time to find solutions of common water sharing related problems. In this connection in Asia a number of cooperative management systems have been established for optimum and equitable distribution of available water resources and in many cases with the provisions for the dispute resolution. Some of these are as follows:-

- ▸ The Mekong River Committee (1957) and its successor the Mekong River Commission.

- ▸ The Treaties of Sarada (1920), Kosi (1954) and Gandak (1959) between India and Nepal.

- ▸ The Indus Water Treaty between India and Pakistan (1960).

- ▸ The Ganges Waters Treaty between India and Bangladesh (1977), and the 1996.

- ▸ Agreement on the Use of Water and Energy Resources of the Syr Darya Basin between Kazakhstan and Uzbekistan. - They have been poorly enforced.

Though most of them are in vogue but they have, if not failed out rightly, have failed to meet the aspirations of all stake holders and more importantly meet the challenges of a very dynamic international environment. India also needs to create global awareness about the water resources in Tibet and build regional pressure that Tibet's water is for humanity and not for China alone. Almost two billion people in South and South East Asia depend on the water resources of Tibet. China need to be sensitised against the present trend of unchecked exploitation of the water resources by her and the implications of her efforts on the continued trajectory of over exploitation which may result into irreparable ecological damage.

There is a need to evolve a comprehensive, widely accepted set of international water laws on utilization of international water channels. The scope of these laws should also have an element for the enforcement of the necessary conflict resolution mechanism which should be independent in nature.

Continued population growth and the impact of global warming along with inadequate conservation and huge wastage are putting enormous pressure on water resources. With no proportional increase in water availability and an ever increasing demand, a water crisis seems imminent. Therefore there is a need to synchronise internal water management measures with external riparian policies. Although India has a comparatively lower per capita water consumption presently but with the rise in the aspirations of the people, shifting of economy from agrarian base to industrial and and finally to service based economy and above all exponential rise in the population calls for more optimal use of existing water resources. Thus there is a need to evolve systems and procedures to leverage technology to ensure more efficient use of available water resources across the entire spectrum of the utilisation.

There is a need to evolve a policy revamp which moves away from a narrowly understood framework of 'water management' to a broad-based and wide-reaching 'water resource management'.[ccxxx] The subtle difference between the two is that while water management amounts to optimum use of available water but the water resource management also entails making of efforts to develop the water sources in such a way that their yield is enhanced without compromising the effectiveness of the management of the available water. This would require, in Indian context, treating river systems, particularly the Ganges-Brahamaputra Meghna (GBM), the Indus and the peninsular rivers in a holistic way and re-orienting hydro diplomacy on a multilateral basis than just a bilateral format in regional context.[ccxxxi] This would entail a shift from sharing waters to sharing benefits.

There is a need to evolve a mechanism in the MEA to take proactive measures to appreciate the emerging conflict and address them well in time. Regional collaborative mechanism like Indus Water Treaty-1960 between India and Pakistan, Treaty of Peace between Israel and Jordan 1994, Agreement for Cooperation for the Sustainable Development of the Mekong river basin 1995 and treaty between India and Bangladesh for sharing of Ganges waters- 1996 are some of the collaborative mechanism which have withstood the test of time.

Creating international or national water commissions to manage shared resources such as river basins can reduce the threat of conflict and promote equitable water sharing. Improved institutional capacity may involve formal legislation, international agreements, and treaties. For example, growing populations, commercial agriculture, electric utilities, and industries in several Southern African countries compete for the water resources of the Zambezi River basin. In the future, supplies may not be sufficient to meet domestic and commercial needs. A Water Sector has been created within the existing Southern African Development Community (SADC), and new initiatives are being carried out in conjunction with the Zambezi River Authority to establish a protocol on shared water courses and to promote integrated water resource management.

Policymakers and the general public need to be educated about water resources and population dynamics, with an emphasis on making human activities sustainable with respect to water availability.

Economic planning should take into account projected population growth and finiteness of the existing water resources with a trend analysis to match the demand versus supply needs at a designated time in future. Plans for growth in the agricultural and industrial sectors must be balanced by the need for sufficient clean water for domestic use and for maintaining healthy ecosystems.

National population policies, sensitive to community and individual needs, can make an important contribution to reduce the pressure on the existing water resources.

National water commissions and river basin authorities should be established to monitor and coordinate water use, and arbitrate between conflicting interests. Commissions and authorities should have the power to create and enforce policies, while recognizing that they must be accountable to the public and responsive to local needs.

Renewable and non-renewable groundwater resources require greater attention. Because groundwater is hidden from sight, it is often neglected in comprehensive policies, and in some countries has been treated as a public good, to be used on a first-come, first-served basis.

There is a need for creation of adequate storage facility with a long term view. Inadequacy of storage facility results into tensions among the stake holders and also population pressure and non availability of land for creation of storage space may further aggravate the tension. Case in point is India, which faces a water storage problem. Its annual demand for water is more than two times the available storage capacity of the existing reservoirs. However building of storage facilities is a time, technology and cost intensive proposition. Also their impact on environment, issues on account of silt accumulation and quality of water in reservoir needs to be studied in detail before undertaking construction of new storage facilities.

Water dispute amelioration is as important, and a lesser costly route as compared to conflict resolution. It has been widely experienced that generally international attention, and resultant financing, is focused on a basin only after a crisis or a flashpoint has been triggered. Such has been the case on the river basins like Indus, Jordan, Nile, and Tigris-Euphrates among many others. As against these mechanisms which emerged post conflicts the case studies of the Mekong and La Plata commissions which are institutional framework for joint management and dispute resolution and were established well in advance of any likely conflict. It is also worth noting that the Mekong Committee's impressive record of continuing its work throughout intense political disputes between the riparian countries and resolving issues well before the flash point could be reached, resulted into overall development of the region. It is indeed a worth emulating endeavour. In this connection generating a data base of all disputes/ conflicts with their reasons is an exercise which would help in evolving the right strategy for dispute resolution.

Existing collaborative mechanism for sharing of hydrological information with respect to flooding, precipitation and likely evolving disasters in case of all -common rivers/ international water channels within the riparian states be strengthened to avoid Parichu type of incident. There should be institutional arrangement under the aegis of SAARC and Indo-China cooperative mechanism. Such a facility should have capability to do research, to predict and to recommend necessary response mechanism well in time.

Tibet is the water Tower of the World in general, but specifically for the South and the South East Asia. But for few like Yangtze, most of the rivers emanating in Tibet flow South/ South Eastward. However it needs to be understood that even Tibet's resources are not in- exhaustible. Human made environmental changes and the global warming are more visible on the Tibetan Plateau than in the Cryosphere (the frozen part of the earth's surface including the polar icecaps). This needs to be understood that it is indeed a resource which we, the present generation is a mere custodian of, and have a bonden duty to hand it over to the next generation. Unfortunately China is trying to appropriate the water resources of Tibet for itself, which needs to be challenged. It is recommended that an international organisation preferably under the aegis of UN fully dedicated to preserve this precious resource be established. This proposed organisation needs to view the issue holistically and permit only those projects which neither cause environmental degradation nor allow unilateral use.

While planning framework for dispute resolution one of the important aspect that needs to be developed is the overall basin development including addressing HR issues and capacity building which will help over all development and economic prosperity which will contribute positively to the easing of tension within the region.

While considering the measures for cooperation and enhancing the water availability, normally the entire energy is spent in addressing the issues based on surface water. It needs to be appreciated that the situation with respect to ground water is even graver. Problem is far more acute in case of aquifers which are of trans-boundary in nature. For example; aquifer in Gangetic basin which stretches across India, Bangladesh and some its tributaries originate in Nepal. This particular basin also suffers due to Arsenic contamination which is to a large extent is on account of over exploitation. In fact there is no law which in any way addresses the utilisation of the ground water of aquifer which is within a country or stretches across the boundary. Country like Bangladesh already suffers on account of this with India not too far behind, because of the excessive contamination of the ground water. It is therefore necessary that charging of aquifer and improving the water quality in the Indian Subcontinent improves. Necessary R&D effort needs to be initiated.

India

Coming specifically to India, river linking projects in India for inter basin transfer be progressed to make sure that the water deficient areas are taken care by the water which in water sufficient areas is presently surplus to the requirement. This should be done in a graduated manner, ie; first within a state, then within a region and only in the end pan Indian approach be considered. The National Water Development Agency (NWDA) was setup in 1980 by the Ministry of Water Resources for Water Development, keeping existing uses undisturbed, honouring existing awards in view, and finally for providing for the reasonable needs of the basin states for the foreseeable future.[ccxxxii] It is understood that plans for Himalayan Rivers and Peninsular rivers separately have already been prepared. It needs to be progressed on priority. After having achieved success in the intra connectivity linkages, similar exercise could also be planned within South Asia for which pre-discussion and working of the feasibility should commence now. It should be planned in a cooperative manner to tackle impending water shortages in future, effectively. Such connectivity will also introduce an element of interdependence between the concerned nations which will reduce the probability of conflicts substantially. In this connection, an effective working model of inter-dependence in the form of Indo- Bhutan Hydro Energy cooperation is worth studying.

India needs to pay special emphasis on Research and Development to evolve those food grain production technologies which economise on use of water and for this collaboration with countries who are pioneers in the field of food grain production with lesser quantity of water. Efforts should also be made to enhance the production of grain and with a planned strategy to increase their consumption. In the field of conservation use of qualitatively graded water for different usages should also be given a consideration. In this connection finiteness of the fresh water needs to be underlined and steady reduction in the availability of water per capita should also be given due thought on account of various reasons which have adequately been covered in Chapter-3. Conversion of sea water to potable water is energy intensive and India is terribly short of energy. Therefore conservation is the best policy which needs to be adopted and enforced if necessary. Research and innovation to enhance the conservation and economise on the use of fresh water should be a continuous exercise.

India needs to constantly evolve policies and frameworks to deal with neighbours so that emerging conflicts are addressed well in time. With Pakistan and China water issues will be far more political and strategic. Water as an instrument and tool of bargain and trade-off will assume predominance because the political stakes are high. Water issues with Pakistan and China have the potential to become catalysts for conflict. Though the importance of politics cannot be discounted in India's water relations with Nepal and Bangladesh, there is however far greater scope to overcome and break political deadlocks through sensible water sharing arrangements and resource development. With Bhutan hydro-relations have been extremely beneficial. Sharing the benefits of river cooperation has given substance to the relationship. The growing confidence has led to a recent agreement between the two countries to develop 10 more hydropower projects with a total capacity of 11,576 MW by 2020 in Bhutan. Recommended options for the specific action which need to be considered for an effective engagement with the neighbours; China, Pakistan, Nepal and Bangladesh are as follows:-

> ▶ **With China-** First and foremost requirement is to go in for a comprehensive treaty with respect to common resources. This framework need not be bilateral but it could be a multilateral arrangement basin wise. Sharing of data and information should be part of such an arrangement. Conflict avoidance can be converted into an opportunity so that all riparian states are benefitted. In any case water hereafter should be part of all future discussion with China and China should not be allowed to exploit the water resources of Tibet in total disregard to the existing

International rules/ protocols and informal understandings. The recent discussion between the new President of People's Republic of China, Xi Jinping and Dr Manmohan Singh, Prime Minister of India during the Durban Conference of BRICS countries (26-27 Mar 2013) on water issues between the two countries is the way ahead.

► **With Pakistan-** Certain stringent technical provisions in the Indus Water Treaty that give Pakistan right to question every proposal envisaged by India for the development of projects on the Western rivers (All within the given provisions of the Indus water Treaty-1960) need to be reviewed and if considered appropriate, a 'modification' of the provisions of the treaty needs to be deliberated. Whether it is done through re-negotiations or through establishing an Indus II Treaty, is a matter of detail which can be examined by both countries, however it needs to be appreciated that modifications of the provisions of the treaty are crucial in case of the Western rivers. Diplomacy and negotiations be used to convince Pakistan to make a common cause with India on the issue of exploitation of Indus River where China is the upper riparian. It is also felt that the water engagement with Pakistan has to be within the overall framework of security structure and at no stage Pakistan be allowed to exploit the generosity of India for actions against India. Case in point is the misuse by Pakistan of water flowing into Pakistan down stream of Madhopur in excess of her authorisation as per IWT provisions.

► **With Nepal-**Nepal is extremely important country not only for the water security of India but also in the overall security matrix of India. Therefore India needs to make a conscious effort to address all issues with Nepal in a manner that overall relations, including water and other security related issues, improve and long standing special relationship is restored. All adjustments should be based on equality keeping in view the sensibilities of Nepal, which on the basis of previous treaties give Nepal an impression that these are unequal. Considering the sensitivity of water relationship and the benefits that can come about, India should invest in Nepal's water infrastructure particularly irrigation and flood control. Identification and feasibility studies on small and medium projects should be undertaken. Small run-of the river projects should be started to build in political confidence. A common cause be attempted for the rivers emanating in China to safe guard the interests of Nepal and India.

- **With Bangladesh-** with Bangladesh, India's approach should be to deal with water issues in the overall political and security context. While the Ganges Treaty is well established, concerns over the sharing of the Teesta and India's construction of the Tipaimukh dam is opening up new fronts in water relations between the two countries. While it is important to continue dialogue with Bangladesh on joint river basins, India needs to look after its own interest as well. Bangladesh also needs to be sensitized on China's long distance transfer of waters of the Brahmaputra.

- **With Bhutan-** The water cooperation model between India and Bhutan is highly successful. Therefore it needs to be further strengthened and besides trying to replicate it with other countries of the Indian Subcontinent an attempt needs to be made to encourage Bhutan to have arrangement with other Indian Subcontinent countries for the power supply.

National water Policy. First national policy was formulated in 1987 which was updated in 2002. The major provisions under the policy are as follows:-

- Envisages to establish a standardized national information system with a network of data banks and data bases.

- Resource planning and recycling for providing maximum availability

- To give importance to the impact of projects on human settlements and environment.

- Guidelines for the safety of storage dams and other water-related structures

- ► Regulate exploitation of groundwater.

- ► Setting water allocation priorities in the following order: Drinking water, Irrigation, Hydropower, Navigation, Industrial and other uses.

- ► The water rates for surface water and ground water should be rationalized with due regard to the interests of small and marginal farmers.

- ► The policy also deals with participation of farmers and voluntary agencies, water quality, water zoning, conservation of water, flood and drought management, erosion etc.[ccxxxii]

A draft national water policy-2012 has been prepared and the main emphasis of this policy is to treat water as economic resource which the ministry claims to promote its conservation and efficient use.[ccxxxiv] This provision intended for the privatization of water-delivery services is being criticized from various quarters.[ccxxxv] The draft has also done away with the priorities for water allocation mentioned in 1987 and 2002 versions of the policy. The other major recommendations are

- ► To ensure access to a minimum quantity of potable water for essential health and hygiene to all citizens, available within easy reach of the household.

- ► To curtail subsidy to agricultural electricity users.

- ► Setting up of Water Regulatory Authority.

- ► To keep aside a portion of the river flow (storage infrastructure) to meet the ecological needs and to ensure that the low and high flow releases correspond in time closely to the natural flow regime.

- ► To give statutory powers to Water Users Associations to maintain the distribution system.

- ► Project benefited families to bear part of the cost of resettlement & rehabilitation of project affected families.

- ► To remove the large disparity between stipulations for water supply in urban areas and in rural areas.

Following aspects are recommended to be included in the policy framework:-

▶ Water be considered as a national asset.

▶ Policy should be able to address the issues of Centre Versus State issues with out resorting to courts. Without diluting the rights of States supremacy of the decisions of the Central Government should be final and binding.

▶ Policy should be able to address the issues of water relations with the neighbours, pollution, environment and R&D.

▶ Building of storage infrastructure be given special emphasis and adequate funds be catered for the same.

Areas for Further Research

following areas are recommended for further research:-

▶ An assessment of the capacity of China to cause water based damage to India in Rivers Sutlej & Brahmaputra.

▶ Evolution of a strategy to use water to meet the strategic aim in Western Theatre.

▶ Evolution of a plan for inter basin transfer of water in a phased manner as part of 'River Linking Project' of the country.

▶ Strategy for recharging of existing ground aquifers.

▶ Plan to exploit the full potential of waters for 'Run of the River' projects under existing provisions of Indus Water Treaty.

Chapter-7
Conclusion

"Water is the driver of Nature.".

- Leonardo da Vinci

The research question which was decided to be examined during the research was whether water was the source of future flash points. Till about middle of 20th Century, there was a concept that the states shall fulfil their water needs through "forceful acquisition and retention of neighboring territories of interest or by restricting the flow of rivers before they cross national borders". Examples are China claiming Tibet, Pakistan claiming J&K, Isreal forcefully occupying Golan Heights and many more. Water conflicts between states sharing a water resource were seen in a zero-sum perspective. However in recent times the line between such an approach and a more cooperative approach is gradually getting blurred but a total cooperative response is still a distant dream.

To keep the focus of the research, after establishing a linkage of water with the past conflicts and a global environment scan, analysis was restricted to only Asia. It was done deliberately because the hypothesis which was being attempted to be validated that Water based conflicts were not only on account of water based disputes but were also associated with other disputes between the two adversaries and also among those who have their own internal problems.

It has been established beyond doubt that the depleting water availability further adversely affected by the burgeoning population, pollution, global warming and above all increase in the demand itself is definitely a major source of conflict amongst nations which have competing requirements. No wonder countries like Pakistan who are already in the category of "Water Scarce" countries are making all out efforts to wrest

Jammu and Kashmir from India, which, she feels, can help her to get her water problems addressed. Similarly China, a "Water Stressed" country wants to hold on to Tibet essentially for the water storage which Tibet has got so that in future when she needs additional water she would have a source available besides controlling water to her adversary being a upper riparian for most of the rivers in the South and South East Asia. In most cases though a dispute resolution mechanism does exist but very rarely it can meet the aspirations of all the stake holders.

Based on an examination of the case studies of the countries of Asia in general and South Asia in particular the hypothesis stands validated. A number of issues have a bearing on the on-going water disputes amongst the nations of the Indian Sub-Continent. Therefore to qualify this statement following aspects need to be taken with account :-

- ▸ The power dynamics in the Subcontinent.

- ▸ The border disputes between Afghanistan and Pakistan, India-Pakistan, India-China.

- ▸ Maritime boundary disputes between India & Bangladesh and India &Pakistan.

- ▸ Economic issues between India & Bangladesh and India & Nepal.

- ▸ Illegal migration from Bangladesh to India.

- ▸ Abetment to cross border terrorism in India by Pakistan and Bangladesh providing sanctuary to elements inimical to India and host of other issues including resentment against the perceived big brother attitude of India have a bearing on the on-going water dispute among the nations of the Indian Subcontinent.

The analysis also brings out further areas which need to be addressed. These are as follows :-

- ▸ An assessment of the capacity of China to cause water based damage to India in Sutlej & Brahmaputra.

- ▸ Evolution of a strategy to use water to meet the strategic aim in Western Theatre.

- ▶ Evolution of a plan for inter basin transfer of water in a phased manner as a part of the 'River Linking Project' of the country.

- ▶ Strategy for recharging of existing ground aquifers.

- ▶ Plan to exploit the full potential of waters for 'Run of the River' projects under existing provisions of Indus Water Treaty.

There is a large and growing literature warning of future "water wars"- they point to water not only as a cause of historic armed conflict, but as the resource which will bring combatants to the battlefield in the 21st century. The historic reality has been quite different. In modern times, only seven minor skirmishes have been waged over international waters-- invariably other inter-related issues also get factored in. Conversely, over 3,600 treaties have been signed historically over different aspects of international waters. 145 in this century alone, many of the stake holders are showing tremendous elegance and creativity for dealing with this critical resource. This is not to say that armed conflict has not taken place over water, only that such disputes generally are between tribes, water-use sectors, or states. What we seem to be finding, in fact, is that geographic scale and intensity of conflict are inversely related.

Nations do not, and probably will not, go to war over water. But neither are international institutions adequately equipped to resolve water disputes. The 145 treaties which govern the world's international watersheds, and the international law on which they are based, are in their respective infancies. ccxxxvi More than half of these treaties include no monitoring provisions whatsoever and, perhaps as a consequence, two-thirds do not delineate specific allocations and four-fifths have no enforcement mechanism. Moreover, those treaties which do allocate specific quantities, allocate a fixed amount to all riparian states but one. That one state must then accept the balance of the river flow, regardless of fluctuations. Finally, multilateral basins are, almost without exception, governed by bilateral treaties, precluding the integrated basin management long-advocated by water managers. In order to fill this institutional gap, suggestions have occasionally been made for the creation of an international body for the resolution of water conflicts.

Water Conflict Chronology List

Date	Parties Involved	Basis of Conflict	Violent Conflict or In the Context of Violence?	Description	Sources
3000 BC	Ea, Noah	Religious account	No: Threat	Ancient Sumerian legend recounts the deeds of the deity Ea, who punished humanity for its sins by inflicting the Earth with a six-day storm. The Sumerian myth parallels the Biblical account of Noah and the deluge, although some details differ.	Hatami and Gleick 1994
2500 BC	Lagash, Umma	Military tool	Yes	The dispute over the "Gu'edena" (edge of paradise) region begins. Urlama, King of Lagash from 2450 to 2400 B.C., diverts water from this region to boundary canals, drying up boundary ditches to deprive Umma of water.	Hatami and Gleick 1994
1790 BC	Hammurabi	Development dispute	No	The Code of Hammurabi for the State of Sumer lists several laws pertaining to irrigation that address negligence of irrigation systems and water theft.	Hatami and Gleick 1994
1720–1684 BC	Abi-Eshuh, Iluma-Ilum	Military tool	Yes	A grandson of Hammurabi, Abish or Abi-Eshuh, dams the Tigris to prevent the retreat of rebels led by Iluma-Ilum, who declared the independence of Babylon.	Hatami and Gleick 1994

Date	Parties	Classification		Description	Reference
circa 1300 BC	Sisera, Barak, God	Religious account; Military tool	Yes	The Old Testament gives an account of the defeat of Sisera and his "nine hundred chariots of iron" by the unmounted army of Barak on the fabled Plains of Esdraelon. God sends heavy rainfall in the mountains, and the Kishon River overflows the plain and immobilizes or destroys Sisera's technologically superior forces.	Scofield 1967
1200 BC	Moses, Egypt	Military tool; Religious account	Yes	When Moses and the retreating Jews find themselves trapped between the Pharaoh's army and the Red Sea, Moses miraculously parts the waters of the Red Sea, allowing his followers to escape. The waters close behind them and cut off the Egyptians.	Hatami and Gleick 1994
720–705 BC	Assyria, Armenia	Military tool	Yes	After a successful campaign against the Halidians of Armenia, Sargon II of Assyria destroys their intricate irrigation network and floods their land.	Hatami and Gleick 1994
705–682 BC	Sennacherib, Babylon	Military tool; Military target	Yes	In quelling rebellious Assyrians in 695 B.C., Sennacherib razes Babylon and diverts one of the principal irrigation canals so that its waters wash over the ruins.	Hatami and Gleick 1994
701 BC	Israel (Judah), Assyria	Military tool; Military maneuvers	Yes	When King Hezekiah of Judah sees that Sennacherib of Assyria is coming in war, he has the water from the springs and brook outside Jerusalem stopped to keep the water from the Assyrians.	Scofield 1967
681–699 BC	Assyria, Tyre	Military tool; Religious account	Yes	Esarhaddon, an Assyrian, refers to an earlier period when gods, angered by insolent mortals, created destructive floods.	Hatami and Gleick 1994

Date	Parties	Type	Violent	Description	Sources
669–626 BC	Assyria, Arabia, Elam	Military tool; Military target	Yes	In campaigns against both Arabia and Elam in 645 BC, Assurbanipal, son of Esarhaddon, dries up wells to deprive Elamite troops. He also guards wells from Arabian fugitives in an earlier Arabian war. On his return from victorious battle against Elam, Assurbanipal floods the city of Sapibel. According to inscriptions, he dams the Ulai River with the bodies of dead Elamite soldiers and deprives dead Elamite kings of their food and water offerings.	Hatami and Gleick 1994
612 BC	Egypt, Persia, Babylon, Assyria	Military tool	Yes	A coalition of Egyptian, Median (Persian), and Babylonian forces attacks and destroys Ninevah, the capital of Assyria. The converging armies divert the Khosr River to create a flood, which allows them to elevate their siege engines on rafts.	Hatami and Gleick 1994
605–562 BC	Babylon	Military tool	No	Nebuchadnezzar builds immense walls around Babylon, using the Euphrates and canals as defensive moats surrounding the inner castle.	Hatami and Gleick1994; Drower 1954
6th Century BC	Assyria	Military target; Military tool	Yes	Assyrians poison the wells of their enemies with rye ergot.	Eitzen and Takafuji 1997
590–600 BC	Cirrha, Delphi	Military tool	Yes	Athenian legislator Solon reportedly had roots of helleborus thrown into a small river or aqueduct leading from the Pleistrus River to Cirrha during a siege of this city. The enemy forces became violently ill and were defeated as a result. Some accounts have Solon building a dam across the Plesitus River cutting off the city's water supply. Such practices were widespread.	Absolute Astronomy 2006

558–528 BC	Babylon	Military tool	Yes	On his way from Sardis to defeat Nabonidus at Babylon, Cyrus faces a powerful tributary of the Tigris, probably the Diyalah. According to Herodotus' account, the river drowns his royal white horse and presents a formidable obstacle to his march. Other historians argue that Cyrus needed the water to maintain his troops on their southward journey.	Hatami and Gleick 1994
539 BC	Babylon	Military tool	Yes	According to Herodotus, Cyrus invades Babylon by diverting the Euphrates above the city and marching troops along the dry riverbed.	Hatami and Gleick 1994
430 BC	Athens	Military tool	Yes	During the second year of the Peloponnesian War in 430 BC when plague broke out in Athens, the Spartans were accused of poisoning the cisterns of the Piraeus, the source of most of Athens' water.	Strategy Page 2006
355–323 BC	Babylon	Military tool	Yes	After the Indian campaigns, Alexander heads back to Babylon via the Persian Gulf and the Tigris, where he tears down defensive weirs that the Persians had constructed along the river.	Hatami and Gleick 1994
210–209 BC	Rome and Cathage	Military tool	Yes	In 210 BC, Scipio crossed the Ebro to attack New Carthage. During a short siege, Scipio led a breaching column through a supposedly impregnable lagoon located on the landward side of the city; a strong northerly wind combined with the natural ebb of the tide left the lagoon shallow enough for the Roman infantry to wade through. New Carthage was soon taken.	Fonner 1996; Gowan 2004

Date	Parties	Type		Description	Source
52 BC	Rome, Gaul	Military tool	Yes	Caesar constructs water-filled ditches as blockade during Siege of Alesia in Gaul, site of modern-day Alise-Sainte-Reine in Côte d'Or near Dijon, France.	Wikipedia ("Battle of Alesia")
51 BC	Rome, Gaul	Military target	Yes	Caesar attacks water supplies during siege of Uxellodunum by undermining one of the local springs and placing attackers near the other. Shortage of water leads to the surrender of the Gauls.	History of War Online 2011
49 BC	France, Rome	Military tool	Yes	At the siege of Marseille, the defenders countered attempts by the Romans to tunnel under their walls by digging a large basin inside the walls, which they filled with water. When the mines approached the basin, the water flowed out, flooding them and causing them to collapse.	Illustrated History of the Roman Empire undated
30 AD	Parties involved: Roman Empire (Pontius Pilate), Jews	Development dispute	Yes	Roman Procurator Pontius Pilate uses sacred money to divert a stream to Jerusalem. The Jews are angered at the diversion and tens of thousands gather to protest. Pilate's soldiers mingle among the crowd and with daggers hidden in their garments, attack the protesters. "A great number" are slain and wounded and the sedition ends.	Josephus 90 A.D.

537	Goths and Rome	Military tool; Military target	Yes	In the sixth century AD, as the Roman Empire began to decline, the Goths besieged Rome and cut almost all of the aqueducts leading into the city. In 537 AD, this siege was successful. The only aqueduct that continued to function was that of the Aqua Virgo, which ran entirely underground.	Rome Guide 2004; InfoRoma 2004
1187	Saladin and the Crusaders	Military tool	Yes	Saladin was able to defeat the Crusaders at the Horns of Hattin in 1187 by denying them access to water.	Lockwood 2006; Priscoli 1998
1503	Florence and Pisa warring states.	Military tool	No: Plan only	Leonardo da Vinci and Machiavelli plan to divert Arno River away from Pisa during conflict between Pisa and Florence.	Honan 1996
1573–1574	Holland and Spain	Military tool	Yes	In 1573 at the beginning of the eighty years war against Spain, the Dutch flooded the land to break the siege of Spanish troops on the town r. The same defense was used to protect Leiden in 1574. This strategy became known as the Dutch Water Line and was used frequently for defense in later years.	Dutch Water Line 2002

Date	Parties	Type	Water as weapon?	Description	Source
1626–1629	Spain, Dutch Republic	Development dispute; Military tool	No	The Spanish Habsburgs attempt to prevent ship traffic on the River Rhine from reaching the Dutch Republic in order to damage the Dutch economy. Plans were also made to divert water from the Rhine to lands under Spanish control to dry up downstream cities in Holland.	Israel 1997; Bachiene 1791
1642	China; Ming Dynasty	Military tool	Yes	The Huang He's dikes breached for military purposes. In 1642, "toward the end of the Ming dynasty (1368–1644), General Gao Mingheng used the tactic near Kaifeng in an attempt to suppress a peasant uprising."	Hillel 1991
1672	French, Dutch	Military tool	Yes	Louis XIV starts the third of the Dutch Wars in 1672, in which the French overran the Netherlands. In defense, the Dutch opened their dikes and flooded the country, creating a watery barrier that was virtually impenetrable.	Columbia Encyclopedia 2000b
1748	United States	Development dispute; Terrorism	Yes	Ferry house on Brooklyn shore of East River burns down. New Yorkers accuse Brooklynites of having set the fire as revenge for unfair East River water rights.	MCNY undated
1777	United States	Military tool	Yes	British and Hessians attacked the water system of New York. "…the enemy wantonly destroyed the New York water works" during the War for Independence.	Thatcher 1827

1804	France, Holland	Development dispute; Military tool	No	Napoleon ordered the construction of a canal between Neuss and Venlo, to connect the Rhine and Meuse rivers, to divert trade from the Batavia Republic to the Southern Netherlands, then under French control. Three-quarters of the canal was completed, but work stopped because of lack of funds.	Israel 1997
1841	Canada	Development dispute; Terrorism	Yes	A reservoir in Ops Township, Upper Canada (now Ontario), was destroyed by neighbors who considered it a hazard to health.	Forkey 1998
1844	United States	Development dispute; Terrorism	Yes	A reservoir in Mercer County, Ohio was destroyed by a mob that considered it a hazard to health.	Scheiber 1969
1850s	United States	Development dispute; Terrorism	Yes	Attack on a New Hampshire dam that impounded water for factories downstream by local residents unhappy over its effect on water levels.	Steinberg 1990
1853–1861	United States	Development dispute; Terrorism	Yes	Repeated destruction of the banks and reservoirs of the Wabash and Erie Canal in southern Indiana by mobs regarding it as a health hazard.	Fatout 1972; Fickle 1983
1860–1865	United States	Military tool; Military target	Yes	General William T. Sherman's memoirs contain an account of Confederate soldiers poisoning ponds by dumping the carcasses of dead animals into them. Other accounts suggest this tactic was used by both sides.	Eitzen and Takafuji 1997
1862	United States Union and Confederate Armies	Military tool	Yes	During the U.S. Civil War, near Yorktown, Confederate forces use dams on the Warwick River to cut off Union troops. "The enemy is pushed behind a .... branch of the Warwick river in which they control the depths of water by dams. McClellan did not intend to pass that stream at that time, or at that point where the skirmish took place. The water was then deepened so that they were measurably cut off.	Hitchcock 1862

Date	Country	Type	Violent	Description	Sources
1863	United States	Military tool	Yes	General Ulysses S. Grant, during the Civil War campaign against Vicksburg, cut levees in the battle against the Confederates.	Grant 1885; Barry 1997
1870s	China	Development dispute	No	Local construction and government removal (twice) of an unauthorized dam in Hubei, China.	Rowe 1988
1870s to 1881	United States	Development dispute	Yes	Recurrent friction and eventual violent conflict over water rights in the vicinity of Tularosa, New Mexico, involving villagers, ranchers, and farmers.	Rasch 1968
1887	United States	Development dispute; Terrorism	Yes	Dynamiting of a canal reservoir in Paulding County, Ohio, by a mob regarding it as a health hazard. State Militia called out to restore order.	Walters 1948
1890	Canada	Development dispute; Terrorism	Yes	Partly successful attempt to destroy a lock on the Welland Canal in Ontario, Canada, either by Fenians protesting English Policy in Ireland or by agents of Buffalo, New York, grain handlers unhappy at the diversion of trade through the canal.	Styran and Taylor 2001
1898	Egypt, France, Britain	Military tool; Political tool	Military maneuvers	Military conflict nearly ensues between Britain and France in 1898 when a French expedition attempted to gain control of the headwaters of the White Nile. While the parties ultimately negotiate a settlement of the dispute, the incident has been characterized as having "dramatized Egypt's vulnerable dependence on the Nile, and fixed the attitude of Egyptian policy-makers ever since."	Moorehead 1960

1907–1913	Owens Valley, Los Angeles, California	Terrorism; Development dispute	Yes	The Los Angeles Valley aqueduct/pipeline suffers repeated bombings in an effort to prevent diversions of water from the Owens Valley to Los Angeles.	Reisner 1993
1908–1909	United States	Development dispute	Yes	Violence, including a murder, directed against agents of a land company that claimed title to Reelfoot Lake in northwestern Tennessee who attempted to levy charges for fish taken and threatened to drain the lake for agriculture.	Vanderwood 1969
1915	German Southwest Africa	Military tool	Yes	Union of South African troops capture Windhoek, capital of German Southwest Africa in May 1915. Retreating German troops poison wells—"a violation of the Hague convention."	Daniel 1995
1935	California, Arizona	Development dispute	Military maneuvers	Arizona calls out the National Guard and militia units to the border with California to protest the construction of Parker Dam and diversions from the Colorado River; dispute ultimately is settled in court.	Reisner 1993
1937	Republican Government of Spain, Spanish Nationalists	Military target	Yes	During the Spanish Civil War, two concrete gravity dams, at Burguillo and Ordunte, are attacked by the Nationalist army, with a 2.5-ton charge placed in an inspection gallery at Ordunte. Some limited damage; repaired 1938–1939.	Pagan 2005

Date	Parties			Description	Sources
1938	China and Japan	Military tool; Military target	Yes	Chiang Kai-shek orders the destruction of flood-control dikes of the Huayuankou section of the Huang He (Yellow) River to flood areas threatened by the Japanese army. West of Kaifeng dikes are destroyed with dynamite, spilling water across the flat plain. The flood destroyed part of the invading army and its heavy equipment was mired in thick mud, though Wuhan, the headquarters of the Nationalist government was taken in October. The waters flooded an area variously estimated as between 3,000 and 50,000 Sq Kms, and killed Chinese estimated in numbers between "tens of thousands" and "one million."	Hillel 1991; Yang Lang 1994
1939–1940	Netherlands, Germany	Military tool	Yes	During the mobilization of the Dutch at the beginning of World War II, 1939–1940, the Dutch attempted to flood the Gelderse Vallei with the New Dutch Water Defence Line, which had been completed in 1885. During the German invasion in May 1940, large areas were inundated.	IDG 1996
1939–1942	Japan, China	Military target; Military tool	Yes	Japanese chemical and biological weapons activities reportedly include tests by "Unit 731" against military and civilian targets by lacing water wells and reservoirs with typhoid and other pathogens.	Harris 1994
1940–1945	Multiple parties	Military target	Yes	Hydroelectric dams routinely bombed as strategic targets during World War II.	Gleick 1993

1940	Finland, Soviet Union	Military tool	Yes	Manipulation of the waters of the Saimaan Canal (Finland) by partisan Finns in order to flood surrounding land and hinder Soviet troop movements during the Soviet-Finnish conflict.	Malik 2005
1941	USSR and Germany	Military target	Yes	The Dnieper hydropower plant in the Ukraine was strategically important throughout World War II and was targeted by both Soviet and German troops. On August 18, 1941, the dam and power plant were dynamited by Soviet troops retreating in front of advancing German forces. The facility was then bombed in 1943 by retreating German troops.	Pagan 2005; NYT 1941; Makarov 2005; Axis History Forum 2004
1941	Germany, Soviet Union	Military tool	Yes	In November 1941, Soviet troops flooded the area to the south of the Istra Reservoir near Moscow in an effort to slow the German advance. Just a few weeks later, German troops used the same tactic to create a water barrier to halt advances by the Soviet 16th Army.	Malik 2005
1941–1943	Germany, USSR	Military target	Yes	World War II inflicted enormous harm to hydroelectricity systems in the Soviet Union. Over two-thirds of the hydroelectric power stations were lost.	Malik 2005
1943	Britain, Germany	Military target	Yes	British Royal Air Force bombed dams on the Möhne, Sorpe, and Eder Rivers, Germany (May 16 and 17). Möhne Dam breech killed 1,200, destroyed all downstream dams for 50 km. The flood that occurred after breaking the Eder dam reached a peak discharge of 8,500 m³/s, which is nine times higher than the highest flood observed. Many houses and bridges were destroyed, and 68 people were killed.	Kirschner 1949; Semann 1950

1944	Germany, Italy, Britain, United States	Military tool	Yes	German forces used waters from the Isoletta Dam (Liri River) in January and February to successfully destroy British assault forces crossing the Garigliano River (downstream of Liri River). The German Army then dammed the Rapido River, flooding a valley occupied by the American Army.	Corps of Engineers 1953
1944	Germany, Italy, Britain, United States	Military tool	Yes	German Army flooded the Pontine Marshes by destroying drainage pumps to contain the Anzio beachhead established by the Allied landings in 1944. Over 40 square miles of land were flooded; a 30-mile stretch of landing beaches was rendered unusable for amphibious support forces.	Corps of Engineers 1953
1944	Germany, Allied forces	Military tool	Yes	Germans flooded the Ay River, France in July 1944, creating a lake two meters deep and several kilometers wide, slowing an advance on Saint Lo, a German communications center in Normandy.	Corps of Engineers 1953
1944	Germany, Allied forces	Military tool	Yes	Germans flooded the Ill River Valley during the Battle of the Bulge (winter 1944–1945) creating a lake 16 Kms long, 3–6 Kms wide, and 1–2 meters deep, greatly delaying the American Army's advance toward the Rhine.	Corps of Engineers 1953
1944	United States, Japan	Military target	Yes	The U.S. bombardment of the Japanese-occupied island in June 1944 targeted water supply points, resulting in severe shortages.	Stewart undated

Year	Parties	Type		Description	Sources
1944	Finland, USSR	Military target	Yes	In June, the Soviet air force attacked the Svir River Dam near Leningrad, then under the control of the Finnish military.	Orlenko 1981; Axis History Forum 2004
1945	Romania, Germany	Military target	Yes	The only known German tactical use of biological warfare was the pollution of a large reservoir in northwestern Bohemia with sewage in May 1945.	SIPRI 1971
1947 onwards	Bangladesh, India	Development dispute	No	Partition divides the Ganges River between Bangladesh and India; construction of the Farakka barrage by India, beginning in 1972, increases tension; short-term agreements settle dispute in 1977–1982, 1982–1984, and 1985–1988, and thirty-year treaty is signed in 1996.	Butts 1997; Samson and Charrier 1997
1947–1960s	India, Pakistan	Development dispute	No	Partition leaves Indus basin divided between India and Pakistan; disputes over irrigation water ensue, during which India stems flow of water into irrigation canals in Pakistan. Indus Waters Agreement reached in 1960 after 12 years of World Bank-led negotiations.	Bingham, Wolf and Wohlegenant 1994
1948	Arabs, Israelis	Military tool	Yes	Arab forces cut off West Jerusalem's water supply in first Arab-Israeli war.	Wolf 1995; Wolf 1997
1948	Arabs, Israel	Military tool	Yes	Water and food supplies were cut off during Arab siege of Jerusalem from December 1, 1947, to July 10, 1948. Arab forces blocked the road to Jerusalem, in an attempt to defeat Jewish Jerusalem.	Collins and LaPierre 1972; Joseph 1960; Wikipedia ("Siege of Jerusalem (1948)")
1950s	Korea, United States, others	Military target	Yes	Centralized dams on the Yalu (Amnok) River serving North Korea and China are attacked during Korean War.	Gleick 1993

Year	Parties	Type		Description	Source
1951	Israel, Jordan, Syria	Military tool; Development dispute	Yes	Jordan makes public its plans to irrigate the Jordan Valley by tapping the Yarmouk River; Israel responds by commencing drainage of the Huleh swamps located in the demilitarized zone between Israel and Syria; border skirmishes ensue between Israel and Syria.	Wolf 1997; Samson and Charrier 1997
1951	United States, Korea	Military target	Yes	The Hwacheon Dam in Korea was completed in 1944. During the Korean War, the facility was used as both a target and a tool by opposing forces. In 1951, it was attacked by aircraft of the U.S. Navy because of the use of the dam by North Korea to flood downstream areas to slow advancing UN forces.	Calcagno 2004; Corps of Engineers 1953
1953	Israel, Jordan, Syria	Development dispute; Military target	Yes	Israel begins construction of its National Water Carrier to transfer water from the north of the Sea of Galilee out of the Jordan basin to the Negev Desert for irrigation. Syrian military actions along the border and international disapproval lead Israel to move its intake to the Sea of Galilee.	Naff and Matson 1984; Samson and Charrier 1997
1958	Egypt, Sudan	Military tool; Development dispute	Yes	Egypt sends an unsuccessful military expedition into disputed territory amidst pending negotiations over the Nile waters, Sudanese general elections, and an Egyptian vote on Sudan-Egypt unification; Nile Water Treaty signed when pro-Egyptian government elected in Sudan.	Wolf 1997

1960s	North Vietnam, United States	Military target	Yes	Irrigation water supply systems in North Vietnam are bombed during the Vietnam War. An estimated 661 sections of dikes are damaged or destroyed.	IWCT 1967; Gleick 1993; Zemmali 1995
1962–1967	Brazil, Paraguay	Military tool; Development dispute	Military maneuvers	Negotiations between Brazil and Paraguay over the development of the Paraná River are interrupted by a unilateral show of military force by Brazil in 1962, which invades the area and claims control over the Guaira Falls site. Military forces were withdrawn in 1967 following an agreement for a joint commission to examine development in the region.	Murphy and Sabadell 1986
1962	Israel, Syria	Development dispute; Military target	Yes	Israel destroys irrigation ditches in the lower Tarfiq in the demilitarized zone. Syria complains.	Naff and Matson 1984
1963–1964	Ethiopia, Somalia	Development dispute; Military tool	Yes	Creation of boundaries in 1948 leaves Somali nomads under Ethiopian rule; border skirmishes occur over disputed territory in Ogaden desert where critical water and oil resources are located; cease-fire is negotiated only after several hundred are killed.	Wolf 1997
1964	Cuba, United States	Military tool	No	On February 6, 1964, the Cuban government ordered the water supply to the U.S. Naval Base at Guantanamo Bay cut off.	Guantanamo Bay Gazette 1964

Year	Parties	Category	In dispute	Description	Source
1964	Israel, Syria	Military target	Yes	HWs of the Dan River on the Jordan River are bombed at Tell El-Qadi in a dispute about sovereignty over the source of the Dan.	Naff and Matson 1984
1965	Zambia, Rhodesia, Great Britain	Military target	No	President Kenneth Kaunda calls on British government to send troops to Kariba Dam to protect it from possible saboteurs from Rhodesian government.	Chenje 2001
1965	Israel, Palestinians	Terrorism	Yes	First attack ever by the Palestinian National Liberation Movement Al-Fatah is on the diversion pumps for the Israeli National Water Carrier. Attack fails.	Naff and Matson 1984; Dolatyar 1995
1965–1966	Israel, Syria	Military tool; Development dispute	Yes	Fire is exchanged over "all-Arab" plan to divert the Jordan River headwaters (Hasbani and Banias) and presumably preempt Israeli National Water Carrier; Syria halts construction of its diversion in July 1966.	Wolf 1995; Wolf 1997
1966–1972	Vietnam, United States	Military tool	Yes	The United States tries cloud-seeding in Indochina to stop flow of materiel along Ho Chi Minh trail.	Plant 1995
1967	Israel, Syria	Military target; Military tool	Yes	Israel destroys the Arab diversion works on the Jordan River HWs. During Arab-Israeli War Israel occupies Golan Heights, with Banias tributary to the Jordan; Israel occupies West Bank.	Gleick 1993; Wolf 1995; Wolf 1997; Wallenstein and Swain 1997

1969	Israel, Jordan	Military target; Military tool	Yes	Israel, suspicious that Jordan is over-diverting the Yarmouk, leads two raids to destroy the newly-built East Ghor Canal; secret negotiations, mediated by the U.S., lead to an agreement in 1970.	Samson and Charrier 1997
1970	United States	Terrorism	No: Threat	The Weathermen, a group opposed to American imperialism and the Vietnam war, allegedly attempted to obtain biological agents to contaminate the water supply systems of U.S. urban centers.	Kupperman and Trent 1979; Eitzen and Takafuji 1997; Purver 1995
1970s	Argentina, Brazil, Paraguay	Development dispute	No	Brazil and Paraguay announce plans to construct a dam at Itaipu on the Paraná River, causing Argentina concern about downstream environmental repercussions and the efficacy of their own planned dam project downstream. Argentina demands to be consulted during the planning of Itaipu but Brazil refuses. An agreement is reached in 1979 that provides for the construction of both Brazil and Paraguay's dam at Itaipu and Argentina's Yacyreta dam.	Wallenstein and Swain 1997
1970	Chinese Citizens	Development dispute	Yes	Conflicts over excessive water withdrawals and subsequent water shortages from China's Zhang River have been worsening for over three decades between villages in Shenxian and Linzhou counties. In the 1970s, militias from competing villages fought over withdrawals.	China Water Resources Daily 2002

Year	Parties	Basis of conflict	Violent conflict or in a military context	Description	Sources
1972	United States	Terrorism	No: Threat	Two members of the right-wing "Order of the Rising Sun" are arrested in Chicago with 30–40 kg of typhoid cultures that are allegedly to be used to poison the water supply in Chicago, St. Louis, and other cities.	Eitzen and Takafuji 1997
1972	United States	Terrorism	No: Threat	Reported threat to contaminate water supply of New York City with nerve gas.	Purver 1995
1972	North Vietnam	Military target	Yes	United States bombs dikes in the Red River delta, rivers, and canals during massive bombing campaign.	Columbia Encyclopedia 2000b
1973	Germany	Terrorism	No: Threat	A German biologist threatens to contaminate water supplies with bacilli of anthrax and botulinum toxin unless he is paid $8.5 million.	Jenkins and Rubin 1978; Kupperman and Trent 1979
1974	Iraq, Syria	Military target; Military tool; Development dispute	Military maneuvers	Iraq threatens to bomb the al-Thawra (Tabaqah) dam in Syria and massed troops along the border, alleging that the dam had reduced the flow of Euphrates River water to Iraq.	Gleick 1994
1975	Iraq, Syria	Development dispute; Military tool	Military maneuvers	As upstream dams are filled during a low-flow year on the Euphrates, Iraqis claim that flow reaching its territory is "intolerable" and asks the Arab League to intervene. Syrians claim they are receiving less than half the river's normal flow and pull out of an Arab League technical committee formed to mediate the conflict. In May, Syria closes its airspace to Iraqi flights, and both Syria and Iraq reportedly transfer troops to their mutual border. Saudi Arabia successfully mediates the conflict.	Gleick 1993; Gleick 1994; Wolf 1997

1975	Angola, South Africa	Military goal; Military target	Yes	South African troops move into Angola to occupy and defend the Ruacana hydropower complex, including the Gové Dam on the Kunene River. Goal is to take possession of and defend the water resources of southwestern Africa and Namibia.	Meissner 2000
1976	Chinese citizens and government	Development dispute	Yes	In 1976, a local militia chief is shot to death in a clash over the damming of Zhang River. Conflicts over excessive water withdrawals and subsequent water shortages from China's Zhang River have been worsening for over three decades.	China Water Resources Daily 2002
1977	United States	Terrorism	Yes	Contamination of a North Carolina reservoir with unknown materials. According to Clark: "Safety caps and valves were removed, and poison chemicals were sent into the reservoir... Water had to be brought in."	Clark 1980; Purver 1995
1978 onwards	Egypt, Ethiopia	Development dispute; Political tool	No	Long-standing tensions over the Nile, especially the Blue Nile, originating in Ethiopia. Ethiopia's proposed construction of dams on the headwaters of the Blue Nile leads Egypt to repeatedly declare the vital importance of water.	Gleick 1991; Gleick 1994
1978 1984	Sudan	Development dispute; Military target; Terrorism	Yes	Demonstrations in Juba, Sudan in 1978 opposing the construction of the Jonglei Canal led to the deaths of two students. Construction of the Jonglei Canal in the Sudan was forcibly suspended in 1984 following a series of attacks on the construction site.	Suliman 1998; Keluel-Jang 1997

1980s	Mozambique, Rhodesia/Zimbabwe, South Africa	Military target; Terrorism	Yes	Regular destruction of power lines from Cahora Bassa Dam during fight for independence in the region. Dam targeted by RENAMO (the Mozambican National Resistance).	Chenje 2001
1980–1988	Iran, Iraq	Military tool	Yes	Iran diverts water to flood Iraqi defense positions.	Plant 1995
1981	Iran, Iraq	Military target; Military tool	Yes	Iran claims to have bombed a hydroelectric facility in Kurdistan, thereby blacking out large portions of Iraq, during the Iran-Iraq War.	Gleick 1993
1981–1982	Angola, Namibia	Military target; Military tool	Yes	Water infrastructure, including dams and the major Cunene-Cuvelai pipeline, was targeted during the conflicts in Namibia and Angola in the 1980s.	Turton 2005
1982	United States	Terrorism	No: Threat	Los Angeles police and the FBI arrest a man who was preparing to poison the city's water supply with a biological agent.	Livingston 1982; Eitzen and Takafuji 1997
1982	Israel, Lebanon, Syria	Military tool	Yes	Israel cuts off the water supply of Beirut during siege.	Wolf 1997
1982	Guatemala	Development dispute	Yes	In Rio Negro, 177 civilians are killed over opposition to the Chixoy hydroelectric dam.	Levy 2000
1983	Lebanon	Terrorism	Yes	An explosives-laden truck disguised as a water delivery vehicle destroyed a barracks in a U.S. military compound, killing more than 300 people. The attack was blamed on Hezbollah with the support of the Iranian government.	BBC 2007
1983	Israel	Terrorism	No	The Israeli government reports that it had uncovered a plot by Israeli Arabs to poison the water in Galilee with "an unidentified powder."	Douglass and Livingstone 1987

1984	United States	Terrorism	Members of the Rajneeshee religious cult contaminate a city water supply tank in The Dalles, Oregon, using Salmonella. A community outbreak of over 750 cases occurred in a county that normally reports fewer than five cases per year.	Yes	Clark and Deininger 2000
1985	United States	Terrorism	Law enforcement authorities discovered that a small survivalist group in the Ozark Mountains of Arkansas known as The Covenant, the Sword, and the Arm of the Lord (CSA) had acquired a drum containing 30 gallons of potassium cyanide, with the apparent intent to poison water supplies in New York, Chicago, and Washington, D.C. CSA members devised the scheme in the belief that such attacks would make the Messiah return more quickly by punishing unrepentant sinners. The objective appeared to be mass murder in the name of a divine mission rather than to change government policy.	No	Tucker 2000; NTI 2005
1986	North Korea, South Korea	Military tool	North Korea's announcement of its plans to build the Kumgansan hydroelectric dam on a tributary of the Han River upstream of Seoul raises concerns in South Korea that the dam could be used as a tool for ecological destruction or war.	No	Gleick 1993

Year	Parties	Type	Violent	Description	Source
1986	Lesotho, South Africa	Development dispute; Military goal	Yes	Bloodless coup by Lesotho's defense forces, with support from South Africa, lead to immediate agreement with South Africa for water from the Highlands of Lesotho, after 30 previous years of unsuccessful negotiations. There is disagreement over the degree to which water was a motivating factor for either party.	Mohamed 2001
1986	Lesotho, South Africa	Military goal; Development dispute	Yes	South Africa supports coup in Lesotho over support for ANC and anti-apartheid, and water. New government in Lesotho then quickly signs Lesotho Highlands water agreement.	American University 2000b
1988	Angola, South Africa, Cuba	Military goal; Military target	Yes	Cuban and Angolan forces launch an attack on Calueque Dam via land and then air. Considerable damage inflicted on dam wall; power supply to dam cut. Water pipeline to Owamboland cut and destroyed.	Meissner 2000
1990	South Africa	Development dispute	No	Pro-apartheid council cuts off water to the Wesselton township of 50,000 blacks following protests over miserable sanitation and living conditions.	Gleick 1993
1990	Iraq, Syria, Turkey	Development dispute; Military tool	No	The flow of the Euphrates is interrupted for a month as Turkey finishes construction of the Ataturk Dam, part of the Grand Anatolia Project. Syria and Iraq protest that Turkey now has a weapon of war. In mid-1990 Turkish president Turgut Ozal threatens to restrict water flow to Syria to force it to withdraw support for Kurdish rebels operating in southern Turkey.	Gleick 1993; Gleick 1995

1991–present	Karnataka, India	Development dispute	Yes	Violence erupts when Karnataka rejects an Interim Order handed down by the Cauvery Waters Tribunal, set up by the Indian Supreme Court. The Tribunal was established in 1990 to settle two decades of dispute between Karnataka and Tamil Nadu over irrigation rights to the Cauvery River.	Gleick 1993; Butts 1997; American University 2000a
1991	Iraq, Kuwait, United States	Military target	Yes	During the Gulf War, Iraq destroys much of Kuwait's desalination capacity during retreat.	Gleick 1993
1991	Canada	Terrorism	No: Threat	A threat is made via an anonymous letter to contaminate the water supply of the city of Kelowna, British Columbia, with "biological contaminates." The motive was apparently "associated with the Gulf War." The security of the water supply was increased in response and no group was identified as the perpetrator.	Purver 1995
1991	Iraq, Turkey, United Nations	Military tool	Yes	Discussions are held at the United Nations about using the Ataturk Dam in Turkey to cut off flows of the Euphrates to Iraq.	Gleick 1993
1991	Iraq, Kuwait, United States	Military target	Yes	Baghdad's modern water supply and sanitation system are intentionally and unintentionally damaged by Allied coalition. "Four of seven major pumping stations were destroyed, as were 31 municipal water and sewerage facilities—20 in Baghdad—resulting in sewage pouring into the Tigris. Water purification plants were incapacitated throughout Iraq" (Arbuthnot 2000). In the first eight months of 1991, after Iraq's water infrastructure was damaged by the Persian Gulf War, the New England Journal of Medicine reported that nearly 47,000 more children than normal died in Iraq and the country's infant mortality rate doubled to 92.7 per 1,000 live births.	Gleick 1993; Arbuthnot 2000; Barrett 2003

1991	Chinese villages of Huanglongkou and Qianyu	Development dispute	Yes	In December 1991, Huanglongkou village and Qianyu village exchange mortar fire over the construction of new water diversion facilities. Conflicts over excessive water withdrawals and subsequent water shortages from China's Zhang River have been worsening for over three decades. (See also entries for 1970, 1976, 1992, and 1999.)	China Water Resources Daily 2002
1991–2001	United States, Iraq	Military target; Military tool	No	United States deliberately pursues policy of destroying Iraq's water systems through sanctions and withholding contracts.	Nagy 2001
1992	Czechoslovakia, Hungary	Political tool; Development dispute	Military maneuvers	Hungary abrogates a 1977 treaty with Czechoslovakia concerning construction of the Gabcikovo/Nagymaros project based on environmental concerns. Slovakia continues construction unilaterally, completes the dam, and diverts the Danube into a canal inside the Slovakian republic. Massive public protest and movement of military to the border ensue; issue taken to the International Court of Justice.	Gleick 1993
1992	Turkey	Terrorism	Yes	Lethal concentrations of potassium cyanide are reported discovered in the water tanks of a Turkish Air Force compound in Istanbul. The Kurdish Workers' Party (PKK) claimed credit.	Chelyshev 1992

1992	Bosnia, Bosnian Serbs	Military tool	Yes	The Serbian siege of Sarajevo, Bosnia and Herzegovina, includes a cutoff of all electrical power and the water feeding the city from the surrounding mountains. The lack of power cuts the two main pumping stations inside the city despite pledges from Serbian nationalist leaders to United Nations officials that they would not use their control of Sarajevo's utilities as a weapon. Bosnian Serbs take control of water valves regulating flow from wells that provide more than 80 percent of water to Sarajevo; reduced water flow to city is used to "smoke out" Bosnians.	Burns 1992; Husarska 1995
1992	Chinese villages	Development dispute	Yes	In August 1992, bombs are set off along a Zhang River distribution canal, collapsing part of the canal and causing flooding and economic losses. Violence continues in the late 1990s with confrontations, mortar attacks, and bombings. Conflicts over excessive water withdrawals and subsequent water shortages from China's Zhang River have been worsening for over three decades.	China Water Resources Daily 2002
1992	Moldova, Russia	Military target	Yes	In June, hostilities between Moldova and Russia in a short but intense conflict included a rocket-artillery attack on the hydroelectric turbines at the Dubossary power station on the Nistru (or Dniester) River.	Malik 2005; Belitser et al. 2009
1993–2003	Iraq	Military tool	No	To quell opposition to his government, Saddam Hussein reportedly poisons and drains the water supplies of southern Shiite Muslims, the Ma'dan. The marshes of southern Iraq are intentionally targeted. The European Parliament and UN Human Rights Commission deplore use of water as a weapon in the region.	Gleick 1993; American University 2000c; National Geographic News 2001

1993	Iran	Terrorism	No	A report suggests that proposals were made at a meeting of fundamentalist groups in Tehran, under the auspices of the Iranian Foreign Ministry, to poison water supplies of major cities in the West "as a possible response to Western offensives against Islamic organizations and states."	Haeri 1993
1993	Yugoslavia	Military target; Military tool	Yes	The 65-meter high Peruća Dam on the Cetina River was Yugoslavia's second-largest hydroelectric facility before the country's breakup with the Croation War beginning in 1991. On January 28, 1993, Serbian/Yugoslav army forces detonated explosives at the dam in an attempt to wipe out Croatian villages and the port city of Omiš. A successful Croatian counterattack allowed military engineers to reach the dam and release water on time to prevent it from bursting, saving an estimated 20,000 to 30,000 civilians.	Gleick 1993; Rathfelder 2007
1994	Moldova, Russia	Terrorism	No: Threat	Reported threat by Moldavian General Nikolay Matveyev to contaminate the water supply of the Russian 14th Army in Tiraspol, Moldova, with mercury.	Purver 1995
1994	United States	Cyber-terrorism	No	The Washington Post reports a 12-year old computer hacker broke into the SCADA computer system that runs Arizona's Roosevelt Dam, giving him complete control of the dam's massive floodgates. The cities of Mesa, Tempe, and Phoenix, Arizona are downstream of this dam. No damage was done.	Gellman 2002; Lemos 2002

1995	Ecuador, Peru	Military tool; Political tool	Yes	Armed skirmishes arise in part because of disagreement over the control of the headwaters of Cenepa River. Wolf argues that this is primarily a border dispute simply coinciding with the location of a water resource.	Samson and Charrier 1997; Wolf 1997
1997	Singapore, Malaysia	Political tool	No	Malaysia supplies about half of Singapore's water and in 1997 threatened to cut off that supply in retribution for criticisms by Singapore of policy in Malaysia.	Zachary 1997
1998	Tajikistan	Terrorism; Political tool	No: Threat	On November 6, a guerrilla commander threatened to blow up a dam on the Kairakkhum channel if political demands were not met. Col. Makhmud Khudoberdyev made the threat, reported by the ITAR-Tass News Agency.	WRR 1998
1998	Angola	Military tool; Political tool	Yes	In September 1998, fierce fighting between UNITA and Angolan government forces broke out at Gove Dam on the Kunene River for control of the installation.	Meissner 2001
1998	Democratic Republic of Congo	Military target; Terrorism	Yes	Attacks on Inga Dam during efforts to topple President Kabila. Disruption of electricity supplies from Inga Dam and water supplies to Kinshasa.	Chenje 2001; Human Rights Watch 1998
1998–2000	Eritrea and Ethiopia	Military target	Yes	Water pumping plants and pipelines in the border town of Adi Quala are destroyed during the civil war between Eritrea and Ethiopia.	ICRC 2003

Date	Country	Type	Violent	Description	Sources
1998–1999	Kosovo	Terrorism; Political tool	Yes	Contamination of water supplies/wells by Serbs disposing of bodies of Kosovar Albanians in local wells. Other reports of Yugoslav federal forces poisoning wells with carcasses and hazardous materials.	CNN 1999; Hickman 1999
1999	Lusaka, Zambia	Terrorism; Political tool	Yes	A bomb blast destroyed the main water pipeline for the city of Lusaka, cutting off water to a population of three million.	FTGWR 1999
1999	Yugoslavia	Military target	Yes	Belgrade reported that NATO planes had targeted a hydroelectric plant during the Kosovo campaign.	Reuters 1999a
1999	Bangladesh	Development dispute; Political tool	Yes	Fifty people are hurt during strikes called to protest power and water shortages. The protests were led by former Prime Minister Begum Khaleda Zia over deterioration of public services and in law and order.	Ahmed 1999
1999	Yugoslavia	Military target	Yes	NATO targets utilities and shuts down water supplies in Belgrade. NATO bombs bridges on Danube, disrupting navigation.	Reuters 1999b
1999	Yugoslavia	Political tool	Yes	Yugoslavia refuses to clear war debris on Danube (downed bridges) unless financial aid for reconstruction is provided; European countries on Danube fear flooding due to winter ice dams will result. Diplomats decry environmental blackmail.	Simons 1999
1999	Kosovo	Political tool	Yes	Serbian engineers shut down water system in Pristina prior to occupation by NATO.	Reuters 1999c
1999	South Africa	Terrorism	Yes	A home-made bomb was discovered at a water reservoir at Wallmansthal near Pretoria. It was thought to have been meant to sabotage water supplies to farmers.	Pretoria Dispatch 1999; IOL News 1999

Year	Country	Category	Violent	Description	Source
1999	Angola	Terrorism; Political tool	Yes	One hundred bodies were found in four drinking water wells in central Angola.	International Herald Tribune 1999
1999	Puerto Rico, U.S.	Political tool	No	Protesters blocked water intake to Roosevelt Roads Navy Base in opposition to U.S. military presence and Navy's use of the Blanco River, following chronic water shortages in neighboring towns.	NYT 1999
1999	China	Development dispute; Terrorism	Yes	Around the Chinese New Year, farmers from Hebei and Henan Provinces fought over limited water resources. Heavy weapons, including mortars and bombs, were used and nearly 100 villagers were injured. Houses and facilities were damaged and the total loss reached one million $US.	China Water Resources Daily 2002
1999	East Timor	Military tool; Terrorism	Yes	Militia opposing East Timor independence kills pro-independence supporters and throws bodies in water well.	BBC 1999
1999	Yemen	Development dispute	Yes	Yemen sends 700 soldiers to quell fighting that claimed six lives and injured 60 others in clashes that erupted between two villages fighting over a local spring near Ta'iz. The village of Al-Marzuh believed it was entitled to exclusive rights from a spring because it was located on their land; the neighboring village of Quradah believed their rights to the water were affirmed in a 50-year-old court verdict. The dispute erupted in violence. President Ali Abdullah Saleh intervened by summoning the sheikhs of the two villages to the capital, and sorted out the problem by dividing the water into halves.	Al-Qadhi 2003
1999–2000	Namibia, Botswana, Zambia	Military goal; Development dispute	No	Sedudu/Kasikili Island, in the Zambezi/Chobe River. Dispute over border and access to water. Presented to the International Court of Justice	ICJ 1999

Year	Country	Type		Description	Source
2000	Ethiopia	Development dispute	Yes	One man stabbed to death during fight over clean water during famine in Ethiopia	Sandrasagra 2000
2000	Central Asia: Kyrgyzstan, Kazakhstan, Uzbekistan	Development dispute	No	Kyrgyzstan cuts off water to Kazakhstan until coal is delivered; Uzbekistan cuts off water to Kazakhstan for non-payment of debt.	Pannier 2000
2000	France, Belgium, Netherlands	Terrorism	Yes	In July, workers at the Cellatex chemical plant in northern France dumped 5,000 liters of sulfuric acid into a tributary of the Meuse River when they were denied workers' benefits. A French analyst pointed out that this was the first time "the environment and public health were made hostage in order to exert pressure, an unheard-of situation until now."	Christian Science Monitor 2000
2000	Hazarajat, Afghanistan	Development dispute	Yes	Violent conflicts broke out over water resources in the villages Burma Legan and Taina Legan, and in other parts of the region, as drought depleted local resources.	Cooperation Center for Afghanistan 2000
2000	India: Gujarat	Development dispute	Yes	Water riots reported in some areas of Gujarat to protest against authority's failure to arrange adequate supply of tanker water. Police are reported to have shot into a crowd at Falla village near Jamnagar, resulting in the death of three and injuries to 20 following protests against the diversion of water from the Kankavati dam to Jamnagar town.	FTGWR 2000
2000	Bolivia	Development dispute	Yes	Massive protests, riots, and violence result from efforts to privatize the water system of Cochabamba, Bolivia.	Shultz and Draper 2009
2000	United States	Terrorism	No	A drill simulating a terrorist attack on the Nacimiento Dam in Monterey County, California got out of hand when two radio stations reported it as a real attack.	Gaura 2000
2000	Kenya	Development dispute	Yes	A clash between villagers and thirsty monkeys left 8 apes dead and 10 villagers wounded. The duel started after water tankers brought water to a drought-stricken area and monkeys desperate for water attacked the villagers.	BBC 2000; Okoko 2000

2000	Australia	Cyber-terrorism	Yes	In Queensland, Australia, on April 23rd, 2000, police arrested a man for using a computer and radio transmitter to take control of the Maroochy Shire wastewater system and release sewage into parks, rivers, and property.	Gellman 2002
2000	China	Development dispute	Yes	Civil unrest erupted over use and allocation of water from Baiyangdian Lake – the largest natural lake in northern China. Several people died in riots by villagers in July 2000 in Shandong after officials cut off water supplies. In August 2000, six died when officials in the southern province of Guangdong blew up a water channel to prevent a neighboring county from diverting water.	Pottinger 2000
2001	Israel, Palestine	Terrorism; Military target	Yes	Palestinians destroy water supply pipelines to West Bank settlement of Yitzhar and to Kibbutz Kisufim. Agbat Jabar refugee camp near Jericho disconnected from its water supply after Palestinians looted and damaged local water pumps. Palestinians accuse Israel of destroying a water cistern, blocking water tanker deliveries, and attacking materials for a wastewater treatment project.	Israel Line 2001a; Israel Line 2001b; ENS 2001a
2001	Pakistan	Development dispute; Terrorism	Yes	Civil unrest over severe water shortages caused by the long-term drought. Protests began in March and April and continued into summer. Riots, four bombs in Karachi (June 13), one death, 12 injuries, 30 arrests. Ethnic conflicts as some groups "accuse the government of favoring the populous Punjab province [over Sindh province] in water distribution."	Nadeem 2001; Soloman 2001
2001	Macedonia	Terrorism; Military target	Yes	Water flow to Kumanovo (population 100,000) is cut off for 12 days in conflict between ethnic Albanians and Macedonian forces. Valves of Glaznja and Lipkovo Lakes damaged.	AFP 2001; BBC 2001b

Year	Place	Category	Yes/No	Description	Source
2001	China	Development dispute	Yes	In an act to protest destruction of fisheries from uncontrolled water pollution, fishermen in northern Jiaxing City, Zhejiang Province, dammed the canal that carries 90 million tons of industrial wastewater per year for 23 days. The wastewater discharge into the neighboring Shengze Town, Jiangsu Province, killed fish and threatened people's health.	China Ministry of Water Resources 2001
2001	Philippines	Terrorism	No	Philippine authorities shut off water to six remote southern villages yesterday after residents complained of a foul smell from their taps, raising fears Muslim guerrillas had contaminated the supplies. Abu Sayyaf guerrillas, accused of links with Saudi-born militant Osama bin Laden, had threatened to poison the water supply in the mainly Christian town of Isabela on Basilan island if the military did not stop an offensive against them.	World Environment News 2001
2001	Afghanistan	Military target	Yes	U.S. forces bombed the hydroelectric facility at Kajaki Dam in Helmand province of Afghanistan, cutting off electricity for the city of Kandahar. The dam itself was apparently not targeted.	BBC 2001a; Parry 2001
2002	Nepal	Terrorism; Political Tool	Yes	The Khumbuwan Liberation Front (KLF) blew up a hydroelectric powerhouse of 250 KW in Bhojpur District January 26. The power supply to Bhojpur and adjoining areas was cut off. Estimated repair time was 6 months; repair costs were estimated at 10 million Rs. By June 2002, Maoist rebels had destroyed more than seven micro-hydro projects as well as an intake of a drinking water project and pipelines supplying water to Khalanga in western Nepal.	Kathmandu Post 2002; FTGWR 2002
2002	Rome, Italy	Terrorism	No: Threat	Italian police arrest four Moroccans allegedly planning to contaminate the water supply system in Rome with a cyanide-based chemical, targeting buildings that included the United States embassy. Ties to al-Qaida were suggested.	BBC 2002

2002	Kashmir, India	Development dispute	Yes	Two people were killed and 25 others injured in Kashmir when police fired at a group of villagers clashing over water sharing. The incident took place in Garend village in a dispute over sharing water from an irrigation stream.	Japan Times 2002
2002	United States	Terrorism	No: Threat	Papers seized during the arrest of a Lebanese national who moved to the US and became an Imam at a Islamist mosque in Seattle included "instructions on poisoning water sources" from a London-based al-Qaida recruiter. The FBI issued a bulletin to computer security experts indicating that al-Qaida terrorists may have been studying American dams and water-supply systems in preparation for new attacks. "U.S. law enforcement and intelligence agencies have received indications that al-Qaida members have sought information on Supervisory Control And Data Acquisition (SCADA) systems available on multiple SCADA-related Web sites," reads the bulletin, according to SecurityFocus. "They specifically sought information on water supply and wastewater management practices in the U.S. and abroad."	McDonnell and Meyer 2002; MSNBC 2002
2002	Colombia	Terrorism	Yes	Colombian rebels in January damaged a gate valve in the dam that supplies most of Bogota's drinking water. Revolutionary Armed Forces of Colombia (FARC), detonated an explosive device planted on a German-made gate valve located inside a tunnel in the Chingaza Dam.	Waterweek 2002
2002	Karnataka, Tamil Nadu, India	Development dispute	Yes	Continuing violence over the allocation of the Cauvery (Kaveri) River between Karnataka and Tamil Nadu. Riots, property destruction, more than 30 injuries, arrests through September and October.	The Hindu 2002a; The Hindu 2002b; Times of India 2002a
2002	United States	Terrorism	No: Threat	The Earth Liberation Front threatens the water supply for the town of Winter Park. Previously, this group claimed responsibility for the destruction of a ski lodge in Vail, Colorado that threatened lynx habitat.	Crecente 2002; Associated Press 2002

Year	Location	Type	Violent	Description	Sources
2002	Botswana, Bushmen	Development dispute	Yes	Botswana's president Festus Mogae sent troops to the Kalahari Desert to destroy wells and empty water sources of indigenous Khoisan (also known as Bushmen), ostensibly in an effort to remove them from their ancestral lands and assimilate them into modern society. Critics blame the government of taking away water rights in favor of mining interests and labeled the government's actions a "siege"; Botswana is condemned by international observers. Against expectations, a band of Bushmen retreat into the desert and survive for years with little outside assistance.	Workman 2009
2003	United States	Terrorism	No: Threat	Al-Qaida threatens U.S. water systems via call to Saudi Arabian magazine. Al-Qaida does not "rule out... the poisoning of drinking water in American and Western cities."	Associated Press 2003a; Waterman 2003; NewsMax 2003; US Water News 2003
2003	United States	Terrorism	Yes	Four incendiary devices were found in the pumping station of a Michigan water-bottling plant. The Earth Liberation Front (ELF) claimed responsibility, accusing Ice Mountain Water Company of "stealing" water for profit. Ice Mountain is a subsidiary of Nestle Waters.	Associated Press 2003b
2003	Colombia	Terrorism; Development dispute	Yes	A bomb blast at the Cali Drinking Water Treatment Plant killed three workers May 8. The workers were members of a trade union involved in intense negotiations over privatization of the water system.	PSI 2003
2003	Jordan	Terrorism	No: Threat	Jordanian authorities arrested Iraqi agents in connection with a botched plot to poison the water supply that serves American troops in the eastern Jordanian desert near the border with Iraq. The scheme involved poisoning a water tank that supplies American soldiers at a military base in Khao, which lies in an arid region of the eastern frontier near the industrial town of Zarqa.	MJS 2003

2003	Iraq, United States, Others	Military target	Yes	During the U.S.-led invasion of Iraq, water systems were reportedly damaged or destroyed by different parties, and major dams were military objectives of the U.S. forces. Damage directly attributable to the war includes vast segments of the water distribution system and the Baghdad water system, damaged by a missile.	UNICEF 2003; ARC 2003
2003	Iraq	Terrorism	Yes	Sabotage/bombing of main water pipeline in Baghdad. The sabotage of the water pipeline was the first such strike against Baghdad's water system, city water engineers said. It happened around seven in the morning, when a blue Volkswagen Passat stopped on an overpass near the Nidaa mosque and an explosive was fired at the six-foot-wide water main in the northern part of Baghdad, said Hayder Muhammad, the chief engineer for the city's water treatment plants.	Tierney and Worth 2003
2003–2007	Sudan, Darfur	Military tool; Military target; Terrorism	Yes	The ongoing civil war in the Sudan has included violence against water resources. In 2003, villagers from around Tina said that bombings had destroyed water wells. In Khasan Basao they alleged that water wells were poisoned. In 2004, wells in Darfur were intentionally contaminated as part of a strategy of harassment against displaced populations.	Amnesty International 2004; Reuters Foundation 2004
2004	Mexico	Development dispute	Yes	Two Mexican farmers had argued for years over water rights to a small spring used to irrigate a small corn plot near the town of Pihuamo. In March, these farmers shot each other dead.	Guardian 2004
2004	Pakistan	Terrorism	Yes	In military action aimed at Islamic terrorists, including al-Qaida and the Islamic Movement of Uzbekistan, homes, schools, and water wells were damaged and destroyed.	Reuters 2004a

Year	Country/Region	Type	Violent	Description	Source
2004	India, Kashmir	Terrorism	Yes	Twelve Indian security forces were killed by an IED planted in an underground water pipe during "counter-insurgency operation in Khanabal area in Anantnag district."	TNN 2004
2004	China	Development dispute	Yes	Tens of thousands of farmers staged a sit-in against the construction of the Pubugou dam on the Dadu River in Sichuan Province. Riot police were deployed to quell the unrest and one was killed. Witnesses also report the deaths of a number of residents. (See China 2006 for follow-up.)	BBC 2004b; VOA 2004
2004	China, United States	Military target	No	A 2004 Pentagon report on China's military capacity raises the concept of Taipei adopting military systems capable of being used as a tool for deterring Chinese military coercion by "presenting credible threats to China's urban population or high-value targets, such as the Three Gorges Dam." China promptly denounces "a U.S. suggestion" that Taiwan's military target the Three Gorges dam, leading to a U.S. denial that it had so urged.	China Daily 2004; Pentagon 2004
2004	South Africa	Development dispute	Yes	Poor delivery of water and sanitation services in Phumelela Township led to several months of protests, including some severe injuries and property damage. No one was killed during the protests, but a few people were seriously injured, and municipal property was extensively damaged.	CDE 2007
2004	Gaza Strip	Terrorism; Development dispute	Yes	The United States halts two water development projects as punishment to the Palestinian Authority for their failure to find those responsible for a deadly attack on a U.S. diplomatic convoy in October 2003.	Associated Press 2004
2004	India	Development dispute	Yes	Four people were killed in October and more than 30 were injured in November in ongoing protests by farmers over allocations of water from the Indira Gandhi Irrigation Canal in Sriganganagar district, which borders Pakistan. Authorities imposed curfews on the towns of Gharsana, Raola and Anoopgarh.	Indo-Asian News Service 2004

2004–2006	Ethiopia	Development dispute	Yes	At least 250 people killed and many more injured in clashes over water wells and pastoral lands. Villagers call it the "War of the Well" and describe "well warlords, well widows, and well warriors." A three-year drought has led to extensive violence over limited water resources, worsened by the lack of effective government and central planning.	BBC 2004a; Associated Press 2005; Wax 2006
2005	Kenya	Development dispute	Yes	Police were sent to the northwestern part of Kenya to control a major violent dispute between Kikuyu and Maasai groups over water. More than 20 people were killed in fighting in January. By July, the death toll exceeded 90, principally in the rural center of Turbi. The tensions arose over grazing and water. Maasai herdsmen accused a local Kikuyu politician of diverting a river to irrigate his farm, depriving downstream livestock. Fighting displaced more than 2000 villagers and reflects tensions between nomadic and settled communities.	BBC 2005; Ryu 2005; Lane 2005
2005	Ukraine	Terrorism	Yes	On April 13, the Kiev Hydropower Station on the Dnieper River received a threat that 40 rail cars filled with explosives had been placed on a portion of levees holding back the reservoir.	Levitsky 2005
2006	Yemen	Development dispute	Yes	Local media reported a struggle between Hajja and Amran tribes over a well located between the two governorates in Yemen. According to news reports, armed clashes between the two sides forced many families to leave their homes and migrate. News reports confirmed that authorities arrested 20 people in an attempt to stop the fighting.	Al-Ariqi 2006
2006	China	Development dispute	Yes	The Chinese authorities executed a man who took part in protests against the Pubugou dam in Sichuan province in 2004 (see China 2004 entry). Chen Tao had been convicted of killing a policeman, but was executed before legal appeals had been completed.	BBC 2006d; Coonan 2006

Year	Country	Category	Conflict	Description	Source
2006	Ethiopia	Development dispute	Yes	At least 12 people died and over 20 were wounded in clashes over competition for water and pasture in the Somali border region.	BBC 2006a
2006	Ethiopia and Kenya	Development dispute	Yes	At least 40 people died in Kenya and Ethiopia in continuing clashes over water, livestock, and grazing land. Fighting occurred in southern Ethiopia in the region of Oromo and the northern Kenya Marsabit district.	Reuters 2006
2006	Sri Lanka	Military tool; Military target; Terrorism	Yes	Tamil Tiger rebels cut the water supply to government-held villages in northeastern Sri Lanka. Sri Lankan government forces then launched attacks on the reservoir, declaring the water Tamil actions to be terrorism. Conflict around the water blockade claimed more than 425 lives in 2006.	BBC 2006b; BBC 2006c; Gutierrez 2006
2006	Israel, Lebanon	Military target; Terrorism	Yes	Hezbollah rockets damaged a wastewater treatment plant in Israel. The Lebanese government estimates that Israeli attacks damaged water systems throughout southern Lebanon, including tanks, pipes, pumping stations, and facilities along the Litani River.	Science 2006; Amnesty International 2006; Murphy 2006
2006	Sudan	Development dispute	Yes	Militia of the Merowe Dam Militia Implementation Unit in the Sudan attacked a gathering of villagers concerned about the community impacts of the dam at a school in Amri village, killing three farmers and injuring more than 50 others.	Bosshard 2009
2007	India	Development dispute	Yes	Thousands of farmers breached security and stormed the area of Hirakud dam to protest allocation of water to industry. Minor injuries were reported during the conflict between the farmers and police.	Statesman News Service 2007
2007	Afghanistan	Military target; Terrorism	Yes	The Kajaki Dam has been the scene of major fighting between Taliban and NATO forces.	Friel 2007
2007	Canada	Terrorism	No	A Toronto man among other things charged after allegedly tampering with bottled water.	Toronto Star 2007

Year	Parties	Type		Description	Source
2007	Burkina Faso, Ghana, and Cote d'Ivoire	Development dispute	Yes	Declining rainfall has led to growing fights between animal herders and farmers with competing needs.	UNOCHR 2007
2007	Israel, Palestine	Development dispute	No	Israel's sanctions against Gaza cause water shortages and a growing public health risk.	Oxfam 2007
2007	Sydney residents	Development dispute	Yes	An Australian was charged with murder, after allegedly killing a man during a fight over water restrictions in Sydney. A number of incidents of similar nature were being reported after a draught of 10 years of drought.	ABC News 2007; Crase 2009
2007	Sudan	Development dispute	Yes	Angry villagers in the Sudan staged protests against Kajbar Dam.	Bosshard 2009
2008	Nigeria	Development dispute	Yes	A protest over the price of water in Nyanya, Abuja, Nigeria resulted in violence.	Yakubu 2008
2008	China, Tibet	Military target; Development dispute	Yes	China launched a political crackdown in Tibet essentially to ensure that the water resources of Tibet remain with China.	Sharife 2008
2008	Pakistan	Terrorism	Yes	In October, the Taliban threatened to blow up Warsak Dam, the main water supply for Peshawar, during a government offensive in the region.	Perlez and Shah 2008
2008	Murulle and Garre clans	Development dispute	Yes	Fighting over boreholes in arid northern Kenya.	Reuters 2008
2009	China and India	Development dispute; Military tool	No	China tries to block a $2.9 billion loan to India from the Asian Development Bank on the grounds that part of this loan was destined for water projects in the disputed area of Arunachal Pradesh.	Wong 2009
2009	Ethiopian Oromia and Somali Regions	Development dispute	Yes	Ethiopian Somalis attack a Borana community in the Oromia region over ownership of a new borehole being drilled on the disputed border.	BBC 2009

2009	Indian Citizens	Development dispute	Yes	Drought and inequality in water distribution in Madhya Pradesh lead to more than 50 violent clashes in the region in the month of May.	Singh 2009
2009	Mumbai residents, Police	Development dispute	Yes	On December 3, police clash with hundreds of Mumbai residents protesting water cuts. Mumbai authorities had resorted to rationing due to shortage.	Chandran 2009
2009	North Korea, South Korea	Political tool	Yes	Without previous warning, North Korea released 40 CUM of water from the Hwanggag dam to causea flash flood on the Imjin River in South Korea.	Choe 2009
2010	Pakistani tribes	Development dispute; Military tool	Yes	More than 100 are dead and scores injured following two weeks of in the Kurram region of Pakistan over irrigation water.	Express Tribune 2010; Associated Press 2010
2010	Afghanistan	Terrorism	Yes	A remote-controlled bombblasted in Eastern Afghanistan.	Associated Press 2009
2010	Mangal and Tori tribes, Pakistan	Development dispute	Yes	A water disputein Pakistan's tribal region leads to 116 deaths.	CNN 2010
2010	India	Development dispute	Yes	Erratic water supply, and eventually a complete cutoff of water in in East Delhi causes a violent protest.	Gosh 2010
Credits					

Source: By Peter Gleik Pacific Institute updated upto Nov 2009 and uploaded on http://www.worldwater.org/conflict.htm

Pictorial Representation Of Water Conflicts Through Ages

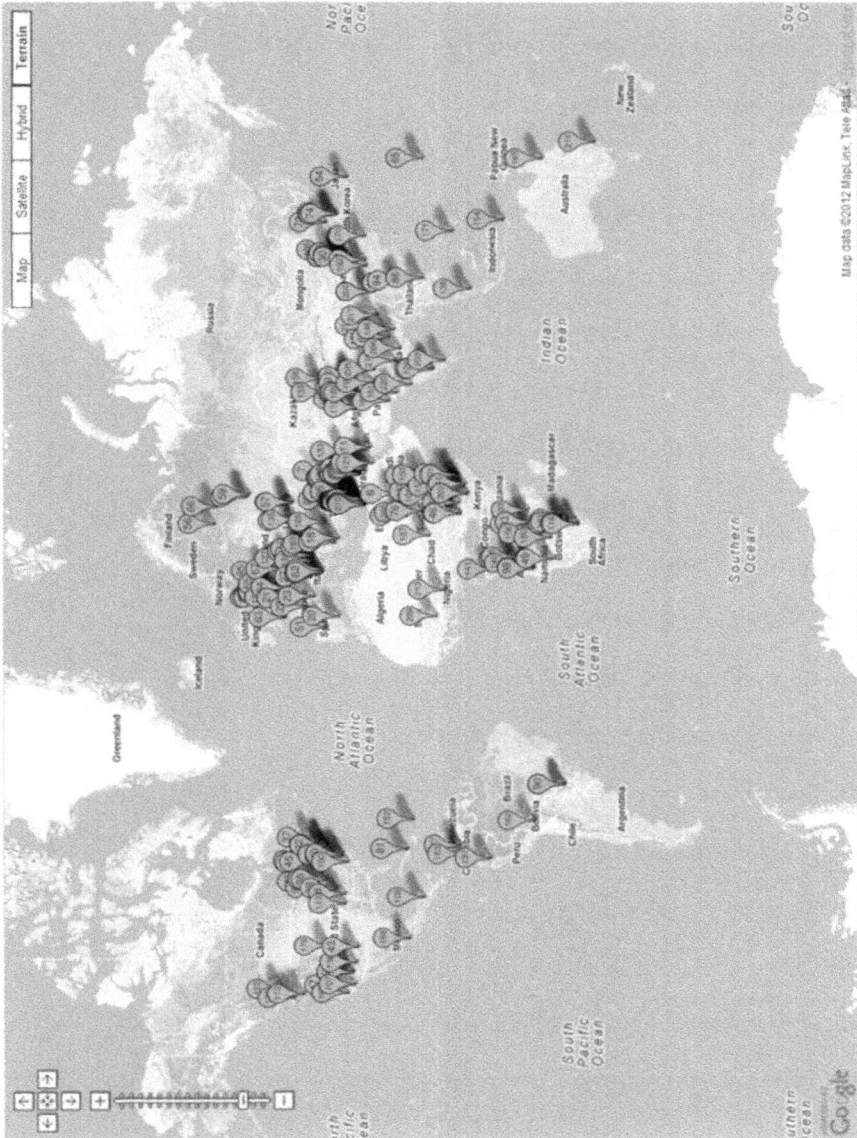

Legend:-

1. God punishes man with six-day storm (3000 BC)

2. Lagash-Umma border dispute (2500 BC)

3. Hammurabi's laws on water (1790 BC)

4. Tigris River dammed (1720–1684 BC)

5. Kishon River flooded in defeat of Sisera (circa 1300 BC)

6. Moses parts the Red Sea (1200 BC)

7. Assyrian king destroys Armenian irrigation network (720–705 BC)

8. Sennacherib razes Babylon (705–682 BC)

9. Hezekiah stops springs in advance of Assyrian Invasion (701 BC)

10. Assyrian king cuts off water of enemy (681–699 BC)

11. Assyrian king dries up enemy's wells (669–626 BC)

12. Khosr River diverted by Babylonians (612 BC)

13. Nebuchadnezzar uses Euphrates River as defense (605–562 BC)

14. Assyrians poison wells of enemies (6th Century BC)

15. Athens poisons enemies' water (590–600 BC)

16. Cyrus diverts the Diyalah River (558–528 BC)

17. Cyrus diverts the Euphrates (539 BC)

18. Spartans poison cisterns of Piraeus (430 BC)

19. Alexander tears down Persian dams (355–323 BC)

20. Rome's siege of New Carthage (210–209 BC)

21. Caesar constructs ditches in Siege of Alesia (52 BC)

22. Caesar attacks water supplies during siege of Uxellodunum (51 BC)

23. Marseille uses water to defend against Roman siege (49 BC)

24. Jewish protestors killed by Roman troops in protest over stream diversion (30 AD)

25. Goths cut Roman aqueducts (537)

26. Saladin cuts off Crusaders' water (1187)

27. Florence plan to cut Pisa's water (1503)

28. Dutch flood land to repel Spaniards (1573–1574)

29. Spain attempts to re-route Rhine River to harm Dutch (1626–1629)

30. China floods rebel peasants (1642)

31. Dutch flood land to repel French (1672)

32. New York water dispute (1748)

33. British attack New York's water (1777)

34. Napolean attempts to re-route Rhine River to harm Dutch (1804)

35. Reservoir destroyed in Canada (1841)

36. Mob destroys reservoir in Ohio (1844)

37. New Hampshire residents attack dam (1850s)

38. Mobs destroy canals in Indiana (1853–1861)

39. US Civil War soldiers poison wells (1860–1865)

40. US Civil War Confederates use dams to cut off Union troops (1862)

41. Levees cut in Vicksburg, Virginia (1863)

42. China removes unauthorized dams (1870s)

43. Water violence in New Mexico (1870s to 1881)

44. Mob dynamites Ohio reservoir (1887)

45. Canal lock destroyed in Canada (1890)

46. France and Britain battle over Nile (1898)

47. Los Angeles aqueduct bombed (1907–1913)

48. Violence over fishing in Tennessee (1908–1909)

49. German troops poison South African wells (1915)

50. Arizona mobilizes troops to protest Parker Dam (1935)

51. Dams attacked in Spanish Civil War (1937)

52. China floods Yellow River to defend from Japan (1938)

53. Dutch flood valley to defend from Germany (1939–1940)

54. Japan's Unit 731 poisons wells (1939–1942)

55. Dams bombed in WWII (1940–1945)

56. Finns use canal water against Soviets (1940)

57. Soviet dam targeted during World War II by Soviets and Germans (1941)

58. Soviets create flood to slow German troops (1941)

59. WWII damages Soviet's hydroelectric dams (1941–1943)

60. German dams destroyed by Allies (1943)

61. Germans use Italian rivers against Allies (1944)

62. Germany floods Pontine Marshes (1944)

63. Germans flood Ay River (1944)

64. Germans flood Ill River Valley (1944)

65. US targets Japanese water supplies in bombardment of Saipan (1944)

66. Soviets attack Finn-controlled dam near Leningrad (1944)

67. Germans pollute reservoir in Bohemia (1945)

68. Ganges divided between Bangladesh and India (1947 onwards)

69. Indus divided between India and Pakistan (1947–1960s)

70. Arabs cut off Jerusalem water (1948)

71. Water and food supplies cut off during Arab siege of Jerusalem (1948)

72. US attacks North Korean dams (1950s)

73. Israel and Syria fight over Yarmouk River (1951)

74. US Bombers Destroy Korea's Hwacheon Dam (1951)

75. Israel and Syria clash over Sea of Galilee (1953)

76. Egypt and Sudan clash over Nile (1958)

77. US bombs irrigation systems in Vietnam (1960s)

78. Brazil and Paraguay clash over Paraná River (1962–1967)

79. Israel destroys irrigation ditches in demilitarized zone on Syrian border (1962)

80. Ethiopia and Somali nomads fight for desert water (1963–1964)

81. Cuba cuts off water to US at Guantanamo (1964)

82. Israel drops bombs over Dan River (1964)

83. British defend South African dam (1965)

84. Palestinians attack Israeli water pumps (1965)

85. Israel attacks over Arab water plan (1965–1966)

86. US attempts to flood Vietnam (1966–1972)

87. Israel attacks Jordan water works (1967)

88. Israel destroys Jordan canals (1969)

89. Alleged plot on US water supply (1970)

90. Argentina v. Brazil, Paraguay on Paraná River (1970s)

91. Violent conflicts over use of China's Zhang River (1970)

92. Attempt to poison Chicago's waters (1972)

93. New York water threatened (1972)

94. US bombs water works in Vietnam (1972)

95. German water supply threatened (1973)

96. Iraq threatens Syria dam (1974)

97. Iraq, Syria mobilize troops over drought tensions (1975)

98. South Africa takes over Angolan dam (1975)

99. Militia Chief shot in China's Zhang River conflict (1976)

100. North Carolina reservoir poisoned (1977)

101. Egypt threatens Ethiopia over Nile plans (1978 onwards)

102. Sudan kills canal protestors (1978–1984)

103. Mozambique targets dam in fight vs. South Africa (1980s)

104. Iran floods Iraqi defenses (1980–1988)

105. Iran targets Iraq hydroelectric dam (1981)

106. Namibia targets Angola pipeline (1981–1982)

107. Plan to poison Los Angeles water (1982)

108. Israel cuts off Beirut water (1982)

109. Guatemala kills dam protestors (1982)

110. Terrorists destroy US military barraks in Lebanon (1983)

111. Terrorists plot to poison Israel water (1983)

112. Oregon water supply poisoned (1984)

113. Cult plans to poison US waters (1985)

114. South Koreans uneasy over North's dam (1986)

115. Lesotho coup partly over water (1986)

116. Lesotho coup partly over water (1986)

117. Angolans attack South African dam (1988)

118. South Africa cuts off black community's water (1990)

119. Turkey's Ataturk Dam a weapon of war? (1990)

120. Violence over use of India's Cauvery River (1991–present)

121. Iraq destroys Kuwait desalination plants (1991)

122. British Columbia water supply threatened (1991)

123. UN considers cutting river flow to Iraq (1991)

124. US destroys Iraq water systems (1991)

125. Chinese villages exhange mortar fire over water diversion (1991)

126. US sanctions against Iraq target water systems (1991–2001)

127. Hungary and Czechoslovakia dispute over Danube (1992)

128. Turkish air base waters poisoned (1992)

129. Serbs cut off water and power to Bosnian cities (1992)

130. Canal on China's Zhang River bombed (1992)

131. Russians attack Moldovan hydroelectric dam (1992)

132. Iraq uses water to silence opposition (1993–2003)

133. Iran threatens west's water (1993)

134. Yugoslavian army destroys dam (1993)

135. Moldova threatens Russian army's water (1994)

136. Arizonan hacks water facility (1994)

137. Ecuador, Peru fight over Cenepa River (1995)

138. Malaysia threatens to cut Singapore's water (1997)

139. Guerillas threaten Tajikistan dam (1998)

140. Angolan rebels, government fight at dam (1998)

141. Congo rebels attack dam (1998)

142. Water plants destroyed in Ethiopia-Eritrea war (1998–2000)

143. Wells contaminated during Kosovo war (1998–1999)

144. Zambia water cut off (1999)

145. NATO targets dam in Kosovo (1999)

146. Injuries at protest in Bangladesh (1999)

147. NATO strikes water facilities in Yugoslavia (1999)

148. Yugoslavia refuses to clear river debris (1999)

149. Serbs cut off water to Pristina (1999)

150. Bomb plot at South Africa reservoir (1999)

151. 100 bodies found in Angolan wells (1999)

152. Puerto Ricans protest US Navy's water use (1999)

153. Chinese farmers fight over water (1999)

154. Indonesian militia dump bodies in wells in East Timor (1999)

155. Villagers killed in Yemen water clash (1999)

156. African nations fight over Zambezi island (1999–2000)

157. Ethiopian killed in water fight (2000)

158. Central Asian nations cut off water to neighbors (2000)

159. French workers pollute river over labor dispute (2000)

160. Violent conflict in Afghanistan (2000)

161. Water riots in Gujarat, India (2000)

162. Riots over privatization in Cochabamba, Bolivia (2000)

163. Terrorist drill gets out of hand in California (2000)

164. Kenyans battle monkeys for drought relief (2000)

165. Australian hacker causes sewage spills (2000)

166. Riots in northern China (2000)

167. Palestinians destroy water supply to Israeli settlements (2001)

168. Unrest over shortages in Pakistan (2001)

169. Water cut off in Macedonian conflict (2001)

170. Chinese protestors block canal (2001)

171. Philippine water poisoned (2001)

172. US bombs Afghan powerhouse (2001)

173. Nepal rebels blow up powerhouse (2002)

174. Italy foils terror plot (2002)

175. Deadly clash in Kashmir, India (2002)

176. Terrorist targets water systems (2002)

177. Colombian rebels bomb dam (2002)

178. Violence over Cauvery River in India (2002)

179. Colorado eco-terrorists threaten water supply (2002)

180. Botswana authorities destroy wells of Kalahari Bushmen (2002)

181. Al-Qaida theatens US water (2003)

182. Bombs found at US bottling plant (2003)

183. Columbian water plant bombed (2003)

184. Iraq attempts to poison water at US base (2003)

185. Water systems damaged in US-Iraq war (2003)

186. Insurgents bomb Iraq pipeline (2003)

187. Sudan targets water in civil war (2003–2007)

188. Mexican farmers shot in duel over spring (2004)

189. Pakistan targets terrorists' water (2004)

190. Terrorists bomb water pipe in India (2004)

191. Police kill dam protestor in China (2004)

192. Taiwan to target China's water in defense? (2004)

193. Violent protests in South Africa (2004)

194. US halts water projects in Gaza (2004)

195. Police kill water protestors in India (2004)

196. Violence over water in Ethiopia (2004–2006)

197. Over 90 dead in Kenya water fight (2005)

198. Soviet troops dynamite Ukranian dam (2005)

199. Armed clashes in Yemen (2006)

200. Dam protester executed in China (2006)

201. Violent water clashes in Somali Region (2006)

202. Water clashes kill 40 in Kenya and Ethiopia (2006)

203. Sri Lankan rebels cut water supplies (2006)

204. Lebanon, Israel target water infrastructure in attacks (2006)

205. Sudanese anti-dam militia attacks school (2006)

206. Injuries at protest in Orissa, India (2007)

207. Battles at Kajaki Dam, Afghanistan (2007)

208. Tampering in Toronto (2007)

209. Conflicts in Burkina Faso (2007)

210. Israel's sanctions against Gaza cause water shortages (2007)

211. Australian man murdered in fight over water restrictions (2007)

212. Violent protests against the Kajbar Dam in Sudan (2007)

213. Violent protests in Nigeria (2008)

214. China cracks down on Tibet (2008)

215. Taliban threatens water supply (2008)

216. Four killed in Kenya over dispute over boreholes (2008)

217. China tries to block loan to India for water projects in territorial dispute (2009)

218. Village attacked in Ethiopian water pipe conflict (2009)

219. Drought and water inequities spark killings India (2009)

220. Man killed in Mumbai protest over water cuts (2009)

221. North Korea dam release kills six in South Korea (2009)

222. Fighting in Pakistan over irrigation water (2010)

223. Bomb in water truck kills 3 in Afghanistan (2010)

224. Pakistan irrigation dispute kills 116 (2010)

225. Violent water protest in India (2010)

End Notes

i http://www.rivervalleycivilizations.com/index.php

ii Aaron T Wolf,"Water policy Vol 1# 2", Conflict & Cooperation along International Waterways, 1998, pp-251, uploaded on www. transboundarywaters.orst.edu/publications/conflict_coop/

iii Dan Smith, Janani Vivekananda," Climate change Conflict and Fragility", Pub by International alert, November 2009 , uploaded on http://www. international-alert.org/pdf/A-climate_of_conflict.pdf

iv Gurr, 1985; Lipschutz, 1989; Homer-Dixon, 1991," WATER RESOURCES RESEARCH, VOL. 40, W05S04, doi:10.1029/2003WR002530, 2004.

v Remans, Wilfried. "Water and War." Humantäres Völkerrecht Vol. 8 #1, 1995.

vi Bullock, John and Adel Darwish. Water Wars: Coming Conflicts in the Middle East. London: St. Dedmundsbury Press, 1993.

vii Allister Heath, Associate Editor of The Spectator and Deputy Editor of The Business, "A priceless commodity", uploaded on www.martinfrost. ws/htmlfiles/aug2006/water_wars.html and

viii Ullman,"Water Resources", pub by Oxford University Press, 1983, pp-142

ix Norman Myers," Environmental Security: What's New And Different" pub by Institute of Environmental Security, 1989, uploaded on www. envirosecurity.org/conference/working/newanddifferent.pdf

x http://www3.interscience.wiley.com /journal/119047944/ abstract ? CRETRY=1&SRETRY=0 Retrieved 2009-01-19.

xi http://www.pacinst.org/topics/global_change/climate_security/indexhtm

xii http://md1.csa.com/partners/viewrecord.php?requester=gs&collection= ENV&recid=4406040&q=%22water+security%22&uid=&setcookie=y es Retrieved 2009-01-19

xiii http://www.stormingmedia.us/75/7593/A759324.html Retrieved 2009-01-19

xiv Jameel M. Zayed, No Peace Without Water – The Role of Hydropolitics in the Israel-Palestine Conflict http://www.jnews.org.uk/commentary/"no-peace-without-water"---the-role-of-hydropolitics-in-the-israel-palestine-conflict

xv http://www.globalpolicy.org/security/natres/waterindex.htm Retrieved 2009-01-19

xvi Ibid iv

xvii Page-1 of "Water Conflicts in South Asia", edited by Toufiq A Siddiqi and Shirin Tahir-Kheli

xviii Anumita Raj, Research Analyst, Strategic Foresight Group, Mumbai," WATER: SECURITY IN INDIA: THE COMING CHALLENGE, pub in Indian Economic Review Jul 2010, Page 160-161

xix   http://www.cgiar.org/enews/june2007/images_06_07/story12c.gif Retrieved 2009-01-19

xx Jameel M. Zayed, No Peace Without Water – The Role of Hydropolitics in the Israel-Palestine Conflict http://www.jnews.org.uk/commentary/"no-peace-without-water"---the-role-of-hydropolitics-in-the-israel-palestine-conflict

xxi World Bank Climate Change Water: South Asia's Lifeline at Risk, World Bank Washington D.C

xxii Survey by Karen Frenken," Irrigation in the Middle East Region in Figures-FTP FAO" uploaded on ftp://ftpfao.org/docrep/fao/012/i0936e/i0936e00.pdf

xxiii Page-12 of "Water Conflicts in South Asia", edited by Toufiq A Siddiqi and Shirin Tahir-Kheli.

xxiv Report of GOI, NCIWRDD, 1999

xxv Human Development Report 2006 Beyond Scarcity: Power, Poverty and the Global Water Crisis (UNDP New York 2006) at 4±5.

xxvi The Millennium Development Goals Report 2008 (UN Department of Economic and Social Affairs New York 2008) at 41. See also UNDP (n 1) at 6.

xxvii United Nations `Adoption of Declaration on the Rights of Indigenous Peoples a historic moment for human rights, UN Expert says' Press Release (Geneva 14 September 2007).

xxviii Ramaswamy Iyer, "The politicisation of water", www.infochangeindia.

org/age, Accessed on February 21, 2006. His other writings include "Rivers of Discord", The Times of India, November 6, 2002.

xxix Alex de Sherbinin, IUCN-The World Conservation Union, " INTRODUCTION: Water and Population Dynamics: Local Approaches to a Global Challenge", uploaded on www.aaas.org/international/ehn/ waterpop/desherb.htm

xxx Postel, S.L., Daily, G.C., and Ehrlich, P.R., 1996. ìHuman Appropriation of Renewable Fresh Water.î Science 192: 785-788.

xxxi United Nations, 1997. Comprehensive Assessment of the Freshwater Resources of the World. New York: United Nations Department of Policy Coordination and Sustainable Development.

xxxii McCully, Patrick, 1996. Silenced Rivers: The Ecology and Politics of Large Dams. London: Zed Books.

xxxiii IDSA Task Force Report," WATER SECURITY FOR INDIA: THE EXTERNAL DYNAMICS", page-25, published by Institute for Defence Studies and Analyses New Delhi, Sep 2010.

xxxiv Effects of Global Warming on Water Resources uploaded on www. theglobalwarmingoverview.com/index.php/effects-of-global-warming-on-waterresources.html.

xxxv Human Development Report 2007/2008 Fighting Climate Change: Human Solidarity in a Divided World (UNDP New York 2007).

xxxvi Third major World Water Development Report, released in March at the World Water Forum in Istanbul,

xxxvii China Daily, Updated February 29, 2008. Accessed November 21, 2008.

xxxviii Aaron T. Wolf, " Conflict and cooperation along international waterways", Water Policy. Vol. 1 #2, 1998. pp. 251-265.

xxxix Pentland, William. "The Water-Industrial Complex," Forbes, May 14, 2008. Accessed November 21, 2008.

xl Hamner, Jesse and Aaron Wolf. "Patterns in International Water Resource Treaties: The Transboundary Freshwater Dispute Database." Colorado Journal of International Environmental Law and Policy. 1997 Yearbook, 1998.

xli http://www.grida.no/aral/maps/geog.htm

xlii Peter Gleick, 1993. "Water and conflict." International Security Vol. 18, No. 1, pp. 79-112 (Summer 1993).

xliii Heidelberg Institute for International Conflict Research (Department of Political Science, University of Heidelberg); Conflict Barometer 2007:Crises – Wars – Coups d'Etat – Nagotiations – Mediations – Peace Settlements, 16th annual conflict analysis, 2007.

xliv Tulloch, James, "Freshwater: lifeblood of the planet", accessed November 21, 2008

xlv www.uruknet.info dated 01 Jun 2006

xlvi Ibid xxxviii

xlvii Ramzan Sabir, " KARBALA CHAIN OF EVENTS", uploaded on http//www. al-islam.org/short/Karbala.htm

xlviii Islamic-Western Calendar Converter Based on the Arithmetical or Tabular Calendar prepared by Institute of History and Foundation of Science uploaded on http://www.staff.science.uu.nl/~gent0113/islam/ islam_tabcal.htm and Gregorian-Hijri Dates Converter uploaded on http://www.rabiah.com/convert/

xlix Maqtal al Husain-The watering Place, pp-152 uploaded on www.al-islam.org/maqtal/41.htm

l "Seven Experts Debate The Past And Present Existence Of Water Wars, Consider The Difficulty Of Owning A Fluid Resource, And Examine The Hot Spots For Future Conflict", pub in SEED magazine.com December 5, 2012

li Yonathan Lupu, "International Law and Waters of the Eupherates and Tigris" uploaded on www.envirozon.info/Ez_Docs/water_resources/ IIET.pdf last up dated on 20 Aug 2007

lii Uzgel I., 1992. GÜVENSİZLİK ÜÇGENİ: TÜRKİYE, SURİYE, IRAK VE SU SORUNU, MÜLKİYELİLER BİRLİĞİ DERGİSİ, 162, p.47-52

liii Muhanad Mohammed, Baghdad,"Turkey lets more water out of dams to Iraq: MP" uploaded on http://www.reuters.com/article/ environmentNews/idUSTRE54M0XG20090523, dated 23 May 2009.

liv AFP Report, "Turkey to up Euphrates flow to Iraq", uploaded on http://www.google.com/hostednews/afp/article ALeqM5giDgd3ukLR8UcfziUQcNToKyM_tw, dated 19 Sep 2009.

lv David Krusch, "The Jordan River" uploaded on http://www. jewishvirtuallibrary.org/jsource/Society_&_Culture/geo/jordanriver. html

lvi Jane Taylor,"Petra and the Lost Kingdom of the Nabataeans" pub by IB Taures Co Ltd, 2002

lvii En.wikipedia.org/wiki/jonathan_aphus

lviii T Naff and RC Matson, "Water in the Middle East, Conflict or Cooperation," Colo, west View, 1984 and quoted by Muther J Hadddadin, "The Jordan river Basin W and Negotiated Resolution", sponsored by UNESCO.

lix Haddadin, M, J. 2001. "Diplomacy on the Jordan: International Conflict and Negotiated Resolution". Pub by Norwell, Mass., Kluwer Academic, pp-16.

lx Encyclopedia Britanica.

lxi Oloo, Adams (2007). "The Quest for Cooperation in the Nile Water Conflicts: A Case for Eritrea". African Sociological Review 11 (1). Retrieved 25 July 20

lxii Ibid xxiii

lxiii Tulloch, James (August 26, 2009). "Water Conflicts: Fight or Flight?". Allianz. Retrieved 14 January 2010.

lxiv Smith D.R. 1995. Environmental Security and Shared Water Resources in Post-Soviet Central Asia. Post-Soviet Geography and Economics, 36(6): 351-370.

lxv Vinogradov Sergei. 1996. Transboundary Water Resources in the Former Soviet Union: Between Conflict and Co-operation, Natural Resources Journal 36 (2): 393-415. Vinogradov Sergei. 1996. Transboundary Water Resources in the Former Soviet Union: Between Conflict and Co-operation, Natural Resources Journal 36 (2): 393-415. And O'Hara Sarah L. 2000. Central Asia's Water Resources: Contemporary and Future Management Issues. International Journal of Water Resources

Development, 16(3): 423-441.

lxvi Ibid xlvi.

lxvii Bedford D. 1996. International Water Management in the Aral Sea Basin. Water International, 21: 63-69.

lxviii http://www.grida.no/aral/maps/geog.htm

lxix Ibid xxxvi

lxx Klötzli Stefan, "The Water and Soil Crisis in Central Asia – a Source for Future Conflicts?" ENCOP Occasional Paper No 11, Center for Security Policy and Conflict Research, Zurich/Swiss Peace Foundation, Berne, 1994

lxxi Hogan Bea, " Central Asian states wrangle over water", Eurasia Net Environment Report uploaded on http://www.eurasianet.org/ departments/environment/articles/eav040500.shtml in 2000 and Grozin Andrei, " Vodnaya kooperatsiya – edinstvenniy vyhod dlya prikaspiiskih stran. Respublika.kz" uploaded on http://www.respublika.kz/archive/ sosedy/world/world07_01.html in 2001.

lxxii Khamidov Alisher. 2001. Water continues to be source of tension in Central Asia. EurasiaNet Environment Report:http://www.eurasianet. org/departments/environment/articles/eav102301.shtml

lxxiii Kansas v. Colorado, 543 U.S. 86 (2004) US Supreme court judgment.

lxxiv Reisner, Mark (1993). Cadillac Desert (revised ed.). Penguin USA. ISBN 0-14-017824-4.

lxxv http://en.wikipedia.org/wiki/California_Water_Wars

lxxvi SALMAN M. A. SALMAN, The World Bank, Washington DC, USA," Water Resources Development, Vol. 23, No. 4, 625–640, December 2007"

lxxvii Bourne, C. (1996) The International Law Association's contribution to International Water Resources Law, Natural Resources Journal, 36, pp. 155 –216

lxxviii Salman, S. & Uprety, K. (2002) Conflict and cooperation on South Asia's international rivers (The Hague: Kluwer Law International).

lxxix Sherk, G. W. (2000) Dividing the Waters—The Resolution of Intestate Water Conflicts in the United States (The Hague: Kluwer Law

International).

lxxx WASSA Analysis.

lxxxi Page-1 of "Water Conflicts in South Asia", edited by Toufiq A Siddiqi and Shirin Tahir-Kheli.

lxxxii Jayashree Nandi, "Poison in our Paani", pub in Times of India, New Delhi addition, dated 02 Dec 2012, page-11.

lxxxiii M Falkenmark, "Meeting Water Requirements of an Expanding World Population", pub by Philosophical Transactions of Royal society, dated 29 Jul 1997, uploaded on www.ncbi.nim.nih.gov/pmc/articles/PMC/1691983/

lxxxiv Malin Falkenmark, "Global Water Issues Confronting Humanity", published in Journal of Peace Research 27, No 2 dated May 1990, pp177-90.

lxxxv Tobias Siegfried, Associate research scientist at the Earth Institute's Columbia Water Center, and an adjunct assistant professor at the School of International and Public Affairs (SIPA),"ibid xxiii", Pub in SEED Magazine.com 05 Dec 12

lxxxvi "UN:World Population ReachesSeven Billion" reported by Al Jazeera dated 31 Oct 2012.

lxxxvii "In Pictures World Food day" reported by Al Jazeera, dated 16 Oct 2012.

lxxxviii Sandra Postel, Director, independent Global Water Policy Project, "ibid xxiii", SEED magazine.com 05 dec2012.

lxxxix Enhance, ArunP (1999),"Hydropolitics in the Third World: Conflict and Cooperation in International River Basins, pub by US Institute of Peace Press, pp 156-158 , retrieved on 24 Apr 2011.

xc Acker, Fabian (2009-03-02). "Taming the Yangtze". IET magazine. [dead link]

xci "Three GorgesUnderground Power Station Electrical and Mechanical Equipment Fully Handed overProduction" (in Chinese), China Three Gorges Corporation retrieved on 08 Jul 2012.

xcii Brahma Chellaney, "Water Asia's New Battle Ground", page-30-31, quoting,Kang Juan,"Water Project Leads to Mass Relocation," Global

Times, February 24,2010; Hu Jiahai, Deputy Director of the Migration Bureau of the Wanzhou District of Chongqing Province cited in Wang Huazhong,"Dam Forces Relocationsof 300,000More",China Daily, Janiuary 21 , 2010.

xciii Brahma Chellaney,"Water Asia's new Battleground", pub by Harper Collins Publishers India, 2011, pp-31.

xciv XINHUA REPORT, "Climate change to reduce water availability, FAO warns" PUB IN HINDU 10Jun 2011, (report originated from Santiago).

xcv Chris Arsenault, "Risk of water wars rises with Scarcity" reported by Al Jazeera 26 aug 2012 and up loaded on www.aljazeera.com

xcvi Rhodri Davies, "Mexico City's Water Crisis, reported by Al Jazeera dated 23 Apr 2012

xcvii Chris Arsenault, "Risk of water wars rises with Scarcity" reported by Al Jazeera 26 aug 2012 and up loaded on www.aljazeera.com

xcviii Chris Arsenault, "Risk of water wars rises with Scarcity" reported by Al Jazeera 26 aug 2012 and up loaded on www.aljazeera.com

xcix "OECD Environmental Outlook to 2030", uploaded on www.oecd.org/ environmentalindicatorsmodellingand outlooks/402000582.pdf

c Ibid ixxi

ci "Report pub by Stolkholm International Water Institute (SIWI)",pp404 for UNO and uploaded on http://www.siwi.org/sa/node.asp?node=159.

cii Ibid lxxi

ciii Ibid lxxi

civ Adel darwish and John Bullock,"water Wars: Coming Conflicts in Middle East", pub by Gollanz, Nov 1993.

cv Brahma Chellaney, "Water Asia's New Battleground", pub by Harper Collins Publishers India during 2011, pp-2.

cvi "World's top 10 exporters and importers of food", http://www.rediff. com/business/slide-show/slide-show-1-worlds-top-10-exporters-and-importers-of-food/20110315.htm, Last updated on: March 15, 2011 08:49 IST

cvii India, China could become net importers of grains by 2050 http://www.

commodityonline.com/news/india-china-could-become-net-importers-of-grains-by-2050-39562-3-39563.html Last Updated : 01 June 2011 at 17:50 IST

cviii Ibid xcv pp-84

cix Sandip Das, Sunny Verma, "Coarse grain farmers harvest a fine margin", pub in Financial Express, New Delhi, 24 Dec 2012

cx A Report from United Nations Department of Economic and Social Affairs, "International Decade for Action 'Water for Life' 2005-2015", uploaded on www.un.org/waterforlifedecade/food_security.shtml and Ibid xcv pp-85.

cxi Ibid ixxxii pp-3

cxii Ibid xivi

cxiii Ibid xivi

cxiv Ibid xivi

cxv Navid Ahdich," Turkey, Dam, Kurds and Conflict within and Between Countries", an ICE Case study No 200 Apr 2007, uploaded on www1.american.edu/ted/ice/kurd-water.htm

cxvi Ibid xivi

cxvii Ibid xivi

cxviii http://envirozan.info Powered by Joomla! G

cxix Endangered Jordan", Dateline World Jewry, World Jewish Congress, September, 2007

cxx Plushnick-Masti, Ramil (10 September 2006). "Raw Sewage Taints Sacred Jordan River". The Washington Post. Retrieved 10 October 2010.

cxxi Klein, Ernest, A Comprehensive Etymological Dictionary of the Hebrew Language for Readers of English, The University of Haifa, Carta, Jerusalem, p.264

cxxii bidl

cxxiii Mehr, Farhang, The politics of water, in, Antonino Zichichi, Richard C. Ragaini, eds.,International Seminar on Nuclear War and Planetary Emergencies, 30th session, Erice, Italy, 18–26 August 2003, Ettore Majorana International Centre for Scientific Culture, World Scientific

Publishing Co. Pie. Ltd., 2004, p.258

cxxiv Ibid liv

cxxv Ibid liv

cxxvi "Appendix C: Historical review of the political riparian issues in the development of the Jordan River and basin management". Murakami. 1995

cxxvii Mehr, Farhang, The politics of water, in, Antonino Zichichi, Richard C. Ragaini, eds.,International Seminar on Nuclear War and Planetary Emergencies, 30th session, Erice, Italy, 18–26 August 2003, Ettore Majorana International Centre for Scientific Culture, World Scientific Publishing Co. Pie. Ltd., 2004, p.259

cxxviii Iskakov and Tabyshalieva,"Cold Winters Upstream, Dry Summers Downstream in Central Asia" dated 30 Jan 2002.

cxxix Michael Wine S, "Grand Soviet Scheme for Sharing Water in Central Asia is Floundering", pub in New York Times on 09 Dec 2002

cxxx Julia Bucknall, Irina Klytchnikova, Julian Lampietti, Mark Lundell, Monica Scatasta, Mike Thurman," rrigation in Central Asia: Social, Economic and Environmental Considerations", pub by The World Bank, February 2003 and uploaded on www.worldbank.org/eca/environment

cxxxi Smith,"Water Conflict in Central asia", pub under arrangement Wageningen University dated 18 jan 07

cxxxii Wegerich,Kai,"The potential for Success Uzbek Local water Management", pub by Centre for Water and Development", SOAS University of London, year of publication 2001.

cxxxiii Ibid lviii

cxxxiv Ibid lxxxvi

cxxxv International Crisis group 2002 b, "Central Asia: water and Conflict", Asia report No 34 dated 30 May 2002

cxxxvi Klötzli Stefan. 1994. The Water and Soil Crisis in Central Asia – a Source for Future Conflicts? ENCOP Occasional Paper No 11, Center for Security Policy and Conflict Research, Zurich/Swiss Peace Foundation, Berne.

cxxxvii Ibid xcii

cxxxviii O'Hara Sarah L. 1998. Water and Conflict in Central Asia. Proceedings of Political Studies Association of the UK annual conference, available at:http://www.psa.ac.uk/cps/1998/ohara.pdf and ibid lviii

cxxix Hogan Bea. 2000a. Decreased water flow threatens cotton crop, peace in region. EurasiaNet Environment Report: http://eurasianet.org/departments/environment/articles/eav080200.shtml

cxl Grozin Andrei. 2001. Vodnaya kooperatsiya – edinstvenniy vyhod dlya prikaspiiskih stran. Respublika.kz: http://www.respublika.kz/archive/sosedy/world/world07_01.html

cxli Ibid xcii

cxlii Chait E.A. 1999. Water Politics of Syr Darya Basin, Central Asia: Question of State Interests. At International Water Resources Association homepage: www.iwra.siu.edu/pdf/Chait.pdf

cxliii Sievers Eric W. 2002. Water, Conflict and Regional Security in Central Asia. New York University Environmental Law Journal, X.

cxliv Prime Sarmiento, "Study reveals extent of Mekong dam food security threat" dated 29 November 2012, uploaded on www.scidev.net/en/south-east-asia/news/study-reveals-extent-of-mekong-dam-security-threat.html

cxlv Ibid cvii

cxlvi Ibid cvii

cxlvii " Vietnam warns of water conflicts", published on 14 Sep 2012 and up loaded on peakwater.org

cxlviii Aaron T. Wolf and Joshua T. Newton," Case Study of Trans boundary Dispute Resolution: Salween River" published by Institute of Water and Water Sheds, Oregon State University

cxlix "water Needs in South Asia: Closing the Demand Supply Gap", edited by Toufiq A. Siddiqi and Shirin Tahir- Kheli, pub by GEE-21, Honululu, Hawaii, December 2004, page-1.

cl Ibid Xcv pp-1

cli Ibid xcv, pp-97

clii UN-Water,"Coping with Water Scarcity: A Strategic Issue and Priority for System-Wide Action," United Nations,New York, August 2006,2 cliii Fourth Assessment of the UN Intergovernmental Panel on Climate Change, reported by Newsweek Magazine dated 27 May 2010.

cliv China, Tibet and the Strategic Power of Water uploaded on www. circleofblue.org/water news/2008/world/china-tibet, on thursday 08 May 2008..

clv Xinhua, "Environment of Roof of the World under Threat", 16 May 2005, posted by the Chinese Ministry of Water Resources on its website; www.mwr.gov.cn/enlish/

clvi Paul Harrison and Fred Pearce, AAS Atlas of Population and Environment (Washington DC: American Association for the Advancement of Science, 2007), "Part2-Ecosystems: Mountains."

clvii Y Ding, S Liu, J Li and D Shangguan, "The Retreat of Glaciers in Response to Recent Climate Warming in Western China", Annals of Glaciology 43, No 1 (2006):97-105; Cruz et al, "Asia".

clviii Science Museums of China, " Yarlung Tsangpo Great Canyon" (Beijing Computer Network Information Centre of the Chinese Academy of Science, n.d.)

clix World Wide Fund for Nature," World's Top 10 Rivers at Risk" (Gland, Switzerland:WWF International, 2006),4

clx Cruz etal., "Asia", pp-469-506.

clxi Part of Preface of ibid xi.

clxii Walter W Immerzeel, Ludovicus P.H. Van Beek and Marc F.P. Bierkens,"Climate Change Will Affect the Asian Water Tower,"Science 328,No5983 dated 11 June 2010, pp-1382-85, DOI:10.1126/science.1183188.

clxiii Ibid cl

clxiv "Water Needs in South Asia Closing the Demand –Supply Gap",coordinated and edited by Toufiq A Siddiqi and Shirin Tahir-Kheli, sponsored by the Carnegie Corporation of New York, pp-9

clxv Ibid clii

clxvi Ibid clii pp20.

clxvii Ibid clii pp-21.

clxviii Ibid clii pp-29

clxix Ibid clii, pp-29

clxx WRSF Consortium (2000). Water Resources Strategy Formulation Study (Phase II). Annx 3: River Basin Planning Frame work; Annx 4: Irrigation; Annx 5: Hydro power; Annx 6: Water Supply and Sanitation.

clxxi Ibid clviii

clxxii Usman Karim," Catastrophic effects of depleting groundwater in Pakistan A Time Bomb Threat ", pub in GUPSHUP Forum on 02 Apr 2007 and uploaded on http://www.paklinks.com/gs/forum.php

clxxiii Usman Karim," Catastrophic effects of depleting groundwater in Pakistan A Time Bomb Threat ", pub in GUPSHUP Forum on 02 Apr 2007 and uploaded on http://www.paklinks.com/gs/forum.php

clxxiv Ibid clii, pp-31.

clxxv Halcrow Rural Management, (1996). OECF Assisted On-Farm Water Management Project, Monitoring and Evaluation Programme, Report on the Second Baseline Season, Islamabad. Federal Water Management Cell, Ministry of Food, Agriculture and Livestock (mimeo)

clxxvi Usman Karim," Catastrophic effects of depleting groundwater in Pakistan A Time Bomb Threat ", pub in GUPSHUP Forum on 02 Apr 2007 and uploaded on http://www.paklinks.com/gs/forum.php

clxxvii Ibid clxii

clxxviii Pakistan's Economic Survey,2001.

clxxix Ibidclii, PP-33

clxxx Ibidclx

clxxxi Ibid clx

clxxxii Ibid clx

clxxxiii Mohammad, Nur (1987),"Rangelands of Pakistan". Kathmandu: ICIMOD.

clxxxiv Ibid clii, pp-81.

clxxxv Ibid xvii, page-26.

clxxxvi Government of India. (1987a). Report of the Ravi Beas Water Tribunal.

clxxxvii Sonu Jain, "Flash Point Babhali", pub in Indian Express dated 16 May 2007

clxxxviii h "National Register for Large Dams". India: Central Water Commission. 2009. pp. 194–197. Retrieved 30 November 2011.

clxxxix Ibid cixviii

cxc Roy Mathew (2 December 2011). "State is unprepared for disasters". State is unprepared for disasters. Chennai, India: Kasturi & Sons Ltd. Retrieved 6 November 2011.

cxci The Kerala Irrigation And Water Conservation (Amendment) Act, 2006.

cxcii "Tamil Nadu not interested in adjudicating Mullaperiyar before panel". The Hindu (Chennai, India). 8 March 2010. ^ "Tamil Nadu not interested in adjudicating Mullaperiyar before panel". The Hindu (Chennai, India). 8 March 2010.

cxciii "Tamil Nadu plea dismissed, empowered panel on Mullaperiyar will stay". The Hindu (Chennai, India). 30 March 2010.

cxciv http://www.thehindu.com/news/national/article3353151.ece Mullaperiyar dam structurally & hydrologically safe: panel

cxcv TP Sreenivasan (in The New York Times' India Ink) ,"The Mullaperiyar Dam dispute between Kerala and Tamil Nadu is unnecessary",| Updated: January 08, 2012 23:58 IST

cxcvi Dr Shaheen Akhtar, " Emerging Challenges To Indus Waters Treaty: Issues of compliance & transboundary impacts of Indian hydroprojects on the Western Rivers", up loaded on http://www.irs.org.pk/f310.pdf

cxcvii Economic Survey of Pakistan, 2009-10, op.cit., (ref.21), p.13.

cxcviii Page 4, "Water Needs in South Asia" coordinated and edited by Toufiq A. Siddiqi and Shirin Tahir-Kheli sponsored by the Carnegie Corporation of New York

cxcix Michael Kugelman, Ahmad Rafay Alam, and Gitanjali Bakshi, "Peace through water", pub in FP dated 02 December 2011.

cc Ibid clxxxv

cci Muhammad Idris Rajput, "Inter Provincial Water Issues in Pakistan", pub by Pakistan Institute of Legislative Development and Transparency dated Jan 2011.

ccii TP Barnett, JC Adam and DP Lettenmaier, "Potential Impacts of a Warming Climate on Water Availability in Snow Dominated Regions", Nature 438, 17 November 2005, pp-306.

cciii A Nishat , Md. Ashfaque Azam and MFK Pasha, "A Review of the Ganges Treaty of 1996", presented at the University of Dundee International Speciality Conference 2001, dated 6-8 Aug 2001.

cciv Md. Nurul Islam and Dr. Q R Islam, "TEESTA RIVER WATER SHARING: A CASE STUDY IN TEESTA BARRAGE PROJECT" uploaded on http://www.watertech.cn/english/islam.pdf

ccv Rajesh tahapa,"Teesta Water Issues: A Few Hard Facts", uploaded on http://www.mingpoonews.blogspot.in/

ccvi WWF. 2003 The Third World Water Forum 2003, 16-21 March 2003, Kyoto, Bangladesh Delegation,Ministry of Water Resources, Dhaka, pp 6-17.

ccvii Upreti BC,"Politics of Himalayan River Waters. India", pub by Nimala Publications, 1993

ccviii Rao, RA and Prasad T, "Water Resources Development of the Indo-Nepal Regio" ,pub in Water Resources Development, 10(2), pp-157-173 during 1994.

ccix Toufiq A Siddiqi and Shirin Tahir-Kheli, "Water Conflicts in South Asia", project sponsored by the Carnegie Corporation of New York, pub by GEE-21, Honolulu, Hawaii, PP-164, dated August 2004.

ccx http://www.internationalrivers

ccxi Uttam Kumar Sinha, "India and Pakistan: Introspecting the Indus Treaty", Strategic Analysis, Vol. 32, No. 6., November 2008, p.965.

ccxii "Hydro Electric Potential in the District", <http://doda.nic.in/others/hydro.htm>

ccxiii Data provided by Indus Waters Commission, Pakistan.

ccxiv Nirupama Subramanian, "Violation of treaty will damage ties: Zardari", pub in The Hindu, New Delhi, 13 October 2008.

ccxv Waqar Gillani, "Troubled waters," The News, 4 April 2010

ccxvi BG Verughese,"The Inconvenient Truth, uploaded on http://.www.

bgverghese.com dated 08 June 2010

ccxvii "Pakistan-India Relations", Pakistan Institute of Legislative Development and Transparency (PILDAT) archived from original on 24 July 2011 and Press Release http://pib.nic.in

ccxviii Ibid ccii

ccxix Asif Ali Zardari, "Partnering with Pakistan", The Washington Post, 28 January 2009, <http://www.washingtonpost.com/wp-dyn/content/article/2009/01/27/AR2009012702675_pf.html>

ccxx "Assef fears war with India over water", The News, Islamabad/ Rawalpindi, 03 January 2010.

ccxxi 'India plans 52 projects to control Pakistan's water', The Nation, Islamabad, 30 March 2010.

ccxxii Ibid ccix

ccxxiii "India 'not responsible for Pak's water woes'" The Kashmir Times, Jammu, 27 March 2010.

ccxxiv Anita Joshua, "Discourse on India-Pakistan water sharing hots up", The Hindu, 4 April 2010.

ccxxv Ibid ccxii

ccxxvi Ibid xcvpp-98.

ccxxvii Food and Agriculture Organisation (FAO) of the United Nations, Country summary fact sheet on Bangladesh, 15 June 2010, Aquastat online database

ccxxviii MS Menon, "Concerns over Chinese barrage on Sutlej", pub in Hindu, 30 July 2006.

ccxxix Arabinda Ghose,"Eagle's Eye: Barrage across Parichu river, pub in Central Chronicle, July 14, 2006.

ccxxx Bernard J Wohlwend, Equitable Utilisation and the Allocation of Water Rights to Shared Water Resources. http://www.aida-waterlaw.org/PDF/EQUITABLE.pdf

ccxxxi Jayanta Bandyopadhyay and Nilanjan Ghosh, "Holistic Engineering and Hydro-Diplomacy in the Ganges-Brahmaputra-Meghna Basin", EPW, Vol.44, No.45, Nov 7-13, 2009 pp.50-60 ccxxxii NDWA &Government of Tamil Nadu (2000),"Proceedings of the Eight National Water Commission, New Delhi, NWDA &Government of Karnataka, 2001,"Proceedings of the Ninth National Wate Convention, New Delhi

ccxxxiii http://en.wikipedia.org/wiki/National_Water_Policy#cite_note-NWP1987-2

ccxxxiv Ibid Note-3.

ccxxxv Ibid Note-4.

ccxxxvi Ibid xxxv

www.ingramcontent.com/pod-product-compliance
Lightning Source LLC
Chambersburg PA
CBHW031413270326
41929CB00010BA/1438